INSIDE THE TORNADO

If you are marketing technology-based products or managing the people who do, then you will find yourself *Inside the Tornado*. Here's what the experts have to say:

"*Inside the Tornado* applies the kind of fresh thinking, sound advice, and pure common sense that global companies—regardless of industry or product offering—will need to survive in a world of constant change. If there is one business book you read this year, this is it!"—David A. Duffield, president, CEO, and founder, People-Soft, Inc.

"A must-read for all participants in high-tech."—Thomas J. Kosnik, consulting associate professor, Stanford Engineering School; visiting associate professor, Harvard Business School

"Moore articulates a marketplace that at once can be cutthroat and incredibly fun. Like Silicon Valley itself, *Tornado* is not for the squeamish."—Dave Bagshaw, vice president of marketing, Silicon Graphics, Inc.

"A must for everyone who wants to realize the phenomenal success of many of America's high-tech companies."
—Yogen Dalal, general partner, Mayfield Fund

"A most fitting sequel to the original masterpiece."
—Dominic Orr, senior vice president, Bay Networks

"Fantastic! The most insightful business book for high-tech businesses available without a prescription!"
—Robert Epstein, vice president, Sybase, Inc.

"Moore's book is one that any executive should read, and read again. It's a pragmatic road map full of examples on how to align strategy continually with the vortex of market change. Terrific stuff."
—Jeff Crowe, president, Edify Corporation

INSIDE THE
TORNADO

MARKETING STRATEGIES FROM
SILICON VALLEY'S CUTTING EDGE

GEOFFREY A. MOORE

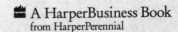

A HarperBusiness Book
from HarperPerennial

A hardcover edition of this book was published in 1995 by Harper-Business, a division of HarperCollins Publishers.

First HarperPerennial edition published 1999.

Designed by Alma Hochhauser Orenstein

The Library of Congress has catalogued the hardcover edition as follows:

Moore, Geoffrey A., 1946–
    Inside the tornado : marketing strategies from Silicon Valley's cutting edge / Geoffrey A. Moore.
        p.   cm.
    Includes index.
    ISBN 0-88730-765-5
    1. High technology industries—Marketing. I. Title.
HC79.H53M66   1995
620'.0068'8—dc20   95-23075

ISBN 0-88730-824-4 (pbk.)

00 01 02 03 ❖/RRD 10 9 8 7

In memory of Patricia C. Moore, who loved literature, had a wonderful way with words, and did her best to pass these gifts on to her son

CONTENTS

ACKNOWLEDGMENTS

This book is an attempt to distill the learning of the past four years of consulting since *Crossing the Chasm* was published. The sources of that learning include a modest amount of published material, none of which I have managed to save or footnote, of which the most valuable are the industry newsletters of Dick Shaffer, Jeff Tarter, and Seymour Merrin, who, along with *Computerworld* and *PC Week* keep me abreast of the industry at large.

But the bulk of this learning has come from colleagues and clients. On the colleague side, my associates Paul Wiefels, Tom Kippola, and Mark Cavender have all contributed significantly to this work at every stage, sharing ideas, critiquing concepts, adding examples, and generally just wising me up when I stray into the ether. If despite their efforts I still have strayed, it is not for their lack of trying.

I'd also like to acknowledge colleagues halfway round the globe, in the Republic of South Africa, who have been applying The Chasm Group methodology to that country's emerging technology sector: Adriaan Joubert, Renier Balt, Herman Malan, and Johan Visagie.

In addition to these associates, there is an informal set of colleagues, many of whom are also consultants, who have taken time from their businesses to critique and advance the argument of this book. These include my daughter Margaret Moore at Regis McKenna Inc., Paul Johnson, a financial analyst at Robertson Stephens, Tom Kucharvy at Summit Partners, Charles Dilisio at KPMG Peat Marwick, Tom Byers, now a con-

sulting professor at Stanford, Andy Salisbury, consulting independently, Tony Morris, also with his own firm, as are Ann
Badillo, Bruce Silver, Phillip Lay, Brett Bullington, and David
Dunn-Rankin. Another support group includes recovering
ex-colleagues from Regis McKenna Inc., including Greg Ruff,
Page Alloo, Glenn Helton, Rosemary Remacle, Karen Lippe,
and Doug Molitor. All of us have proven unemployable by anyone other than ourselves—which will surprise no one at RMI.
And a third comes from colleagues in the public relations field,
including Sabrina Horn, Maureen Blanc, Simone Otus, and
Pam Alexander.

Still further support has come from the venture capital
community, including the firms of Accel Partners, The Charles
River Group, Atlas Partners, St. Paul Venture Capital, The
Mayfield Fund, and Institutional Venture Partners. I owe a
special debt to this last group for incubating The Chasm Group
in their office space for a year, and I'd like to convey special
thanks to Reid Dennis, Pete Thomas, and Norm Fogelsong for
their kind attentions.

Participating on the boards of companies has also provided
numerous lessons, and I would especially like to acknowledge
Carl Herrmann and Walt Pounds at Solbourne, Tom Quinn at
Gyration, and Richard Furse at PC Upgrades.

And then there are the clients. While colleagues advise and
friends support, clients teach. I have had the privilege of working with close to a hundred different client groups in the past
four years who have brought to our relationship not only great
problems but wonderful insights into how to solve them. Of
these, the many people of Hewlett-Packard, too many to name
individually, have had a special impact on this book, as well as
earned a special place in my heart. I would just like to acknowledge Bonnie Paradies and Darleen Bevin for helping to shape
this entire relationship. It has been phenomenally rewarding to
me, and I deeply appreciate it.

Individuals who stand out from other client engagements
are so numerous that I no doubt will neglect to recognize many
deserving people. Of the ones that come immediately to mind,
I'd like to give special thanks to Steve Jobs of NeXT Inc., Scott

Silk at Unisys, Jeff Miller and Rob Reid at Documentum, Dave and Al Duffield at PeopleSoft, Bernard Hulme at SCO, Dominic Orr at Bay Networks, Peter Strub at AT&T, Gerry Greeve at Intel, Mark Hoffman and Bob Epstein at Sybase, Richard Probst and Stew Plock at Sun, Franki D'Hoore and Evert Polak at ASM Lithography, Dan Metzger at Lawson Software, Pat Maley at Client Systems, Heather McKenzie at Crystal Services, Rob Reis at Savi, and Al Miksch at Tektronix.

To these and to that one other special person that I have forgot to name but meant to, thank you for the challenges, the insights, and the friendship.

And then there are the people that support writers in the midst of these journeys they insist upon. These include Jim Levine, my literary agent, and Kirsten Sandberg, my editor. At the Chasm Group this labor falls on the shoulders of one of the most delightful colleagues one could wish for, Angelynn Hanley. And elsewhere . . .

Elsewhere is the province of Marie, who has continued to make my life an adventure lo these many years of marriage together. It is she who makes it all worthwhile in the end, and seeing the world through her eyes renews it for me daily. In this she has our three delightful children in cahoots with her, Margaret, Michael, and Anna. I am truly blessed, and delighted to be so.

INTRODUCTION

When I'm writing a book, I typically save the introduction for last, the theory being it's much easier to tell people where you're going once you can see where you've been. But being able to write a second introduction some four years after the book's initial publication—now that's a special treat. For this way I get to incorporate and respond to feedback from a variety of people, *all without having to write another book!* It's a labor-saving device indeed.

The feedback on *Inside the Tornado* has been deeply gratifying. The high-tech industry, particularly in the United States, has embraced its key concepts and made its core metaphors common vocabulary for assessing the maturity of emerging markets and the status of vendors within them. The Chasm Group has made the book the platform for its primary practice offerings and in so doing has grown from three to six partners, and now we are in the process of adding affiliates. That practice is rapidly becoming international, with the book being translated into Chinese, Japanese, Korean, French, German, and Portuguese, with clients on six continents and affiliates on three. The book is also used as a standard text at Stanford, Harvard, MIT, Northwestern, and a host of other business and engineering graduate schools, so that a new generation of entrepreneurs is coming into the market already versed in its ideas. It is hard for me to imagine an author asking for more, and I very am grateful for this response.

That being said, feedback isn't much use if it does not also point out opportunities for improvement. Virtually every model in the book has undergone some level of metamorphosis over the past four years, as the pressure of real-world consulting engagements force contradictions and flaws to the surface. For the time being my colleagues and I have been able to contain these learnings in updates to our PowerPoint library of slides. They have not yet overflowed these banks, but no doubt they eventually shall, at which point I'll put them into a revised edition and test the industry's support once more.

There has been, however, one tsunami of change in the form of the Internet and the emergence of e-commerce that simply cries out to be addressed at this juncture. But before so doing I must issue a word of warning: to apply the ideas in this book to the Internet marketplace, I have to assume that you as a reader are already familiar with them! Unless you are clairvoyant, this seems a bit presumptuous. So, unless you are picking up this book for a second read, let me first of all say welcome; second, say thank you for buying the book and giving it your time; and third, suggest you dog-ear this very page right now and skip to Chapter One. Then, at the end of the book, if you are still willing, come back and finish here at the beginning, taking the introduction as an afterword.

[Interlude, during which first-time readers peruse the remainder of the book, and other readers pass on to the next paragraph.]

Ah, there you are. Welcome back. OK, now that we're all on the same footing, let's get down to a really key question: according to the index, in the entire manuscript of *Inside the Tornado* the Internet is referenced precisely three times. How in the world did I completely miss what will arguably be the grandest tornado of all time? Well, all I can say is that it's a gift.

But in my defense, the manuscript deadline was June 1995, a full six months before Netscape released Navigator 1.0. At that time it certainly felt like the Internet would be the "next big thing," but I for one had no ideal how quickly and comprehensively it would happen.

As of this writing, it is approaching the end of 1998, and there is no sector of the American economy that has been untouched by the Internet. Internationally, on the other hand, the pace of adoption has been substantially slower, gaited by the gradual deregulation of the telecommunications industry. Nonetheless, to put things in the vocabulary of this book, we are witnessing a worldwide series of tornadoes, and I think we are far enough into it to project a trajectory of where things might go next.

First, to review how far we have come, in 1996 and 1997 we witnessed the first Internet tornado, focused on the browser. In this competition Netscape Navigator was virtually a gorilla at birth, skyrocketing to more than 80 percent market share in the hypergrowth market. That lead should have been insurmountable, it should have institutionalized Netscape as the de facto standard, conferred upon it gorilla status, and set up its shareholders for very long-term gains. What happened?

Microsoft made a brilliant strategic response and then executed it with draconian efficiency. The key strategy was to clone the Netscape browser, not compete with it. Microsoft, in other words, played *monkey*, not *chimp*, to this dangerous gorilla threat. By so doing, it was able to co-opt the very market Netscape was creating. However, a clone response alone would not have been enough because Netscape still had the gorilla's right to set extensions to the standard going forward, in the manner that Intel has used to maintain its lead over AMD and National Semiconductor, for example. But here a strategic flaw in Netscape's plan emerged: the technology of the browser was not all that difficult to reverse engineer. As a result Microsoft caught up to Netscape's lead in less than a year, with its Internet Explorer 3.0 reaching parity. This then allowed it to compete head to head—still using monkey tactics—to win major deals on price, where the "price" was *free*.

Meanwhile Microsoft's underlying strategy began to emerge, along the following lines:

1. No one can beat a gorilla on its own turf, but
2. Netscape's turf has to ride on top of our turf, the Windows operating system, so
3. Let's incorporate the browser into Windows and thereby
4. Defeat the gorilla by dissolving its turf.

Once this strategy became evident, it was "game over" for the browser wars. Everyone could see that Microsoft's play was undefeatable, and Netscape's stock plunged virtually overnight.

As a consequence, our society has begun an extended debate on the implications of this strategy and its outcome, one that will force all of us to rethink our understanding of competition, monopoly, restraint of trade, economic freedom, capitalism, regulation, political and social responsibility, and the like. The issues are deeply intertwined and hugely complex, and no single set of rulings will be definitive. Rather it will be part of an ongoing cultural adjustment to the larger movement from an asset-based economy to an information-based one. But in the meantime, the hypergrowth of the Internet continues, and we cannot let its opportunities slip from our grasp.

The second Internet tornado, hitting full force in 1997 and still raging as of this writing, is the explosion in web sites. Whereas the killer app for the browser tornado was, well, browsing, the killer app here is taking advantage of all those browsing eyeballs by letting them look at you. For corporations a web site has become a necessary address, a place to stage its public information, an anteroom if you will to the buildings proper. As the leverage in web sites became clear, IT professionals readily yielded to their deployment, thinking no doubt that the wave of change could be held at bay here, giving everyone some time to settle down and approach future changes more deliberately.

But no. Almost instantaneously internal corporate users became caught up in what was the original purpose of the web—to share information among related working groups—and the real web site explosion happened under the banner of the *intranet*. The intranet, prodded by email, has now become the internal information pathway of choice for all high-tech companies and for technology-enabled services such as banking and brokerage. It is a testimony to the success of this deployment that most people, in these sectors at any rate, already are feeling glutted by this new arrival.

Both the public Internet and the internal intranet tornadoes have driven demand for web servers and software, not to mention Internet connectivity, all of which has driven infrastructure players like Cisco, Sun, Microsoft, and Netscape to prominence. At the same time, the Internet has also driven the transformation of electronic mail from proprietary software from Lotus and Microsoft to a simple common Internet email protocol. And as this new world of unified addressing emerges, email itself is becoming a tornado market force in its own right, driving traffic volumes up dramatically (thanks in large part, unfortunately, to spamming), and creating a whole new market in directory services.

Huge increases in traffic, in time, are impacting everyone's networks. As organizations seek to offload this deluge, they turn to colocating facilities like Exodus or to complete outsourcing from a value-added internet service provider such as an MCI/Worldcom or a GTE/BBN. These institutions' networks, in turn, impinge upon the publicly switched telephone network—our voice heritage—which is hopelessly swamped by what looks, to it, like an epidemic of phone callers who simply won't hang up. That in turn is driving more infrastructure innovation—and dramatic merger and acquisition activity—as voice switch and data communications vendors seek to match up systems for the new world. NorTel buying Bay Networks appears to be no more than the opening move in what looks to be an extended game.

All this tornado activity to date has been driven almost exclusively by the three information-sharing killer apps of browsing, web publishing, and email. At this stage of market evolution, the infrastructure players are the key competitors, with the rest of high-tech serving primarily as the first bowling alley of pragmatic adopters. As 1998 comes to a close, however, we are seeing two other bowling alleys come onto the scene—telecommunications itself, and financial services—where the killer apps are, respectively, customer care and electronic financial transactions. In both cases we are seeing the beginnings of a second series of tornadoes, this one emerging not from investments in infrastructure but rather investments in *applications*.

The customer service implications of the Internet are simply huge. In technology-based businesses, the Internet has already become the first stop in customer support. Combined with email, and backed up by customer service applications from Vantive, Clarify, Baan (Aurum) and Siebel (Scopus), web-based support systems are already reengineering the way companies interact with business partners, with interactions with end customers not far behind. All this in turn will become part of a series of tornadoes in the customer relationship management and supply chain management areas. In every case what we are seeing is the grafting of a new communications medium onto business processes that are externally focused—the complement of all the back office automation that has been driven by replacing internal systems in preparation for the year 2000.

As application vendors get swept up in the Internet tornado market forces, they must review their fundamental strategic assumptions. Bowling alley strategy is best for most application vendors most of the time. Tornado forces, however, reward marketshare "land grabs." The problem is that rapid customer acquisition is fundamentally in conflict with complex business process reengineering, and so application companies are torn between losing out to a competitor or underservicing a valuable customer. The fundamental lesson of tornado marketing, however, is clear on this part: beat the competition first, apologize to the customer later.

In the domain of financial services, in additional to customer care applications, we are also seeing the emergence of commercial transaction processing—real e-commerce. Thus on-line portfolio management, a customer service, is being paired with on-line stock trades, a transaction service. This slight break in the dike portends gargantuan flooding to come. Historically, two infrastructures have developed to support traditional transaction processing—the Verifone network for consumer credit cards, largely from MasterCard and Visa, and the EDI protocol for purchase order processing between companies in the same supply chain. Both will be overwhelmed and assimilated by the coming Internet-based tide. Vendors in each category must begin "creative self-destruction" in order to compete effectively for their own future. There is no more challenging management task than, as the folks at H-P like to put it, "eating your own lunch."

Consumer e-commerce, however, is currently stuck on a pre-sales challenge, that of adopting its shopping mechanisms—not its buying mechanisms—to the web. More specifically, it's a catalog problem. For style-differentiated retail items, the problem is largely photogenic—paper catalogs represent the pinnacle of photo finishing, towering over the lowly image resolution available on the web. Moreover, most retail customers access the web via dial-up connections that have limited bandwidth and will continue to do so for many years to come. And finally, attractive as the Internet is as a source of new prospects, it represents a very small portion of the total retail traffic. All this has combined to make investing in on-line retail a patchy rather than universal phenomenon for the foreseeable future.

That being said, where these exigencies can be got around, there are huge market share grabs under way. The poster child for such efforts is Amazon.com, and it is worthwhile to see just how many unique attributes have contributed to its astounding success. First, as many have noted, books are one of the few retail items that do not have to be "tried on" in some way before purchase. So shopping is not significantly impaired coming to the store on-line. Second, the catalog problem had already been solved by the industry's existing distributors—it had to be converted for on-line use but not assembled for the first time. Third, while book *shoppers* will continue to frequent bookstores, book *buyers* like the convenience of *not* going. Fourth, the book buyer demographic is particularly strong in business people who access Amazon.com not from home but from work—at much higher network speeds, creating a much more user-friendly transaction. And, fifth, book buying does not require purchasers to release confidential personal information, something that can challenge other commercial transactions. And sixth, the inventory, distribution, and returns systems for book buying and selling that Amazon.com leverages were also already in place from its inception.

Now, to be sure, Amazon.com has done a superb job at reinventing the consumer buying experience for the on-line world, making its site a "must-view" for anyone else seeking to conduct e-commerce. But other companies need to carefully vet their own whole product to make sure it too can make the transition.

The other glitch that is slowing the adoption of e-commerce is on the business-to-business side, where the challenge is to front-end existing enterprise systems for customer registration, order management, credit checking, inventory availability, logistics management, and billing and collections. For companies run off a simple integrated package, this is predominantly an interface and security challenge. But for companies that comprise multiple heterogeneous systems, this is a showstopper. There is simply too much complexity, both initially and in maintenance over time, to retrofit this overlay. That portends, in time, yet another tornado as the whole world swaps out client/server infrastructure for web-enabled.

And so, with Internet commerce deferred for a prolonged interval, we can also expect all its extended implications to be deferred as well, many of which have been build around the promise of one-to-one marketing. While that premise is compelling, it must remain dormant until the order transaction flow has been fully Internet enabled.

In the meantime, the e-commerce market's growth and focus is shifting from the product providers, who have profited heavily from the infrastructure tornadoes, to the service providers, who have the upper hand in the coming application phase. There are two fundamental classes of service providers— professional services, typically consultancies, which focus on bringing up new systems, and transaction services, typically sites, which focus on using the new systems to the end-customers' benefit. The former should be thought of as *technology-enabling* services, the latter as *technology-enabled*.

With the tectonic shift toward an information economy, the demand for Internet-enabled suppliers is hugely backlogged, and the talent pool to work off that backlog is scarce indeed. As a result, professional services firms that historically have been valued at one times revenues now have valuations five or six times that. This shift in valuation permits aging companies who have failed to introduce compelling new *products* to redefine themselves as consulting firms with compelling new *services*. As long as widespread demand continues to be wedded to inherent complexity, demand in this arena will be effectively unlimited, and the competition, as in all tornadoes, will be won by those who are best able to leverage supply.

Once any infrastructure is substantially deployed, power shifts from the builders—the professional services firms—to the operators, or what we have come to call the *transaction services* firms. The key to the transaction services model is that the requisite infrastructure has already been assimilated (keeping support costs down) and amortized (minimizing ongoing investment). Unfortunately, neither of these conditions is even remotely approximated by the current state of the Internet. As a result, transaction services companies are at present operating at extraordinary deficits, and all are forced to raise money in a kind of Ponzi scheme that, hopefully, gets renewed by the emergence of stable conditions before it runs out of capital-raising capabilities. Downturns in the world economy, such as the one currently threatened, put such funding mechanisms severely at risk, and investors will need ironclad stomach linings to survive the coming years. That being said, where the infrastructure has stabilized (at least for now), one can find some of the most highly valued companies in high-tech today—Yahoo!, America Online, and Amazon.com being the most visible.

Nonetheless, the sweet spot for transaction revenues is Main Street, a time when the core technology has been commoditized, and companies differentiate based on the variety and customer fit of the offers they can field. With this realization we can close by summarizing the findings as follows:

- For every stage of the Technology Adoption Life cycle, there is an optimal business model:

    —Early Market: Professional services

    —Bowling Alley: Application products

    —Tornado: Infrastructure products

    —Main Street: Transaction services

- The Internet market tornado, however, is so powerful that it has sucked all four models into its vortex.
- Thus each model has its own peace to make with the tornado, and indeed since there are multiple tornadoes within the general one, to make with each of these as well.

In light of the above, our consulting practice at The Chasm Group, which has traditionally been targeted at product companies, no longer can sustain that focus. The product/service interchange has become so fundamental to navigating the Internet-impacted waters that every company needs to retain some flexibility to "go the other way." This represents the single biggest change in perspective since *Inside the Tornado* was written, and since the author did not have it then, I ask that you the reader bring it with you now.

And with that, I wish you all the best as you go out into the world and invent this new economy.

PART ONE

THE
DEVELOPMENT
OF
HYPERGROWTH
MARKETS

CHAPTER 1

THE LAND OF OZ

At the beginning of *The Wizard of Oz*, Dorothy and Toto are caught up inside a tornado, swept away from their mundane world of Kansas, and deposited into the marvelous land of Oz. This miraculous form of ascension is also reenacted from time to time on our own public stock exchanges.

Consider the following:

- **Compaq Computers**, which in recent years has overtaken IBM as the leader of the Intel-based PC market, grew from zero to $1 billion in less than five years.
- Ditto for **Conner Peripherals**, the disk-drive storage company who slipstreamed Compaq's hypergrowth by supplying it, as well as many of its competitors, with low-cost Winchester hard drives.
- Over a six-year period from 1977 to 1982, **Atari**'s home game business doubled in size every year, driving the company from $50 million to $1.6 billion in revenues.
- In successive years during the mid-1980s, **Mentor Graphics** grew from $2 million to $25 million to $85 million to $135 million to $200 million.
- For the *entire decade* of the 1980s, **Oracle Corporation** grew at an annually compounded rate of 100 percent.

- More recently, **Cisco Systems** and **Bay Networks** have appeared out of nowhere to become billion-dollar companies—leaders, respectively, in the network router and the network hub markets. We didn't even know what routers and hubs *were* until just a few years ago.
- In the seven years prior to 1992, **Sony** shipped their first ten million CD-ROM players. The next ten million were shipped over the following *seven months*, and the ten million after that in the following five months.
- **Hewlett-Packard**'s PC printer business, a $10 billion enterprise in 1994, shipped its first product a scant ten years earlier.
- And finally, **Microsoft** in less than fifteen years has grown from a boutique language software company focused on BASIC to the richest and most powerful software company in the world.

Such are the market forces generated by *discontinuous innovations*, or what more recently have been termed *paradigm shifts*. These shifts begin with the appearance of a new category of product that incorporates breakthrough technology enabling unprecedented benefits. It is immediately proposed as the natural replacement for a whole class of infrastructure, winning early converts and enthusiastic predictions of a new world order. But the market is a conservative institution, and it presses back against the new changes, preferring to stay with the status quo. For a long time, although much is written about the new paradigm, little of economic significance happens. Indeed, sometimes the innovation is never embraced, falling back into some primordial entrepreneurial soup, as did artificial intelligence in the 1980s and pen-based computing in the early 1990s. But in many other cases there comes a flash point of change when the entire marketplace, under the pressure of continually escalating disequilibrium in price/performance, shifts its allegiance from the old architecture to the new.

This sequence of events unleashes a vortex of market demand. Infrastructure, to be useful, must be standard and global, so once the market moves to switch out the old for the new, it wants to complete this transition as rapidly as possible. All the pent-up interest in the product is thus converted into a massive purchasing binge, causing demand to vastly outstrip supply. Companies grow at hypergrowth rates, with billions of dollars of revenue seeming to appear from out of nowhere.

We have seen this happen again and again in our own lives. Take communications. After the better part of a century being content with letters, telegrams, and telephones, we have in the past thirty years adopted touch-tone phones, direct-dial long distance, Federal Express, answering machines, fax machines, voice mail, e-mail, and now Internet addresses. In every case, until a certain mass was reached, we didn't really need to convert. But as soon as it was, it became unacceptable not to participate. As members of a market, our behavior is invariable: we move as a herd, we mill and mill and mill around, and then all of a sudden we stampede. And that is what creates the tornado.

Nowhere has the tornado touched down more often in the past quarter-century than in the computer and electronics industry. In the domain of business computing, it began with the proliferation of the IBM mainframe, which won worldwide support as the first major computing infrastructure standard. Then, in the space of less than a decade beginning in the late 1970s, three new architectures arose to challenge and displace that paradigm: the minicomputer, the personal computer, and the technical workstation, and we came to know a whole new set of companies, including DEC, HP, Sun, Apollo, Compaq, Intel, and Microsoft. In conjunction with these three architectures came a communications networking paradigm shift that moved from the centralized hub-and-spokes approach of mainframe-centric computing to the decentralized world of Local Area Networks interconnected via Wide Area Networks, and we met companies like 3-Com, Novell, Cisco, and Bay Networks. And concurrent with both these shifts, virtually all of our software, from the underlying operating systems to the databases, to the applications and the tools that build them, was overthrown or reworked, in most cases more than once, driving companies like Oracle,

Sybase, Lotus, Ashton-Tate, and WordPerfect into our consciousness.

Yet during this same period we still bought most of our cars from General Motors, Ford, and Chrysler. And we flew United or American or Delta. And we drank Coke or Pepsi or Dr Pepper. While some sectors, in other words, were generating whole industries out of thin air, creating hordes of market leaders from early unknowns, others continued along relatively familiar paths—*because they did not introduce discontinuity into their infrastructure paradigms*. The car you drive today is not materially different from one driven forty years ago. Ditto for the air transportation and the soft drinks. By contrast, high tech's insistence on repeatedly swapping out all its infrastructure is exceptionally expensive, and more than one corporation has challenged the whole rationale behind this behavior. But there is a dynamic in operation that gives people little choice. All computing is built atop an underpinning of semiconductor-based integrated circuits, which has the remarkable property of dramatically increasing its price/performance far faster than anything else in the history of our economy. In the 1970s, the rate was already an astounding order of magnitude every ten years. In the 1980s it decreased to an order of magnitude every seven years. In the middle of the 1990s the time has compressed to three and a half years. By the end of the decade microprocessor-based systems will increase ten times in power every 2.5 years. And there is no foreseeable end in sight.

This phenomenon has an extraordinarily destabilizing effect on every industry within the high-tech sector. All high-tech products ultimately take their value from software, and the software written at any point in time must work within the power constraints of the current or soon-to-be-shipped hardware. But after only a few short years, another order of magnitude of additional power has come on the scene, making these same design constraints obsolete. New products, designed to the new performance vectors, incorporate software that simply blows away the old reference points. Their new capability translates into the kind of competitive advantages that stimulate virtually any business customer—better communications, faster time to market, more efficient transaction processing, deeper understanding of their customers, earlier detection of trends. You name it, it now appears within reach.

To be sure, nobody currently enjoying success with their old paradigm really wants to change. Everybody agrees that there is already too much cycling and recycling of high-tech products, and that we would be better served if we could just take a brief time out and catch our breath. But all the while the semi-conductor engine keeps rumbling beneath our feet, and at some point the attraction of dramatically escalated capabilities simply overwhelms the inclination not to change, and despite everyone's best intentions, yet another tornado gets under way.

Each one of these changes generates massive new influxes of spending, as if we were to build up and then tear down our cities over and over again. These new pools of capital, in turn, create some of the fiercest economic competition on the planet, in part because winning or losing is compressed into such a short span of time. And with each revolution, it seems, it is not the old guard but rather a whole new set of players who are swept into prominence, redrawing the boundaries of the high-tech marketplace and realigning the power structures that dominate it.

We're Not in Kansas Anymore

By anybody's standards, this is business played by a new set of rules, with upside potential to glut anyone but a venture capitalist's appetite. At the same time, we should also note that there is a dark side to this story, an information highway littered with bankrupt companies, massive layoffs, derelict buildings, obsolete products, crippled customers, and surly investors. It is not Easy Street where we have landed but more like Tombstone or Dodge City, a place where money and power change hands quickly, and the first order of business is not to end up on Boot Hill.

Given all this, given the cataclysmic and catastrophic impacts, and given that the distribution and redistribution of wealth on the planet is so deeply influenced by what is happening within this crucible of the high-tech marketplace, we simply must get a better grip on how the forces that drive these tornadoes operate.

For those who work within the high-tech sector, or who manage investments in these companies, this imperative translates into a series of deceptively simple questions:

- What can we do during a tornado to best capitalize on our opportunity?
- How can we tell when one is coming, and what can we do to prepare?
- How can we sense when it is ending, and what should we do then?
- Finally, going forward, how can we reframe our strategic management concepts to better accommodate tornado market dynamics in general?

It is the intent of this book to answer these questions in some detail, and to do so specifically in the context of examples drawn from current developments in the high-tech sector.

At the same time, there is another class of executives outside high tech who can also expect to profit from delving into these issues, those working in *high-change* sectors where discontinuous forces are driving an analogous kind of reengineering to their infrastructures. These include:

- **Financial services.** As the financial markets have learned in the harshest possible way, speculating in derivatives and other exotic financial instruments is a highly discontinuous innovation.
- **Insurance.** With competitors chipping away at their customers with innovative financial alternatives, regulators hounding them about premiums and profitability, and their sales practices under attack in court, reengineering has become the order of the day here.
- **Health care.** The story here is *capitation,* the limiting of reimbursement to fixed fees for procedures, creating a new goal of health care providers—not to get decapitated.

- **Aerospace and defense.** Downsizing in the aftermath of the cold war, along with broad redefinition of defense strategies, is forcing this sector to reengineer the old businesses and migrate others into the commercial sector—massively discontinuous changes.
- **Utilities.** What deregulation did to the airlines in the 1980s is now in the offing for the power companies in the 1990s. This will create tornadoes of opportunity and destruction.
- **Pharmaceuticals.** With revenues impacted by capitation, and new products dependent on a discontinuous source of innovation, biotechnology, this industry is undergoing high change.
- **Retailing.** The advent of an entire electronic back-office infrastructure is fusing the links of the retail supply chain as never before, driving reengineering of these relationships as well as providing huge data sources for analyzing market behavior.
- **Publishing.** This used to mean putting words on paper. Enough said.
- **Broadcasting.** The boundaries among broadcasting, telephony, computer software, publishing, and entertainment have all collapsed into a digital pool of images that will rewrite the rules in this industry over the next ten years.

Because the examples in this book come primarily from the consulting practices of myself and my colleagues, they are heavily weighted toward high tech. Readers involved in the industries noted above, however, will find the patterns in these examples familiar, and I hope you can glean from them insights you can translate into new approaches to your own industry's concerns. High tech, in other words, can be seen not only as a sector of interest in its own right but also as a crucible in which a whole new class of business strategies are being born.

A Map of Oz

This book sets out to build a map of the new landscape and then to explore its implications for setting business strategy.

The map is built atop the Technology Adoption Life Cycle, a model of market development introduced some forty years ago by Everett Rogers and his colleagues, which describes how any community absorbs a discontinuous change. Within the outlines of this terrain, we will isolate and name six different regions or stages in the life cycle, inflection points where market forces drive companies to change strategies dramatically or be left behind.

The first two of these stages were the subject of a prior book, *Crossing the Chasm*. For the convenience of the reader the contents of that book, and a general grounding in the life cycle model, are summarized in the following chapter. This material is sufficient to bring up to speed new readers whose primary focus is market developments beyond the chasm. Readers whose interests lie earlier in the life cycle should consult the earlier work.

Once past chapter 2 this book focuses on the next three stages of the life cycle, the mainstream market stages where all high-tech wealth is created. Working to uncover the forces that shape market development at each stage, and showing how companies can align themselves with these forces to win market leadership positions, we shall see a disconcerting pattern assert itself repeatedly:

The winning strategy does not just change as we move from stage to stage, it actually reverses the prior strategy.

That is, the very behaviors that make a company successful at the outset of the mainstream market cause failure inside the tornado and must be abandoned. And similarly what makes companies successful in the tornado causes failure and must be abandoned once that phase of hypergrowth is past. In other words, it is not just the strategies themselves that are cause for note but also the need to abandon each one in succession *and embrace its opposite* that proves challenging.

As we come to understand the logic of these reversals, much of the confusion that has traditionally surrounded high-tech marketing can be dispelled. For too long people have *known* that such and such a tactic either always works or can never work. They have known this because they witnessed it first-hand in a previous assignment, and it is this experience they are bringing to bear on the current situation. The truth, how-ever, is that virtually all well-established strategy models work well in some situations and cause failure in others, so the real skill is less in knowing the strategy than in sorting out the situations to which it actually applies.

By the end of Part One we will have worked our way through these issues, and we will then, in Part Two, focus our newfound understanding on four major areas of business strat-egy that are profoundly impacted by the Technology Adoption Life Cycle's forces:

- Strategic partnerships
- Competitive advantage
- Positioning
- Organizational leadership

Each of these areas shares a common concern with the dis-tribution of power, and the theme of the last half of the book is that over the life cycle the nature and locus of marketplace power shifts and evolves in characteristic ways.

In the context of *strategic partnerships,* we will trace how over the life cycle power transfers from the service providers to the product suppliers and then back again, and how this circuit impacts relationships among partnering companies, and what implications that has for shaping strategies. In the context of *competitive advantage,* we will explore the interaction among leaders, challengers, and followers, showing how each enjoys a period of advantage as the mainstream market moves through its stages, thereby discovering when one should go forward boldly and when one should hang back and conserve resources. All this in turn will shape the way we look at *positioning,* not so much as an exercise in customer communications but rather as a set of ritual behaviors by which we assert our rightful place within the hierarchy of power relationships that govern a mar-ket at any given moment.

Throughout this entire process we will see pillars of cherished wisdom confirmed at one stage of the life cycle only to be overthrown at the next, forcing us into continual shifts in strategic emphasis as established product lines mature and new ones emerge. Indeed, since multidivisional organizations of any size can expect to be fielding products at many if not all stages of the life cycle at the same time, top management must learn to entertain and support contradictory marketing principles, even within a single meeting! This is clearly no game for anyone who has one way of doing things and sticks to it. And that in turn will lead us to the final topic in question, *organizational leadership*.

The demands for frequent and dramatic change inherent in the life cycle cause painful dislocations for individuals as well as for companies. And frankly, few of us are up to them. What we will see by the end of this book is that there is no easy way around this problem. It does improve matters, however, to have a clear way of stating the challenge, a vocabulary with which executive teams can confront the situation squarely, assess each other's strengths and weaknesses, and do their best to move the reins of power into the right hands at the right time. For the way out of this forest, we shall find, lies in the realization that what we may fall short of being able to accomplish as individuals, we can yet accomplish as teams.

All told, *Inside the Tornado* is a book born out of business experiences specific to the high-tech sector and, like much that is written by Americans, has a distinctly U.S.-centric point of view as well. At the same time, however, its lessons go far beyond the borders of any one industry or any one country. What my global traveling has taught me over the past few years is that the Technology Adoption Life Cycle is a universal phenomenon, and the forces that operate so distinctly in high-tech markets shape our lives just as pervasively, if perhaps more subtly, elsewhere. In that spirit, then, whether your field is high tech or just high change, I invite you to take part in the chapters that follow.

CHAPTER 2

CROSSING THE CHASM— AND BEYOND

Virtually all contemporary thinking about high-tech marketing strategy has its roots in the Technology Adoption Life Cycle, a model which grew out of social research begun in the late 1950s about how communities respond to *discontinuous innovations*.

Truly discontinuous innovations are new products or services that require the end user and the marketplace to dramatically change their past behavior, with the promise of gaining equally dramatic new benefits. Applied to marketing, the model postulates that when a marketplace is confronted with the opportunity to switch to a new infrastructure paradigm— from typewriters, say, to word processors—customers self-segregate along an axis of risk aversion, with the risk-immune *innovators* moving to the forefront, asking—even demanding—to be first to try out the new opportunity, while the risk-allergic *laggards* retreat to the rear of the line (quills still firmly in hand). In between, the model identifies three additional communities—the *early adopters, early majority,* and *later majority.*

Graphically, the model is represented as a bell curve:

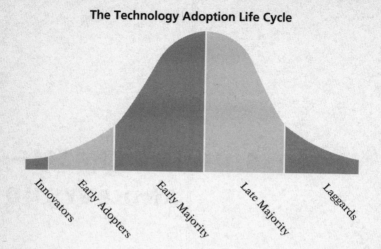

The Technology Adoption Life Cycle

Innovators   *Early Adopters*   *Early Majority*   *Late Majority*   *Laggards*

Each of the segments in the bell curve represents a standard deviation from the norm. Thus the early and late majority are one standard deviation from the norm, each comprising about a third of the total population, while the early adopters and laggards are two and the innovators three standard deviations away. The idea is that change will be adopted from left to right, with each constituency coming to the fore in sequence.

Prior to encountering this model, high-tech marketers were in desperate need of help. Most of us had grown up in a business environment where excellence in marketing was defined in reference to Procter & Gamble. In attempting to apply that company's approach to high tech, we were thrashing about miserably. In particular, the tools for marketing communications just weren't working right, and whenever we went to people for advice, they kept chastising us for making our messages too long, too complicated, and, well, too nerdy. When the Technology Adoption Life Cycle came upon the scene, we were delighted, because it helped explain why our communications got such enthusiastic responses from some customers and such chilly ones from others.

In order to make this model truly ours, we relabeled each of the five constituencies as follows:

1. **Innovators = *Technology enthusiasts*.** These are people who are fundamentally committed to new technology on the grounds that, sooner or later, it is bound to improve our lives. Moreover, they take pleasure in mastering its intricacies, just in fiddling with it, and they love to get their hands on the latest and greatest innovation. And thus they are typically the first customers for anything that is truly brand-new.

   Virtually all organizations support techies. In your own family there is likely to be one—and only one—person who can program the answering machine, set the clock on the VCR, and figure out the espresso machine. Same is true at the office. Who do you go to when you can't get the computer to work right? That is your techie.

   From a marketing point of view, particularly in business-to-business sales, there is really only one drawback to techies: they don't have any money. What they have instead is influence. The reason we spend so much time with them is that they are the gatekeepers to the rest of the life cycle. If they pan a new product, no one else gives that product a second glance. Only with their endorsement can a discontinuous innovation get a hearing, and so we often "seed" (read "give") products to this community to gain their support.

2. **Early Adopters = *Visionaries*.** These are the true revolutionaries in business and government who want to use the discontinuity of any innovation to make a break with the past and start an entirely new future. Their expectation is that by being first to exploit the new capability they can achieve a dramatic and insurmountable competitive advantage over the old order.

   Visionaries have an extraordinary influence on high tech because they are the first constituency who can and will bring real money to the table. In so doing, they provide at least as much seed funding for entrepreneurs as does the venture capital community. And because they tend to love the limelight, they also help publicize the new innovation, giving it a necessary boost to succeed in the early market.

But for all this there is a quid pro quo. Each visionary demands special modifications that no one else would dream of using, and quickly these demands begin to overtax the R&D resources of the fledgling enterprise. Sooner or later this forces companies to seek out a different kind of customer, one who really just wants what everybody else wants, a customer known as the pragmatist.

Taken together, technology enthusiasts and visionaries make up the *early market*. Although their personal motives are quite different, they are united by their drive to be the first, the techies desiring to *explore* and the visionaries desiring to *exploit* the new capability. No one else in the Technology Adoption Life Cycle has any interest in being first, as you can see from the remaining profiles:

3. **Early Majority = *Pragmatists*.** These people make the bulk of all technology infrastructure purchases. They do not love technology for its own sake, so are different from the techies, whom they are careful, nonetheless, to employ. Moreover, they believe in *evolution* not *revolution*, so they are not visionaries, either—indeed they shy away from them. Instead, they are interested in making their companies' systems work effectively. So they are neutral about technology and look to adopt innovations only after a proven track record of useful productivity improvement, including strong references from people they trust.

Pragmatists are the people most likely to be in charge of a company's mission-critical systems. They know this infrastructure is only marginally stable, and they are careful to protect it from novel intrusions. As such, they prove to be a tough nut to crack when the time comes for them to underwrite shifting to the new paradigm.

When they finally do make this shift, pragmatists prefer to buy from the market leader for two reasons. First, everyone else in the market makes their products work with the leader's, so while the leader's product may not be the best one, systems built upon it are going to be the most reliable. Second, the market leader attracts many third-party companies into its aftermarket, so that even when the leader is not responsive to customer requests, the marketplace as a whole is. As a result, pragmatists have determined that customers of market-leading vendors get a better overall value from the market.

4. **Late Majority = *Conservatives*.** These customers are pessimistic about their ability to gain any value from technology investments and undertake them only under duress—typically because the remaining alternative is to let the rest of the world pass them by. They are very price-sensitive, highly skeptical, and very demanding. Rarely do their demands get met, in part because they are unwilling to pay for any extra services, all of which only reconfirms their sour views of high tech.

   Conservatives nonetheless represent a largely untapped opportunity for high-tech products, holding out the promise of a horde of new customers who can be brought into the market if handled with care, albeit presenting deep challenges to the vendors who elect to serve them. The key to winning their business and profiting is to simplify and commoditize systems to the point where they just work. Conservatives, in other words, are happy to buy several dozen of the world's most advanced microprocessors, as long as they are deeply embedded inside a BMW.

5. **Laggards = *Skeptics*.** These are the gadflies of high tech, the ones who delight in challenging the hype and puffery of high-tech marketing. They are not so much potential customers as ever-present critics. As such, the goal of high-tech marketing is not to sell to them but rather to sell around them.

Linked all together these five profiles make up the Technology Adoption Life Cycle. The idea of developing the market by working from one profile to the next provided the basis for high-tech marketing strategy in the 1980s. The desired progression went as follows:

- Begin by seeding new products with the *technology enthusiasts* so they can help you educate the *visionaries*.
- Once you have captured the *visionaries'* interest, do whatever it takes to make them satisfied customers so that they can serve as good references for the *pragmatists*.
- Gain the bulk of your revenue by serving *pragmatists*, ideally by becoming the market leader and setting the de facto standards.
- Leverage success with the *pragmatists* to generate sufficient volume and experience so that products become reliable enough and cheap enough to meet the needs of the *conservatives*.
- As for the *skeptics*, leave them to their own devices.

Introducing the Chasm

Unfortunately, as logical and attractive as this strategy appeared in theory, in actual practice it did not work very often. Specifically, companies kept stumbling every time it came to making the transition from the visionaries to the pragmatists. The problem was that these two groups, although adjacent on the adoption life cycle, are so different in terms of underlying values as to make communication between them almost impossible, as the following comparison illustrates:

Visionaries	Pragmatists
Intuitive	Analytic
Support revolution	Support evolution
Contrarian	Conformist
Break away from the pack	Stay with the herd
Follow their own dictates	Consult with their colleagues
Take risks	Manage risks
Motivated by future opportunities	Motivated by present problems
Seek what is possible	Pursue what is probable

Perhaps the easiest way to epitomize the differences between these two groups is to contrast the way they use the phrase "I see." When visionaries say "I see," they do so *with their eyes closed*. That's how visionaries *see*. Pragmatists, on the other hand, like to see with their eyes open. They don't trust visionaries for the same reasons that they don't trust people who want to navigate using *the force*.

In short, visionaries think pragmatists are pedestrian, and pragmatists think visionaries are dangerous. As a result, visionaries, with their highly innovative—not to say hare-brained—projects do not make good references for pragmatists, and market development, instead of gliding across this transition point, stalls. Unfortunately, by the time that high-tech firms were getting this far into the market, they were so highly leveraged financially that any hiccup (and this stall tended to hit more like a whooping cough) would throw them into a tailspin—or, as we came to call it, *into the chasm.*

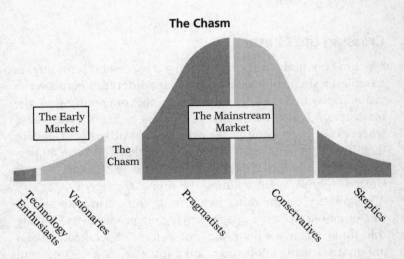

The Chasm

The idea of the chasm is a simple one. It says that whenever truly innovative high-tech products are first brought to market, they will initially enjoy a warm welcome in an *early market* made up of technology enthusiasts and visionaries but then will fall into a *chasm*, during which sales will falter and often plummet. If the products can successfully cross this chasm, they will gain acceptance within a *mainstream market* dominated by pragmatists and conservatives. Since for product-oriented enterprises virtually all high-tech wealth comes from this third phase of market development, crossing the chasm becomes an organizational imperative.

Unfortunately, too few innovative products were actually getting across. What was happening instead was that investors, flushed with the results of early-market acceptance, became impatient to see an immediate transition into a high-growth, high-profit mainstream marketplace. That, after all, was what the life-cycle model predicted. When they got chasm results instead, they assumed that management was somehow at fault, and in trying to correct these faults, they ended up more often than not destabilizing operations to a point from which they could never recover.

Fortunately, as the chasm idea has caught on, this is all beginning to change.

Crossing the Chasm

The fundamental strategy for making a successful "crossing" is based on a single observation: the main difference between the visionaries of the early market and the pragmatists in the mainstream is that the former are willing to bet "on the come" whereas the latter want to see solutions "in production" before they buy. That is, when a visionary sees that you have 80 percent of the solution to her problem, she says, "Great, let's get started right away on building the other 20 percent together." A pragmatist, on the other hand, says, "Wait a minute—aren't *you* supposed to be the one improving *my* productivity? I'll buy this thing when it's done but not before." Specifically, what pragmatists want, more than anything else, is a 100 percent solution to their problem—what we came to call the *whole product*.

The idea of the whole product has been around for some time, having initially been popularized by Theodore Levitt at Harvard and subsequently getting a lot of exposure in Silicon

Valley from Bill Davidow's *Marketing High Technology*. In the context of the chasm, however, it took on a radically simplified meaning. Basically, the whole product became defined as *the minimum set of products and services necessary to ensure that the target customer will achieve his or her compelling reason to buy*. In this light, we saw that high-tech companies were prolonging their stays in the chasm because they were unable, or unwilling, to commit to taking any particular whole product all the way through to this level of completion.

Here's what would happen instead. The high-tech enterprise, sensing it was in the chasm, and realizing that the customer needed more than just the bare product itself, would set out to address this problem. Instead of focusing on a single target customer, however, management would invariably recoil from putting all its eggs in one basket. Instead, it would target four or five likely candidate segments with the idea of focusing intensively on whichever opportunity caught fire first.

This decision was followed by a round of customer visits with major customers from each of the target segments, during which "wish lists" of requirements were painstakingly extracted and recorded. These lists were then reviewed by a product marketing council made up of marketing and engineering managers who would extract from them the common themes, the most broadly requested enhancements. These were the "nuggets," or key requirements, which defined the next release. In this way, when the next release came out, true to its intent, it had something for everybody.

Unfortunately, however, it had *everything* for nobody. That is, no one group ever got 100 percent of its whole product requirements fulfilled. We never finished any one customer's list. *But that is precisely the requirement that pragmatists insist upon before they purchase.* Pragmatists therefore would praise our efforts, pat us on the back, but they would not buy our product. So after a round of development, which in turn required a round of funding, the company garnered a round of applause, but alas, not a round of sales.

It was only then that some of us came to the counter-intuitive—indeed horrifying—realization that *the only safe way to cross the chasm is in fact to put all your eggs in one basket.* That is, the key to a winning strategy is to identify a single beachhead of pragmatist customers in a mainstream market segment and to accelerate the formation of 100 percent of their whole product. The goal is to win a niche foothold in the main-stream as quickly as possible—that is what is meant by *crossing the chasm.*

An Example

When *Crossing the Chasm* was written, all its examples were drawn from companies who had crossed the chasm more or less inadvertently. That is, since we did not have a specified concept for this transition period (although many savvy investors and executives knew about it intuitively), it was hard to have an explicit strategy for negotiating the passage. Subsequently, however, companies have had a chance to incorporate these ideas into their plans with good success. One such company is Documentum.

Documentum is in the document management software business with high-end systems that were originally designed at Xerox. Virtually unknown until 1994, it had spent the early part of the 1990s in the chasm, limping along at a few million dollars per year in revenues, taking on a new visionary every year, with nothing much to show for it. In 1994, it came out of nowhere to become the overwhelmingly dominant supplier of systems to the pharmaceutical industry, beginning with the specific niche of Computer Aided New Drug Approval (CANDA). How was it able to do this?

At the end of 1993, in a series of management meetings, Documentum's executive team reviewed some eighty or so candidate beachhead segments. From these they narrowed it down to their target based on five criteria:

1. Is the target customer well funded and are they readily accessible to our sales force?
2. Do they have a compelling reason to buy?

3. Can we today, with the help of partners, deliver a whole product to fulfill that reason to buy?
4. Is there no entrenched competition that could prevent us from getting a fair shot at this business?
5. If we win this segment, can we leverage it to enter additional segments?

In the case of pharmaceutical companies, there was no question that they were well funded, and the target customer for this application is readily accessed, being a specific department whose sole job is to handle regulatory submissions. So it passed the first hurdle.

As to the compelling reason to buy, over the life of a typical patented drug, revenues average $400 million per year. Patents last for seventeen years, but that period starts with patent award not regulatory approval. Every day of delay from that point on costs the drug company $1 million in lost revenue opportunity. That felt compelling enough for the team at Documentum.

It was the whole product that was the real challenge. The CANDA document set typically ranges from 200,000 to 500,000 pages, coming from scores of different sources, some computerized, many not. Documentum focused all its systems development and all its whole product marketing on pulling this specific set of highly diverse sources together. To do so it had to draw heavily on partnership resources from much larger vendors like Sun, Oracle, and CSC (Computer Sciences Corporation). But from their experience with a project funded by a visionary at Syntex, the company could see this was feasible, and so the segment passed this test.

As to competition, while other competitors were far bigger, more technically accepted, with more established user groups, none had really stepped up to the entire CANDA challenge. Through its special efforts Documentum felt it would be able to fundamentally change the economic equation and communicate that fact to the economic buyers.

And finally, if it won the CANDA application in pharmaceutical, it could readily expand forward both into other departments within pharmaceutical, such as manufacturing and R&D, as well as other FDA-regulated industries such as medical equipment and food processing.

What was the result of all this? In the space of a year, from the go-ahead in first quarter of 1994 to the end of that calendar year, Documentum garnered 30 of their top 40 target customers. In the same space of time their closest competitor won only one. Their revenue run-rate for that year tripled and is on target to triple again. They are the unquestioned market leader in this segment, which gives them far more influence than their size warrants. They can never be dislodged from this marketplace, indeed cannot, from the pharmaceutical industry's point of view, be allowed to go out of business. As such, they are now set up to attack the market from a position of strength and have strong prospects for market expansion. Such is the power of crossing the chasm.

The key point to close with here is the powerful impact on market development of gaining one's first niche in the mainstream. To cite another example, consider the difference between the current status of pagers and pen-based personal digital assistants in the market today. Most people don't carry either. But if you ask someone, If you carried a pager, do you think it would work?, most people answer yes. When asked the same question about a PDA, most answer no. When asked why, they point to the fact that they have seen certain categories of people use pagers routinely—doctors, LAN administrators, and other people on call—whereas they do not know any group of people that uses PDAs routinely. As a result, they are much more willing to consider adopting the former than the latter. This is a key part of the reasoning behind gaining a beachhead. Not only does it gain you some immediate customers, it also makes it much easier for all future customers to buy in.

Beyond the Chasm

Inside the Tornado is focused on mapping the marketplace beyond the chasm. It focuses on three subsequent stages in the life-cycle model, as illustrated by the following figure:

The Landscape of the Technology Adoption Life Cycle

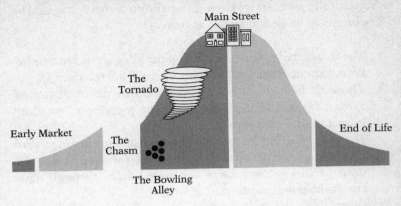

The map divides up the landscape into six zones, which are characterized as follows:

1. *The Early Market,* a time of great excitement when customers are technology enthusiasts and visionaries looking to be first to get on board with the new paradigm.
2. *The Chasm,* a time of great despair, when the early-market's interest wanes but the mainstream market is still not comfortable with the immaturity of the solutions available.
3. *The Bowling Alley,* a period of niche-based adoption in advance of the general marketplace, driven by compelling customer needs and the willingness of vendors to craft niche-specific whole products.
4. *The Tornado,* a period of mass-market adoption, when the general marketplace switches over to the new infrastructure paradigm.
5. *Main Street,* a period of aftermarket development, when the base infrastructure has been deployed and the goal now is to flesh out its potential.
6. *End of Life,* which can come all too soon in high tech because of the semiconductor engine driving price/performance to unheard of levels, enabling wholly new paradigms to come to market and supplant the leaders who themselves had only just arrived.

The thesis of this book is that business strategy must change dramatically as marketplaces move through these stages. The key points of its argument are as follows:

- The forces that operate in the bowling alley argue for a niche-based strategy that is highly customer-centric (chapter 3).
- Those in the tornado push in the opposite direction toward a mass-market strategy for deploying a common standard infrastructure (chapter 4).
- Then on Main Street market forces push back again toward a customer-centric approach, focusing on specific adaptations of this infrastructure for added value through mass customization (chapter 5).
- Given these dramatic reversals in strategy, it is imperative that organizations be able to agree on where their markets are in the life cycle (chapter 6 and the end of Part One).
- In the meantime, the economic cataclysm of the tornado deconstructs and reconstructs the power structure in the market so rapidly that simply understanding who is friend and who is foe becomes a challenge (Part Two, chapter 7).
- Within this newly emerging market structure, companies must compete for advantage based on their status within it (chapter 8).
- Positioning in this context consists of a company taking its rightful place in the hierarchy of power and defending it against challengers (chapter 9).
- And finally, moving fluidly from strategy to strategy is the ultimate challenge of any organization, demanding an extraordinarily flexible response from its management team (chapter 10 and the close of Part Two).

With these directions in one hand, and our map in the other, we can now set out to follow our Yellow Brick Road.

IN THE BOWLING ALLEY

For Dorothy to get to the Emerald City of Oz, she had to journey through a number of strange lands. Just so for the high-tech enterprise, which having just left the chasm and established itself on a beachhead, is now invited to proceed further into—*a bowling alley?* Well, yes, if only to make a point.

The bowling alley represents that part of the Technology Adoption Life Cycle in which a new product gains acceptance from niches within the mainstream market but has yet to achieve general, widespread adoption. The goal of bowling alley marketing is to keep moving toward the tornado, to progress from niche to niche developing momentum. Each niche is like a bowling pin, something that can be knocked over in itself but can also help knock over one or more additional pins. As in bowling, so in marketing—the more pins, the more points—so what this chapter is intended to illustrate is a leveraged approach to niche marketing.

But why focus on niches in the first place? Why not just leap into the tornado? The answer is twofold. First, for many customers there is still plenty of life left in the old paradigm you are displacing. They might see the attractions of the new paradigm you are offering, but they have no compelling reason to move. Since infrastructure changes of any kind always entail hidden consequences, this part of the market instinctively holds back.

Second, although you have crossed the chasm and proven that for at least one niche you have a whole product that can displace the old paradigm, you have yet to prove that your new offering is *generalizable*. That is, a prime reason for focusing on a niche when crossing the chasm was to simplify the construction of the whole product. To transition now to a general-purpose whole product, which a tornado market requires, entails considerable additional work, both inside your own company and in recruiting a much larger set of partners and allies to develop a more complex and rich solution set.

When word processing, for example, first entered the marketplace, based on office minicomputer systems from Wang and others, it got niche adoption among law firms, government agencies, consultancies, and other organizations that generated a lot of boilerplate writing. Most other companies, looking at the purchase price, the extra staffing, and the training required, simply stuck to their typewriters. The same sort of history may be tracked for spreadsheets, which were initially adopted by financial professionals only (Lotus 1-2-3's primary early competitor on the IBM PC was an elaborate financial modeling package called Context MBA) or portable computers like the original Compaq, which were used initially almost exclusively by technical sales support professionals doing on-site demos, or DEC VAXs, which were originally for engineering professionals only, or for pagers, which were initially adopted primarily by doctors on call.

During this stage of the adoption life cycle, in other words, the general populace does not actually adopt the new paradigm, but it does get exposure to it. This helps soften up the mainstream market to participate at a later date in the hypergrowth of the tornado. But there is still great benefit in the present moment because bowling alley niche markets represent profitable repeatable business, and entrepreneurial enterprises can therefore fund themselves for the first time out of working capital, focusing on the discipline of making a profit and continuing to enhance and cost-reduce their offerings for future expansion.

Niches at this stage of the market are not large enough to support multiple vendors, nor are they comfortable doing so. They want instead to rally around a single vendor who has a highly application-specific solution tailored to their particular issues. To truly secure a segment, therefore, you must expel all other competitors and establish yourself as the dominant market leader.

This is not as hard as it may seem. By definition, given where you are in the life cycle, you have a terrifically innovative product. All you have to do is focus it on a segment of customers who have a compelling reason to buy, some pressing need they are currently unable to fulfill. You "enable" these customers by committing to finish their "wish list," completing their particular whole product, in return for which they give you their business. And once enough of them do that, word gets around that there is this company out there with a great new approach, and then they *all* give you their business. This same word-of-mouth mechanism also works to ward off any late-coming competitors because it has labeled you as the "right" vendor, a status you will keep for life (or at least until the next paradigm shift).

This is how the graphic arts community responded to Apple's desktop publishing offering, how Wall Street has responded to the trader workstations supplied by Sun and Sybase, how the banking community responded to Tandem Computers for Automated Teller Machines, and how the film industry is currently responding to Silicon Graphics. These are no fly-by-night commitments. Each can be expected to last a decade or more—a lifetime of loyalty in Silicon Valley years—representing as they do the considered and purposeful action of a group of pragmatist customers ensuring that their industry has the proper infrastructure with the proper support.

In short, being in the bowling alley means you have arrived in the mainstream market. You are "for real." Your product is endorsed by "real customers" (not visionaries), and it is obvious to everyone that with loyal customers like these you are not going out of business any time soon. Congratulations are in order.

At the same time, however, your status is not quite that of a fully established company, such as a Compaq, an Intel, or a Novell. These companies are defined as market leaders in the PC, microprocessor, and LAN markets, respectively. Their markets are defined by their *products*. Yours is not. Instead it is defined by your *customer's application*. At this stage, in other words, it is a desktop publishing market and not a PC market that Apple has won, an automated teller market and not yet a fault-tolerant computer market for Tandem, an entertainment market and not yet a 3-D workstation market for Silicon Graphics.

Unlike the tornado, then, where the product category itself becomes the reference point, in the niche markets of the bowling alley it is really the customer's market, not yours. This has important implications for strategy. You must understand that your power in the marketplace, while not nil, is adjunct. You are not yet really a player, more a protégé, with your niche-market customers being both your sponsors and your protectors. You must not stray from their protective umbrella too soon.

As your sponsors, these customers will testify to your value within their domain and afford you a plausible introduction into other niche markets that have some commerce with them. And as your protectors, they will stick by you, giving you the lion's share of their business even when you may not have the best product available, thereby providing you with some breathing room in a tight competitive race and a place to retreat in rough times. If you have not yet achieved your highest ambitions, you do, for the first time in the life cycle, have lasting friends and allies.

The Impact of Market Leadership

Now why are these companies being so kind to you? It is because they perceive you as their *market leader*, and their behavior is a measure of the status that pragmatist customers give to that title.

Pragmatists value foundations of order and stability on top

of which they can erect and evolve continuously improving systems. Markets without clear leaders lack such foundations and thus are inherently unstable. As of this writing, for example, there are no clear leaders in the object-oriented database or desktop video conferencing marketplaces, and not surprisingly there are no pragmatists investing in either one.

This is not for lack of interest. Most pragmatist IT (Information Technology) executives will tell you they see great value in both these technologies and fully expect them to be adopted broadly in their companies at some future date. But today, lacking a clear leader, these markets have no point of reference for standards, architectures, or vision. Without such guideposts it is impossible to make decisions with long-term implications—precisely the kinds of decisions pragmatist customers of high tech find themselves having to make all the time. As a result, these customers sit on the fence—they watch, they go to seminars, they talk to each other, but they do not adopt.

Once a clear market leader is established, on the other hand, order naturally emerges in a free-market system. The first thing that happens is that third parties realign themselves to be compatible with and complementary to the market leader's products and interfaces. Why? Because the leader has *created a market* for them. That is, every customer who has purchased the market leader's platform now becomes a potential aftermarket customer for their products or services as well. And as these third parties sell their products, an increasingly complete and valuable whole product grows up around the architecture specified by the market leader. Customers in turn are able to leverage this increasingly rich infrastructure to accomplish more and more buying objectives, thereby magnifying the return on their initial investment manyfold, which in turn drives more sales, attracting still more contributing elements to an ever-expanding whole product family.

In this kind of emerging market, these same partners and allies are naturally reluctant to support a second, less successful platform simply because it does not afford the same kind of leveraged opportunity. To be sure, if the market goes on into the tornado, these vendors will come back to work with secondary players—the volume they offer in that case will be sufficient to pay back the investment—but even then these platforms will always get second-class treatment. Which means the customer will get a second-class whole product. Which is one of the main reasons why most pragmatists not only buy from market leaders but are willing to encourage and reward these leaders with highly favorable treatment.

To be specific, pragmatist-dominated markets give the market leader an extraordinary set of competitive advantages, which they deny to all other competitors. This begins with the right to charge more money for the same product, even when that product may have a bug in it, as Intel's Pentium chip recently had, but which nonetheless continued to sell at a 33 percent premium over a bug-free clone from NexGen. Moreover, since market leaders like Intel are by definition shipping the highest volumes, they also enjoy the lowest cost per unit. Highest price plus lowest cost is a formula that is good for margins.

But it gets even better. Market leaders enjoy lower cost of sales because pragmatist customers *expect* to buy the market-leading product. Everyone else has to sell harder and longer if they are going to overcome this expectation. And because the leader is creating a burgeoning aftermarket for third parties, it does not have to pay to win their support—indeed, it can often charge these parties a fee, as Oracle does, for example, to port its database to any computer platform. Not so for the also-rans—indeed, they are lucky if they do not have to *pay* to get porting support. And so the list of advantages grows and grows. Whether it be in distribution, publicity, recruiting, or customer access, the market leader gets demonstrable, bankable advantages over every one of its competitors.

Once you understand how this system works, becoming a market leader becomes a fixation. Indeed, the prize of all prizes is to become a market leader in a tornado. But that goal is premature at this stage. The market is not yet ready to buy in as a whole. It still has too much invested in the old paradigm and will drag its feet for some time to come. If you try a broad frontal assault now, you will only consume your resources in advance of the real opportunity. Instead, it is time to focus on winning niches of the marketplace made up of customers who are marginalized under the old paradigm, not well served by it, and who find themselves under pressure to reengineer their businesses to become more competitive. These segments are very susceptible to conversion, a place where you can make rapid progress immediately, and at the same time gain strategic advantage for the upcoming tornado market battle.

The Example of PeopleSoft

Consider a company like PeopleSoft, the client/server software company that entered the market initially through the niche of Human Resources systems. The management team at People-Soft knew that the big wins in client/server applications would eventually come not from HR but from more mainstream business applications like financials, order processing, manufacturing, and the like. But they saw that it would take time for the market to feel comfortable entrusting such "mission-critical" systems to the new paradigm. An HR application, on the other hand, represented a much less risky place for customers to make their first move. PeopleSoft also knew from its past experience that the human resource function had been characteristically underserved by the marketplace while at the same time put under increasing pressure to reengineer itself for the next century. Here was a receptive and underserved end-user community ready to champion the PeopleSoft cause to an IT department that was looking for a safe test bed for its first foray into client/server systems.

So this is where PeopleSoft staked out its turf. Within a short time they were able to catapult themselves to a clear position of market leader in client/server HR systems, winning more than 50 percent market share. Because of their focus on this niche's compelling reasons to buy, PeopleSoft from the outset was able to charge a premium price, which means that HR has been a highly profitable business for them, allowing them to fund additional product and market initiatives. At the same time, because HR applications represented a safe way for major corporations to gain experience with client/server systems, it has also proved to be an exceptionally high-growth business. And finally, because HR applications led the first major breakthrough in client/server systems adoption, the company gained a reputation as a market leader in the entire client/server market—gaining them an amount of publicity that was out of proportion to their size but certainly not unwelcome.

Today, from this bastion of strength, PeopleSoft is venturing out into the broader client/server business systems marketplace with financial and manufacturing products. In this larger market, PeopleSoft is a small player when compared to the likes of an Oracle or an SAP. The former company had an early lead, in part because it had a financials application already in the market, in part because its database is the number one choice for supporting client/server applications. The latter company, SAP, headquartered in Germany, has recently taken the U.S. market by storm. Its 1994 performance in this category captured the market lead with a 34 percent share. A billion-dollar company like Oracle, SAP's performance in the client/server applications market grew from 1993 revenues of $140 million to a 1994 total of $367 million, a tornado-class 262 percent year-to-year growth.

In a head-to-head competition, without mitigating factors, one would expect PeopleSoft, at this time passing through the $100 million mark, would be blasted from the market by competitors with overwhelming advantages in investment capability and distribution channel size. Despite this mismatch, however, PeopleSoft *cannot be dislodged from the competition!* Their foothold as the unquestioned market leader in client/server HR affords them permanent access to the larger client/server marketplace, and no one can block it. That is, any company that is seriously interested in both human resources and financials will actively seek out a proposal from PeopleSoft, regardless of whose system they finally choose. That is the sales benefit that any established market leader gets. What PeopleSoft must do is focus intelligently on one or more classes of customers for whom a combined HR and financials solution, with strong HR capabilities, is the winning choice.

Such maneuvering for high ground is the essence of all marketing strategy. The key point here is that niche market leadership can be an extraordinary strategic asset as one moves out into broader market expansion, because it establishes a strong base of operations. The idea is not to settle down in the niche but to leverage it forward, to use it to bowl over additional niches, with the ultimate "strike" being a tornado-market victory.

With this strategy of keeping an eye toward the tornado in mind, let us turn to a company that is a little further along in the process—Lotus Development Corporation, with its product Notes.[1]

The Example of Lotus Notes

Notes represents one of the most extraordinary marketing achievements in recent years. Here is a product whose very nature is so hard to capture that to this day Lotus executives stumble on categorizing it. For a long time, they tried to define it in terms of "groupware," but ironically what has actually transpired is the opposite—it is now groupware that has come to be defined by Notes.

What Notes and its inventor, Ray Ozzie, brought to the world was a fundamentally new experience in information sharing based on a deliberate violation of the oldest law of database management. That law said that the first and most important function of a database was to stop the proliferation of files containing the same data by consolidating it all in a single place where it could be updated and controlled by a single piece of database management software.

Notes does just the opposite. At regularly scheduled intervals every Notes server communicates with every other Notes server it is linked to and asks, "What new information do you have that I don't?" All such data is then immediately swapped. Files don't just proliferate—they metastasize! It is a crazy way

---

[1] It is testimony to the high change of high tech that, between the galleys and the final printing of this book, Lotus has been acquired by IBM.

to manage data—but it turns out it is a fabulous way to share information. The reason is simple: at the end of the day, every one on any Notes server in the linkup knows what everyone else knows—all without anybody having to explicitly e-mail anything to anyone.

This technology is called *replication,* and it has become one of the hottest new ideas in database software, being adopted by Oracle and Sybase in their databases and eliciting a competitive response from Microsoft called Exchange. Today Notes holds a commanding edge against these competitors, however, despite their greater size and scope, and we shall see from our study of tornado market dynamics that it is highly improbable that it will ever be displaced as market leader in this category. Our focus at present, however, is to see how Lotus got into this highly favored position.

When Notes was first introduced, it was presented as a new paradigm for enterprise-wide communications and as such won the endorsement of visionaries like Sheldon Laube at Price Waterhouse, who bought 10,000 licenses of the product, arguably before it was really out of beta. But subsequently it languished in the chasm, an exciting new paradigm to be sure, and one that people wanted to keep an eye on, but far too difficult to describe, much less to implement, for any self-respecting pragmatist to readily adopt it. Moreover, it represented the daunting challenge of proliferating and supporting yet another whole new infrastructure—way too much to take on if one could avoid it.

To cross the chasm the Notes team moved their focus down from an enterprise-wide vision of corporate communication to the level of business solutions specific to particular functions. The first of these was global account management, with a specific focus on worldwide accounting and consulting firms, where they could leverage their Price Waterhouse experience. The compelling reason to buy was to give these firms enhanced account activity coordination on highly visible projects and proposals within the intensely political world of their *Fortune* 500 clients. In such an environment, having the latest news on who said what to whom can readily make the difference between success and failure, so it did not take long for the end users of the product to endorse it strongly. The whole product for this application, fortunately, was not much more than Notes itself.

From here it was a short step to global account management for any sales team, particularly within the high-tech sector, where e-mail had already paved the way for communicating on-line. Then, as the communication elements of the solution began to emerge, Lotus was able to migrate to another business function, customer service, especially in high-tech companies, where again, having up-to-date information on late-breaking events can decide whether an account is under or out of control, but where open and free information dissemination can also support creative solutions to problems coming from unin-tended—or rather unspecified—collaboration. From these niches yet another dimension emerged—incorporating the customer into the Notes loop. Now all of a sudden whole new opportunities for getting closer to the customer sprang up.

At the same time another form of "market contagion" was at work. The global account teams who started everything off were, of course, working with their clients. These clients began to get wind of the system and then get on the system, such that when the project team was done, and it was time to unplug Notes, they could not let go of it. From their point of view, it had become key to allowing geographically dispersed project teams to better coordinate their activities, most notably in R&D and product launches. So now, with multiple functions in the organization, some externally focused, others internally, the enterprise-wide vision of communication begins to look more and more plausible. What else, after all, have we all been calling for all these years, if not better communication?

In other words, Notes, even though as of this writing it has no strongly established competition, is already into the tornado phase of its market development. Attendance at its third-party user conference, LotuSphere, is growing at 100 percent per year as more and more companies want to get on what promises to be a highly lucrative bandwagon. *Computerworld*, that bastion of the pragmatist majority, has repeatedly given it front-page status. Mind you, the whole product for Notes still lags considerably. At present it still does not scale well to enterprise-level applications, the application environment is still immature, and there are as yet too few third-party applications that have been tested to the comfort of a pragmatist buyer. Nonetheless, end users are simply demanding this new style of information sharing, and so IT, despite its better judgment, is getting swept up into winds of change.

And all this is traceable back to a cascade of niche markets developing one on top of another, an effect illustrated by the *bowling pin model*.

The Bowling Pin Model

The purpose of the bowling pin model is to approach niche market expansion in as leveraged a way as possible, to bowl toward the tornado. Each niche, you will recall, requires its own whole product to be fully complete before it can adopt the new paradigm. At the same time, it finds it much easier to buy in if vendors can supply references from an "adjacent niche," one within which it already has established word-of-mouth relationships.

If we go after niches at random, driven solely by sales opportunity, there is no such leverage at all. Each whole product must be built from scratch, and it is only chance if some prior customer is referenceable. But look what happens when we build this principle into the core of our market development strategy:

Bowling Alley Market Development

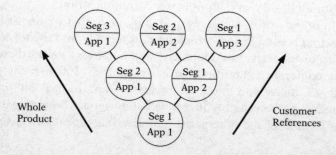

The head bowling pin in this model corresponds to the beachhead segment, the one that was the complete focus of the crossing-the-chasm effort. Every other pin is "derived" from this head pin. Let's look at this in the context of a specific example.

Apple in the Bowling Alley

In the case of the Apple Macintosh, Segment 1 was *in-house graphic artists* and Application 1 was *desktop publishing*. The idea then became to leverage two key assets from success in that segment to facilitate entry into related segments.

The first of these was *customer references*. Staying within the graphic artist community, after desktop publishing, which grew up around Aldus's Pagemaker, additional applications evolved including desktop presentations, around MacDraw first and then Aldus's Persuasion and Microsoft's PowerPoint, and then file sharing and e-mail to enhance exchanges with client groups. These applications were much easier to bring on-line because the customer segment was already familiar with the Macintosh, and people could watch others use it, try it out themselves, and then adopt knowing there was someone else around who could help them when they got in trouble.

At the same time, another form of market development leverage is also at work, this one based on extending the *whole product*. Desktop publishing was fine for in-house artists, but it needed extensions in order to serve agency-based graphic artists in advertising and publications. As these higher-end capabilities came on-line, the whole product went through another series of mutations, focused on color separation and pre-press requirements, to be adoptable by professional publishers. Each extension of the whole product, however, built on previous work and on already established relationships with third parties. As a result it grew much more rapidly than would otherwise have been possible.

Now, Apple did not use the bowling alley model to drive its marketing strategy. It more or less fell into it by chance, with the help of some strong marketing allies and some good executive judgment. The goal nowadays is to achieve these same effects by planning. To do this, let us revisit the case of Documentum.

You will recall the company crossed the chasm by focusing all its energies on the pharmaceutical segment and the CANDA application. Here is one plausible way it might proceed from there:

Sample Bowling Alley Strategy

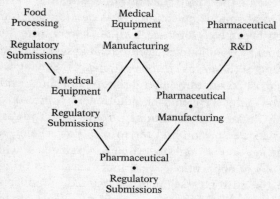

The idea behind this map is simply to leverage the assets acquired by winning the first beachhead. Thus, if we have become the darling of the pharmaceutical industry for regulatory submissions, and they have already gone through the adoption process for an advanced document management, let us now bring to them ways they can extend that capability to their other functions. In manufacturing, they have regulatory demands to track drugs by lot, and in R&D they have literature search needs that go well beyond what other industries require. To be sure, such extensions would demand additional whole product investment, but they could build on the infrastructure already in place.

Similarly, taking the regulatory affairs application outward into medical equipment and food processing—other industries governed by the Food and Drug Administration—offers leverage, this time based on cloning the whole product. Again, there would be modifications required, typically calling for simplification and cost reduction as one moves into markets with less compelling reasons to buy, but all made possible by leveraging the sunk costs of the initial whole product R&D.

Finding additional leverage is critical to high-tech strategy for the simple reason that whole product creation is an expensive and time-consuming process. Indeed, if one never got beyond the initial beachhead segment, it is questionable whether these customers alone could ever pay back the full investment it took to secure them in the first place. But if one can take that same investment and, with modest additional work, secure entirely new niches, now one has a terrifically profitable proposition. That, of course, is the goal of bowling pin strategy.

Whenever you see companies expanding by bowling pin strategy, as long as they can continue to find new applications for their sustainable whole product leverage, they are virtually undefeatable. It is just too hard for a competitor to match their whole product's total value, given that market standards and third party support have already formed around the architecture of the incumbent leader. Conversely, whenever you see companies abandoning their historic sources of whole-product leverage in order to enter new markets, they become exceptionally vulnerable. This is because they are so used to having an unfair competitive advantage, they cannot see that they no longer have that protection. We can see this principle working itself out in recent developments with Sun Microsystems.

The Example of Sun

Sun got its start in the early market by introducing a paradigm shift from proprietary to open systems. This was an extraordinarily visionary concept, championed by Sun's resident technology enthusiast, Bill Joy, and its resident business visionary, Scott McNealy. The entire Unix community rallied around this flag. That being said, however, not one pragmatist moved an inch.

To gain entry into mainstream markets, Sun attacked a number of niche markets including Computer Aided Software

Engineering (CASE), Computer Aided Design (CAD), and technical publications. In each case it was able to leverage software in the public domain to accelerate the development of its whole product offerings. Later on, it launched additional initiatives, specifically into ECAD (CAD for the electronics industry, focused on semiconductor and systems design), scientific computing (such as molecular modeling for chemistry), and Geographical Information Systems (GIS) for a variety of mapping applications. In all these arenas Sun succeeded admirably.

Somewhere along the line, as these bowling pins began crashing into one another, the marketplace converted from a set of verticals to a single horizontal category—*the technical workstation marketplace*. That is, Sun's own *product* category became the dominant *market* category. Workstations were no longer an adjunct to some other established market but had become a market in their own right.

As we shall see in the next chapter, this is a key tornado signal. Whatever company is leading in market share when this happens becomes institutionalized as that new market's leader. In Sun's case, while Apollo had been in the *product category* well before Sun and had shown terrific results, when the *market category* finally became visible, it was Sun, not Apollo, that was in the lead, and it was Sun, not Apollo, that garnered all the benefits of market leadership.

So far the market played well to Sun's strengths and vice versa. But two subsequent developments have exposed weaknesses in Sun's position. First, although a strong market for commercial Unix servers has emerged in the 1990s, Sun's technical desktop orientation, both in its factories and in its field sales force, has kept it from being competitive. That market has instead gone to HP, with challenges from IBM, DEC, and AT&T, all displacing the earlier successes of Sequent and Pyramid— with Sun nowhere near as visible as one would have expected, given its size and strength. At the same time, as Sun has tried to expand its workstation paradigm to intercept the PC's growth, it has been cut off by the surprising price/performance acceleration from Intel and Microsoft. This has created a "No Vacancy" sign on all but a few commercial desktops and threatens indeed to invade Sun's traditionally unchallengeable technical domain.

What happened here? One way to put it is to say that once Sun leapt from the bowling alley into its first tornado—the technical Unix market—it abandoned its niche market approach in order to serve massive demand. So far, so good. When it came, however, to going outside that domain, Sun tried to extend its tornado tactics to encompass the new territories of commercial servers and commercial desktops. This did not work. Here's why.

In neither case was the Sun whole product complete, and in neither case was it positioned as the incumbent market leader. In the case of servers, it badly lacked legacy system integration on the product side and on the service side it lacked a sales and support capability appropriate to large commercial installations. In the case of the commercial desktop, it lacked an appropriate accommodation with the legacy of Microsoft DOS and Windows applications. To be sure, it worked hard on this problem, introducing its own software to emulate Windows as well as supporting third parties like Insignia solutions with its Soft PC product line. But the IT community in *Fortune* 500 companies has been too often burned in the past by emulated environments and so refused to accept these accommodations.

As a result, Sun is having to rethink its whole position in the marketplace and its strategy for going forward. In so doing, it needs to keep in mind the following principles for bowling alley strategy as it seeks to penetrate market spaces that are not part of its traditional hegemony.

Two Principles Even a CEO Should Know

The first principle of bowling alley strategy is never attack a segment whose current expenditures on your category of product exceed your current annual revenue. Or, to put it in the playground vernacular: *Pick on somebody your own size.* Here's why.

In the bowling alley, looking forward to the tornado, your primary goal is to get your architecture adopted as the market-leading standard in as many niches as possible. It is a bit like competing in a primary election. Each niche validates your solution, both literally, in the sense that it proves out your whole product, and figuratively, in that it shows that another constituency has thrown its support to your standard. The goal is to capture a bandwagon of support heading into the key nomination period, when the tornado market elects its leader.

Now, to be sure, winning a California– or New York–size segment has more impact than winning the nomination of an Alaska or an Hawaii, but winning any one state is far superior to showing up second or third in a whole series of them. So it is with market leadership. To gain any one of these bowling-alley-primary votes, you must achieve clear market dominance within a specific segment. As long as the market remains fragmented or there is another competitor with an equally valid claim to the lead, you have not won anything. Or rather, you have won a lot of things but none that speak to your tornado longings.

To dominate a segment typically means winning 40 percent or more of its new business over the past year to eighteen months. At that level of success—assuming your closest competitor is well behind you—word of mouth in the marketplace starts spreading the message that you are the market leader. Once that happens, you can expect your share of the following twelve months' sales to increase to well beyond 50 percent. Pragmatists, more than anything else, want to buy what other pragmatists have bought.

So, the goal is 40 percent or more of a segment's purchases over the next twelve months. This already sets some limits on strategy. If the segment is already well served by another vendor, already has an established market leader, you have no chance of displacing that vendor in this time period. So we must be seeking an underserved segment that is actually not investing heavily at this time, there being no effective solution to its problem, but that would invest heavily if one appeared on the scene.

These are two key bowling pin target criteria, then:

1. The segment has a compelling reason to buy, and
2. The segment is not currently well served by any competitor.

Taken together, these two guarantee you an open field. Now the question is, how big a field can you handle?

To answer this question, look at your business plan. How much have you targeted to ship all told in the next year? Let us suppose it is $10 million, just because that is an easy figure to do math with. The next question is, what percentage of that $10 million will come from the target segment? Not 100 percent, I can assure you, not unless your product only works for one application, in which case there should be no near-term tornado aspirations in your future plans anyway. So let us assume instead that you really motivate your sales force and focus your marketing and that 60 percent of your revenue comes from your target. That equates to $6 million, which is 40 percent of $15 million, which is the maximum amount of spending in the next year your target segment can do and still have you end up the dominant supplier to it.

And that's for your first target segment. As you consider your second target—and bowling alley strategy pretty much implies you have already knocked over the head bowling pin—you may expect to have even less of your total resources to commit to the new segment because a lot will still be tied up completing and extending commitments in your first niche. Hence the rule of thumb is: Don't attack any segment bigger than you are; pick on somebody your own size.

Here is where companies flushed with their early bowling alley successes tend to make a serious strategic error. Feeling the momentum from their initial segment, they underestimate what it will take to win over the next new segment and thus underinvest in their attack on it. This has the impact of creating demand for the new category of solution but not fulfilling it, which means *it creates a market for some other competitor.*

Now, often as not, these competitors are as clueless as we are, and the company gets away with this mistake. Indeed, one can even choose to bet that competitors are out of position to handle the problem, thereby allowing yourself to stretch your resources across more segments, increasing your vulnerability but also increasing the territory captured if no one catches you out in the interim. But the key point to grasp here is that you are taking a serious risk, and you should not do so lightly or, more important, ignorantly.

The safe path—if there is such a thing in business—is to overinvest when invading any new segment, seeking to accelerate your rise to market leadership, and then to divert resources as soon as the position is achieved. The challenge here is to have a superbly engineered whole product so that you can fulfill this newly created demand without having to tie yourself down with ongoing customization commitments. That is the only way to keep resources free to reallocate.

So, one of the key criteria to use when selecting target segments in the bowling alley is, are they small enough—not big enough—to serve our strategic ends? If they are not, it does not mean you should not sell to these customers. It just means you cannot gain market leadership status from them. They should instead be treated as opportunistic sources of revenue and not as stepping-stones toward a generalizable market leadership position.

The Second Principle

The other key principle in bowling alley strategy is to focus market development efforts on the end-user community, not on the technical community. Specifically, you want to enlist the support of the *economic buyer*, the line executive or manager in the end-user organization who has profit-and-loss responsibility for the given function your product serves. Conversely, you should not expect to secure primary sponsorship from the IT professionals, specifically the IT director, responsible for the enterprise's overall infrastructure deployment and maintenance. Here's why.

In the bowling alley, you are asking a company to adopt a new paradigm in advance of the rest of the market. This is not in the interests of the IT department. It means extra work for them, and it exposes their mission-critical systems to additional risk. A far better strategy for them is to stay with their current paradigm a while longer, experimenting with the new one off-line, but not embracing it. That way they get the best of both worlds, minimizing disruption and shock while preparing for a future transition. Given this, it is simply bad strategy to ask these technical buyers to champion you at this time.

Instead you must turn to the end-user community and specifically to the economic buyers within it. These people are normally the bosses of the end users you want to actually use your system, and you are specifically seeking the subset that is underserved by the current IT systems in place. Here's how you approach them:

- You offer to use your innovative product to break the back of some heretofore unsolvable problem that is costing them money.
- You gain their attention by showing them that this problem is inherent in the current IT infrastructure's paradigm for supporting their end users.
- You then show that you can solve this problem readily because your new paradigm effectively redesigns the end-users' work flow to eliminate the problem's root cause.
- At the same time, you show how you have thoroughly studied their particular application requirements, so that not only do you have the core product necessary to bring off this miracle, you have the whole product as well.
- By methodically working through all the elements of this whole product, demonstrating your deep familiarity with their business, you overcome their pragmatist resistance and gain their sponsorship.

Now please note that this same series of offers could have been presented to the technical buyers who would certainly have understood and appreciated them. It is just that it would not have been in their interests to act on them, not yet anyway.

Nor, interestingly enough, would it necessarily have been in the interests of the end users who report to the economic buyer. From their point of view, the old paradigm is more familiar and secure. In the short term, with the learning curve required to come up to speed on the new one, they are actually going to be less effective. So they may resist you as well. It is only the economic buyer, who has to pay the ongoing cost of the status quo but can no longer afford to do so, who can be counted on to be unequivocally supportive of change at this time.

This helps explain the success of vertical marketing—and the failure of horizontal marketing—during the bowling alley. If you market a technology-based product horizontally, as globally deployable infrastructure, you do so using terminology that is most familiar to technical buyers. As a consequence, they are the ones to whom the rest of the company cedes decision-making authority. After all, this is *their turf*. As we have just noted, however, it is bad strategy to play on this turf during the bowling alley. Conversely, if you market your product vertically, focusing on the economic impact of application issues specific to particular business functions in particular industries, then you frame the opportunity in a vocabulary that increases the authority of the economic buyer. Now you have moved the purchase decision onto their turf, which is where you do want to play.

This principle helps explain why a company like Lotus has been so successful with an innovative product like Notes while companies like Hewlett-Packard and NeXT have proved far less successful with equally innovative products like NewWave and NextStep. Five years apart in their entry into the marketplace, these latter two products represented extraordinary leaps in technology at the time of their introduction. NewWave is now no more, and NextStep has yet to achieve broad market success, certainly not of the scope of Notes. The reason, in both cases, I would argue, is that their marketing has been predominantly horizontal. This, in turn, has been largely an outgrowth of each enterprise being led by an extraordinary visionary—in the case of HP, by Bob Frankenberg, who subsequently moved on to be CEO of Novell, and in the case of NeXT, by Steve Jobs.

Visionary leaders are gifted by their ability to communicate to the rest of the world the enterprise-wide implications of paradigm shifts, and they find great success and reinforcement in the early market, where their technology-based vocabulary resonates with technology enthusiasts and fellow visionaries. But this same vocabulary, as we have just seen, sets up the wrong approach for crossing the chasm and entering the bowling alley because it plays into the hands of the pragmatist IT staff and away from gaining the needed support of line executives. It is not that these visionary leaders cannot tone it down for pragmatists. They can indeed do this, but what they cannot do is fully commit to any single niche. To them that is like taking the number system in its entirety and committing to only one operation, say addition, and then only with even numbers divisible by four. It just doesn't make sense.

But of course it does make sense if you are an auto dealer taking inventory on the number of tires on your lot, a blacksmith planning to shoe a herd of horses, or a facilities manager arranging chairs for a bridge tournament. It is just this sort of localization that is required to shift the locus of power in the purchase decision from the general case, which is supervised by infrastructure buyer, to the specific case, which is governed by the local economic buyer. Now, to be sure, at the end of the day, the two must cooperate to move forward, so what we are really talking about here is not an either/or situation but rather a subtle shift of power. Nonetheless, it is a critical shift of power, and without it bowling alley strategy cannot succeed.

To sum up, the bowling alley requires the sponsorship of the economic buyer to overcome the technical buyer's—and potentially the end-users'—reluctance to support a new paradigm in advance of the rest of the market. In order to elicit this support, you must frame the buying issues in vocabulary that economic buyers can sponsor, otherwise they will defer to the domain expertise of the technical buyer. Taking a vertical marketing approach accomplishes this objective, whereas taking a horizontal approach defeats it.

Two Rewards from Bowling Alley Strategy

The purpose of the bowling pin model is twofold—make money now and accumulate credits toward being declared a market leader in a future tornado.

First, to the immediate goal, your priorities are to grow your business, increase your profits, and further develop your whole product. Your market focus is niche, your selling style is consultative (typically via a direct sales force or a well-educated indirect one), and your differentiation is segment-specific expertise. You are a true partner to your customer, and your customer knows you as such.

At the same time, you should always have in mind the longer-term goal, to emerge as the market leader when the market does go into the tornado. The occasion for this occurring is the moment it becomes more efficient and more effective for the marketplace to reorganize itself away from niche markets and rally instead around the emerging product category. This reorganization occurs at the outset of the tornado. At that time, the name of the market category itself will have been kicking around for some time—people will have been *talking* about this market for years—but it is only now that in fact it *becomes* a market, because it is only now that a sufficient amount of visibly predictable future wealth has amassed to make it worthwhile to generate a new market institution.

In the world of internetworking, for example, before there were the two currently dominant market categories of *hubs* and *routers*, there was a period when companies sold *bridges*, and then *routers*, and then a combined entity called for a while a *brouter*. All during this period, sales were being made, companies coming into and going out of the market, consolidations occurring—but there was no stable market in place. Instead, it was all handled as an adjunct to the LAN market. But with the rise of Cisco Systems, in particular, as well as Bay Networks and Cabletron, too much wealth got concentrated into too small a space to treat that space as an adjunct entity. As Senator Everett Dirksen used to say, "A billion here, a billion there, pretty soon it adds up to real money."

When the sales of a given category of product add up to real money, the market shifts its underlying organization to accommodate a new market category. At this time, whichever company has the lead in market share, becomes the declared market leader. The actual shift occurs during the tornado, but the preparation for winning this contest occurs during the bowling alley. It is here that the decisions are made that catalyze or cripple your chances.

It is perhaps easier to see this when it *doesn't* happen, than when it does. Take the pen-based computer market, for example. Despite all the attention, conversation, investment, and promotion it attracted a few years ago, it clearly does not exist today. In the terms of this book, it has yet to cross the chasm. What happened instead is that the major players within this market—Go Corporation, Momenta, and Microsoft—all tried to bypass the bowling alley and land right in the middle of the tornado. They *declared* a market, when in fact no such economic institution existed. Rather than utilize the protective covering of vertical markets, in other words, rather than nurture their whole products in private and emerge only when they had been fully hardened, rather than develop primary-election momentum, they all tried to *go horizontal* from the outset. Why? Because that's where the big money is, of course.

Sadly, such premature entrances into the mainstream are crippling, permanently. As the companies in artificial intelligence proved in the prior decade, any alleged market that burns through that much money—in the case of pen-based computing, perhaps $100 million in five or so years—and produces no sustainable market institution as a result, simply does not recover, even when the technology later becomes capable of delivering on the hype. The forces in the market cannot regroup, wiser and more ready, because they have already been disbanded. The market category name itself is now so discredited that no one wants to be associated with it. Thus the pen, when it finally does become useful, will have to shuffle into the market with downcast eyes, embarrassed by a past that frankly it did not deserve.

All this has transpired for want of spending some time in the bowling alley. Did bowling alley opportunities exist? Absolutely! Express-mail tracking, field-based insurance claims adjudication, home patient care nursing, car rental communications—all are actively using the technology today. Any one of these could readily have served as a head pin in a bowling pin array. No, the issue was not, and almost never is, opportunity availability. It is rather one of *patience*. And that is an attribute which puts bowling alley strategy directly at odds with the dynamics of venture investment.

Venture returns, as we shall see in the next chapter, come from one and only one source—winning first place in the tornado competition. Two of the three major pen-based computing companies were venture backed and rushed ahead way too fast because they were afraid that if they did not do so, others would get there first and they would lose out in the upcoming tornado competition. Microsoft then rushed in, as much as anything to defend its desktop position. Of the three, it was the only one who could afford to lose—indeed, given its status as the leader of the status quo infrastructure, its biggest win arguably would come from the entire category collapsing, as it did.

Lost in all this rush, particularly lost on the venture-backed companies, was the wisdom of the old Italian proverb, *"Festina lente"*—"Make haste slowly." You simply cannot rush past gestation. The bowling alley is not necessarily a slowing down—it can in fact be the fastest way to the tornado. It is a bit like mountain climbing. If you think you can get from the start to the top and back in one day, then there is no advantage to taking it slowly. But if you think it could take a lot longer than that—that in fact it might depend on getting the timing of the start just right, as tornado market development normally does—then the fastest way to the top begins with setting up a good base camp. That is what the bowling alley can provide.

The venture community should also recognize that bowling alley success is the best way for fledgling firms to get off the dole. That is, many VC's assume multiple rounds of funding, including some based on successive rounds of devaluation, because their funded companies do not make becoming finan-cially self-sufficient a critical intermediate milestone. Instead, they make the race for the tornado the only milestone. This not only denies them the staging benefits of a good base camp, it gives them no chance to internalize the disciplines of profitabil-ity, of making their own way in the world not by magic but by dint of hard work. When things do go wrong, when the wheels do come off, as they always must in the tornado, these firms have little to fall back on.

Overall, then, there is very little to lose and a lot to gain from a bowling alley approach. Vertical market niches are great places to make money. By focusing on a target niche to a degree that competing companies in your product category are either unwilling or unable to match, you can exclude even the toughest competitor. Moreover, by taking the time to understand in depth the true dynamics of a particular niche's value chain, you can be far more successful in transforming the potential in your high-tech solution into actual realized profits—first for your customer, and then by extension, for yourself. This in turn makes niche markets natural hosts for value-based pricing, which is the most profitable form of pricing there is. Add to this that each vertical market supports its own highly efficient communications infrastructures, including a strong word-of-mouth channel, and watch your cost of marketing communications plummet. Add to this that, once a niche settles in on its market-leading solution, its loyalty lasts to the grave, and you can see why marketing professionals have long been advocates of this approach.

And yet, despite all of the above, vertical or niche marketing is, to use Shakespeare's phrase, "A custom more honored in the breach than in the observance." Why isn't it more prevalent?

The Case *Against* Bowling Alley Strategy

There are at least four *good* reasons why bowling alley strategy gets rejected and at least one really *bad* one. Let's get the bad one out of the way first. As we have already noted, the most visible form of high-tech marketing success is winning the tornado competition. To achieve this victory you must forego niche marketing. Therefore, if tornadoes equal success, and if that success excludes niche marketing, then niche marketing must be for chumps. Q.E.D.

No matter that life is not always a tornado. No matter that vertical marketing, when applied in advance of the tornado, can actually increase your chances of becoming the market leader once the tornado hits. No matter that *after* the tornado, as we shall see in chapter 5 on the Main Street phase of technology adoption, niche marketing will again become a key tool for growing markets and sustaining margins. Nope. If Bill Gates didn't use it for DOS or Windows, then we don't want to be associated with it, either.

Okay. That's the bad reason. Set that aside because there are four *good* reasons why vertical marketing strategies have not led to broad mainstream market success. They are:

1. *People are typically in too much of a hurry to execute bowling pin strategies properly. As a result, they have a well-earned reputation for not working.*

   This is the most common failure mode in niche marketing. Companies give lip service to it but simply do not engage the marketplace with anything like the commitment needed. Instead, they rewrite the first few paragraphs of their data sheets ("Report-writing software for banking!"), add three or four overheads to their canned sales pitch, buy a list of prospects in the segment, send out a mailing, gain a sale or two out of the process, and then move on to something else six months later.

   The problem here is that these companies are executing vertical marketing as if it were a sales promotion tactic instead of a *territory capture game*. The only way to get a proper return from vertical marketing is to become the number one vendor within the target segment. To achieve such success requires a whole product commitment that solves a critical problem for the niche and at the same time differentiates you from other vendors in your product category. This is not just a talk-the-talk ploy; it is instead a walk-the-walk strategy. Companies that do the former and not the latter get puny results, which in turn qualifies them to impugn any future suggestions they should take a vertical approach: "We tried that—it doesn't work for our type of product."

2. *Companies fall in love with their first few niches and settle down in them for life. They forget all about the tornado.*

I am of two minds regarding this outcome. As long as the market never reaches tornado potential, this should probably be viewed as a very smart trade-off. Every year you understand your target customers' business problems better and better, and every year you can gain an even stronger hold on their loyalty. You can actually refine your whole product, something the rest of high tech is always trying to find time to do but is never able to. After a few years, you "know everybody," and eventually you are incorporated into the segment's own trade associations and business networks. And most important, as long as there is no tornado, you are the best value provider in the marketplace and as such can enjoy the best profit margins. For established companies, these margins can be very good indeed.

The key issue then is, will there ever be a tornado? One market that becomes very interesting to discuss in this light is Geographical Information Systems (GIS). The current market leader is Earth Sciences Research Institute (ESRI), provider of the ArcInfo product line. For the past several decades it has dominated a series of niche markets serving geologists, map makers, agriculturists, real estate developers, military personnel, civil engineers, environmentalists, town planners, police departments, HMO program designers, and market researchers. ArcInfo's original file formats have long been the GIS de facto standard for sharing information, despite the fact that they are by now arcane and unwieldy. This means that when anyone adds a new product to the market it automatically becomes part of ESRI's whole product. At the same time, Jack Dangermond, its founder and chairman, has become so wired into the infrastructure of these markets that he has access to virtually every sales opportunity, as well as almost any strategic alliance in formation. In sum, his is a very strong position, one from which no company can realistically expect to remove him.

As fortified as this position is, however, if the GIS market ever does move into the tornado phase, then ESRI is probably going to lose its market leadership position. Here's why.

As we shall see in the next chapter, one of the keys to tornado success is to relentlessly simplify the whole product in order to make it more suited to general-purpose use and easier and less costly to deploy and maintain. All of this goes directly against the grain of bowling alley values, built around value-added channels of distribution providing niche-specific solutions. It is rare that a traditional vertical market leader can readjust itself to meet such a radically opposing set of demands.

Not only does the market leader have too great a stake in business as usual to want to make such a transition, everything in its experience to date tells it that such a transition is wrong, and that its customers will never go for it. And in a sense this is absolutely true: for some time to come this company's traditional customer base will not go for it. However, a huge new customer base, heretofore not even part of the market, will go for the new approach, and over time the sales to these new customers will dwarf the entire sales to date in the marketplace, and the company that gets the bulk of these new sales will become the new market leader going forward.

In the case of GIS this new customer base could come from marketing and sales organizations incorporating mapping into their basic information infrastructure. Sales territory design, sales performance analysis within territory, product acceptance analysis within territory, marketing communications planning—all these functions could glean new insights if they were able to see their data geographically displayed. To date, given the complexity of GIS, these groups have done without. Now, however, these mapping functions are for the first time showing up on people's desktops as new features built into the next generation of spreadsheets.

The question is, is sales and marketing data analysis and presentation a "killer app" for GIS. If it is, then corporations will start to demand greater and greater use of this software. ArcInfo systems are simply too complex and require too much value-added reseller assistance to deploy at tornado rates. Instead, companies like Strategic Mapping and Map-Info will have the advantage, and it will be one of them, or some other competitor yet to emerge, and not ESRI, that will be the gorilla.

How can making this error be prevented? Keep focused on the tornado and do not settle down into the bowling alley as a way of life. Treat the bowling alley as a phase—serve the market during this period, as described above, but do not build a company that locks itself into this business model. Keep a fine weather eye out for shifts in the wind. Finally, expect your tornado product to be *less* than, not *more* than, your bowling pin solution set, and look for ways to pare down rather than build up to create this offering.

3. *Companies get trapped by the lure of recurrent service revenues and never design a pared-down product that could break free from the need for value-added service support.*

This problem is closely related to the previous one, but the danger it poses is sufficiently subtle as to warrant separate treatment. Niche market solutions, particularly at their outset, require a heavy dose of *services* as well as *product*. Over time, however, these services should be designed into the product in order to reduce overall whole product cost and improve consistency and quality. So far, so good.

A difficulty arises, however, when the same firm that should be designing services out also has a stake in keeping them in, since they are providing attractive profit margins. Now when the product team decides, for example, that it can design out training, the services team cries foul: "We are making $1,000 per day with these classes—*don't touch them!*" Sure enough, the product teams get the message, and they don't object. Designing out the training wasn't that interesting a project in the first place. Instead, they take the opportunity to design in more complexity: a) because it makes the product more powerful and hence more fulfilling to make, and b) because it gives the service people even more work to do. This increasing escalation of functionality and service requirement will keep a product category in the bowling alley forever.

The lesson here is simple: If your service business is providing margins that are both cushy and sustainable, you are likely to protect it rather than design it out. That's fine, as long as you realize there is a cost. In other words, you are probably paying for this luxury by forsaking the tornado market opportunity. That is not always a bad decision—it just ought to be a conscious one.

4. *The structure of consumer markets does not support bowling alley strategy.*

The great attraction of the bowling alley is that it lets a fledgling company in a new product category focus its scarce resources within a relatively protected environment in order to grow and temper its whole product and develop a base camp of loyal customers. All the while the company is also making good money, since, within the confines of its targeted niche, the value of its solution warrants a whole product price point far higher than a general volume market would support. Sadly, this strategy is not typically available to support *consumer market* innovations. Here's why.

First, consumer markets are wedded to low-cost, commodity-oriented distribution channels. These channels unlike, say, VARs (Value Added Resellers) cannot field the focused expertise needed to penetrate a niche market with a brand-new whole product. But this is exactly the type of service and support expertise that products in a bowling alley market need.

Second, consumer markets cannot support scaling down from initially high introductory prices via a series of gradual price reductions over several generations of product, whereas industrial markets can. That is, in an industrial market, products can be successful at virtually any price point, provided the return warrants the investment. By carefully choosing one's bowling pins, one can scale from a relatively price-insensitive head pin where the value received is very high indeed, toward follow-on pins where the value, while not as great, is still higher than in the general market, leading eventually to the tornado, where the value for the general-purpose user is relatively low but still exceeds the now sufficiently reduced price. This scalability of customers makes industrial markets very conducive to bowling pin approaches.

Consumer markets, on the other hand, don't work this way. To be sure, they can get off to a good start with the technology enthusiasts and the prestige buyers, both of whom will purchase at relatively high prices just to be the first people to get the new toy. But after winning their business, there is no place to go next. Everyone else will hold back until the price point gets to a level typical for the category. For a long time vendors invest to lower their price points at high cost to themselves and at no return—witness the prolonged pain in the CD-ROM market, for example, until prices finally dipped down to a consumer-acceptable level. Of course, when this magic price barrier is broken, and a tornado hits, all is forgiven. But there is no safe intermediate haven, so if you get the timing wrong—and there is precious little data for getting it right—you can go broke before the tornado hits.

This is the challenge that the company 3DO is facing as of this writing. Its high-end game graphics capabilities offers an exciting consumer market opportunity, but it is *very expensive* to get started. The company has had to go public without a proven market because it had no way to generate sufficient working capital from continued private investment. Now its investors are all holding their breath to see if its CEO, Trip Hawkins, can start a 3DO tornado before the money runs out.

One way out of this dilemma, suitable for some products, is to cross the chasm in the business marketplace and then "go consumer" after the price point gets down to consumer levels. That is what the ink-jet printer business did at Hewlett-Packard. Ink-jets started life as low-cost alternatives to laser printers for small businesses. This, in itself, was a good living. But after they got under $800, they became attractive as a work-at-home printer, something that really took off after they got below $500. Now, at under $300, they can be marketed as consumer electronics, for incorporation into a home edutainment system or to send off to college with a departing child.

Conclusion

Niche marketing, the discipline that defines the bowling alley, has been badly misunderstood by high-tech firms fixated solely on the tornado. It is in fact a compelling strategy for managing the transition from the chasm to the tornado. Specifically, niche markets

1. *Simplify the whole product challenge* at a time when the fledgling enterprise and its partners cannot field a general-purpose whole product. As a result one can earn pragmatist customers immediately instead of having to wait for another round of development.
2. *Are inherently profitable,* with value-based pricing based on price points set by the inefficient status quo your solution is displacing. As such they can help a fledgling enterprise become self-funding, allowing it more control over the timing of its assault on the tornado market.
3. *Represent capturable territories* of loyal customer constituencies. As such they will sponsor your architecture in the upcoming de facto standards war of the tornado.
4. *Can be leveraged* so that victory in one segment cascades into victories in adjacent segments. If the cascade effect is pronounced enough, it can actually generate the tornado.

Of the many reasons why high-tech companies have failed to avail themselves of bowling alley strategy, the most significant is their inability to give up an R&D-based product-centric perspective and adopt a customer-based application-centric one. That is what vertical marketing requires—letting yourself be an adjunct to another industry's market in lieu of insisting on being the center of attention. If you examine the ego structures of high-tech's leading executives, you will find this is not their strong suit.

But this is not about ego. It is about money. And anyway, giving up the spotlight in the short term is a tactic for retaking it later on. There is no shame in being ambitious. The only shame is in not winning, especially when winning may be right within your grasp.

With that thought in mind, let us now turn to how to win in the tornado phase of the market.

INSIDE THE TORNADO

I am sometimes asked, why a *tornado?* Isn't that a rather destructive metaphor for what, after all, is the promised land to which all high-tech business plans aspire? Can't you couch it in more attractive terms, something more along the line of a roller coaster, perhaps, or some other theme park ride? I mean, for goodness sake, don't you know anything about *marketing?*

Well, here's my problem. Tornadoes, when they occur, *are* destructive. They obliterate the old paradigm with swift ferocity. They catapult companies into market positions using forces that the companies themselves are barely aware of. They thrust one company into a position of market leadership, showering it with benefits, while forcing every other company to play a secondary backup role. They drag people into working ten, twelve, fourteen hours a day five, six, and seven days a week—only to discover, come the following Monday, that their To-Do lists are longer, not shorter. The pressure everywhere is to keep up with tornado demand, to drive every process, every supplier, every employee to the limit, and to fear every other company as a competitor. The only rewards of working in a tornado are power and money, and it does not take too many years of this to realize there might be more to life.

Having said all that, however, one must always come back to

the money. If tornadoes are destructive, they are also creative, generating new wealth where none was present before. New wealth means new industries, new jobs, new promotions, higher salaries, and better standards of living. And for the customers, the new infrastructure will allow them to redefine and reengineer their businesses, not to mention their personal productivity and leisure pursuits as well. Thus life does go forward with each paradigm shift, and there are few of us who, having absorbed the new technology, then want to give it up.

So let us just say that tornadoes are a force to be reckoned with. What makes them feel so destructive, in part, is that they happen so quickly. So a better question to ask might be, Why is there this furious acceleration in the market? What makes the winds of change wrap themselves into a tornado frenzy instead of just working themselves out as a steady breeze?

What Causes Tornadoes?

To understand tornado market dynamics we must shift our view from *economic buyers*, who hold the key to bowling alley success, and focus instead on the *infrastructure* or *technical buyers*, the people in charge of deploying and maintaining our basic support systems. These people are charged with providing reliable and efficient infrastructure by virtue of which we can transact, analyze, monitor, create, communicate, collaborate, and so forth. These systems are always in need of modification, and they are never able to keep up with our end-user demands, inspiring feedback from us that ranges from the curious to the querulous to the downright quarrelsome. And that is what life in an Information Technology department is like on a good day.

Then along comes a new paradigm, a discontinuous innovation that promises to break the IT backlog, delight the end users, and usher in an age of prosperity and competitive advantage. The IT department has heard this before. Of course, it is their responsibility to look at it, which they are interested in doing, but their instincts all say it is too soon to adopt, too soon for the next paradigm shift. They are like career military families who, having just settled down into some reliable routines and relationships, dread having to make yet another move. Yet each year the new paradigm lurks closer and closer. What are they to do?

In a classic human response, they form support groups. IT professionals are expert at networking with each other, even across company and industry boundaries if need be, to discuss the ramifications of the latest technology. These groups are united by a need to answer a single question: *Is it time to move yet?* As we have already noted, being pragmatists they will operate like herd animals, and now they have gotten nervous because some unknown scent is in the air. Should they ignore it or should they stampede? Anxiously they glance back and forth at each other: Are you making the move? Is she? Should I?

If the IT community moves too soon, they incur all the trials of early—which is to say premature—adoption, devoting precious resources to debugging systems that a few years later would come already debugged, committing themselves to write in-house protocols that end up being incompatible with the eventual de facto standards, and stretching themselves thin running systems in parallel until the new paradigm is reliable and robust enough to shoulder the load alone. If they move too late, on the other hand, they expose their company to competitive disadvantages as others in their industry operate at lower cost and greater speed by virtue of their more efficient infrastructures. Worst of all, if they move way too late, as often happens to conservatives, they run the risk of getting trapped in end-of-life systems that, with alarming rapidity, become almost impossible to maintain as the staff and the companies that used to support them move on.

So IT executives find themselves continually balancing alpha and beta risk, being defined as any pair of risks that are inversely proportional to each other. Let us say that alpha in this case is the risk of switching too early, beta of switching too late. For a long time alpha far exceeds beta, and the herd is at peace. But as the paradigm shift approaches, so alpha and beta approach each other, creating the instability that precedes a flash point change in the marketplace. We have moved, in other words, from the relatively low-anxiety state of a *tornado watch*—conditions are such as to make a tornado possible—to the high-anxiety state of a *tornado warning*—the tornado is coming, it's just a question of where it will touch down first.

These tornado signals have their impact on the pragmatist herd. As a way of coping with this tension, they reach agreement about three principles:

1. *When it is time to move, let us all move together.*

   Pragmatists want to all move at once to minimize the risk of moving either too early or too late. When the herd migrates, the industry must follow, and thus no one gets caught out lacking support. Also, whatever protocols get adopted at that time will be the go-forward de facto standards.

2. *When we pick the vendor to lead us to the new paradigm, let us all pick the same one.*

   Picking a common vendor, which has the side effect of driving that company to becoming the market leader, ensures a clear reference point for the de facto standards. Moreover, pragmatists like to stay on the beaten path. They know that market leaders are always the safe buy, always get the best third-party support, and they know they can always find people who have experience with that technology.

3. *Once the move starts, the sooner we get it over with the better.*

   The goal in any infrastructure swap-out is to collapse the transition time in order to minimize the disruption for end users and the stress of having to maintain parallel infrastructures, not to mention having to build temporary bridges between them. The sooner everyone can be settled into the new home, the better.

It is these three principles operating in conjunction that create the tornado. The principle of moving together causes a massive number of new customers to enter the market all at once, swamping the existing system of supply. This in turn causes some pushing and shoving as companies jockey to get their share of vendor attention. That they all want the same product creates a further intensification of demand around a single vendor, along with more pushing and shoving. That they all want to get this over with as soon as possible just drives the thermometer that much higher. And finally, because they feed off each other's behavior, there is a feedback loop operating that whips the entire market up into a frenzy, so that what started out as an orderly migration quickly degenerates into a stampede.

The Significance of the Tornado

The market consequence of this stampede is that, virtually overnight, demand dramatically outstrips supply, and a huge backlog of customers appears. The financial implications of this backlog are hard to overstate. For not only does it represent a massive sales opportunity in and of itself, it also represents an even larger follow-on market opportunity. That is, since switching costs in high tech are so high, once customers settle on a particular vendor, they rarely switch. So each sale gained in a tornado really should be looked at as an annuity, and the total number of sales a company can garner while the tornado is in process sets the limits of their installed base and thus the boundary conditions on their future revenue from that marketplace.

In sum, the tornado is a hugely significant time. It is also a bit confusing for the marketing department. They are used to defining their value to the company as creating demand, but in a tornado there is no need for this service. So what should the marketing strategy be now?

To put it as succinctly as possible—*just ship!*

Don't segment. Don't customize. Don't commit to any special projects. Just ship. It is like a sardine run. You don't bait hooks, you just stick in your bucket, pull them out, and go back for more. Do anything you can to streamline the creation, distribution, installation, and adoption of your whole product. The more friction you can avoid, the more throughput you can achieve. Focus on supply chains and quality to ensure that as you ship you do not get caught up in returns. Don't focus on the customer, in other words; focus on yourself. You, not they, are the gating item in this market.

In the process of acting out this scenario, of participating in a customer-capture game that makes the Oklahoma Land Rush seem tame by comparison, companies reorganize the market-place, and power shifts from the service leaders to the product leaders and eventually to the distribution channels. The entire order of business set up during the bowling alley is blasted away, and a new order is created.

What is the significance of the new order? To answer this question, we need to look ahead to the close of the tornado period. At that time, a typical market share pattern will look like the following:

Post-Tornado Market Share by Revenue

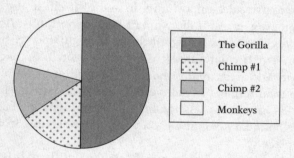

The pie chart indicates that one company has emerged as the dominant market share leader, what Jeff Tarter, software indus-try analyst and editor of *SoftLetter*, likes to call the "gorilla." In addition, one or two other companies have emerged as strong competitors, albeit clearly subordinate. These companies are the "chimpanzees." (Trout and Ries, in a variant of this idea, argue that eventually all but one of these chimpanzees will die off, and that all markets revert ultimately to a two-primate race.) Finally, a whole lot of other companies have been sucked into the vortex of tornado demand, opportunistically seeking a small piece of the pie, and these are the "monkeys."

This pattern is generated by the compulsion of pragmatist customers to create and support a market leader. Without such a leader, as we noted in the previous chapter, the marketplace never really stabilizes, standards remain dangerously fluid, and long-term decisions are so risky as to become virtually impossible to make. So pragmatists will have their leaders—and the mechanism for ensuring that this comes to pass is a simple one: they simply make sure that they buy from the same vendor as their fellow pragmatists are. They do this by staying in close communication with one another, which in turn helps explain why word-of-mouth marketing is so critical to high-tech market leadership.

Now, once pragmatists start buying one particular company's products en masse instead of another's, the process is self-reinforcing. People in decision theory call this an *information cascade*. If you are a pragmatist, and you have to make a difficult decision, and you know that a number of pragmatists have already faced this decision, and that the bulk of them chose **A**, then you will be very inclined to also choose **A**. Indeed, the more that **A** is chosen, the more you will be so inclined, until it is no longer an issue. **A** has simply become *the* choice.

Thus from the population seeking gorilla nomination, once the winning candidate has been identified, it is easy to see how it outstrips its fellow competitors quickly. But how come it got picked in the first place and not some other vendor now destined to become a chimp? Simply put, it had the market momentum and the leadership position at the right time. The previous year it might have been someone else who was in the lead, and if the tornado had started that year, then that company would have been the gorilla. In sum, although there are a number of things a company can do to increase its attractiveness as a gorilla candidate, and still more things it can do to ensure it can meet the demands placed on the gorilla-elect, there is still an element of timing and luck in this equation.

Once the gorilla is identified, the self-reinforcing mechanisms of tornado purchase decisions ensure that company will get all the sales it can process. The upper limit on this number appears to be about 75 to 80 percent—the shares of Microsoft in PC operating systems and Intel in PC microprocessors. At that point markets get nervous about having no alternative at all and work to support minority stakes for companies like Apple's Macintosh and IBM's OS/2 in the PC operating system market and AMD, Cyrix, and Nexgen in the Intel-compatible microprocessor market. The lower limit on the gorilla's size, on the other hand, is a function of its ability to ship. If this lower limit falls below a critical mass, say a 35 to 40 percent share, then the market can become unstable because the top vendor cannot sustain a sufficient lead to enforce the de facto standards. This is what happened to Apollo during the original technical workstation tornado, and it opened the way for Sun to steal the prize. Anywhere in between, however, the gorilla simply processes sales.

And these sales shower down in abundance, as if the whole forest were raining bananas. Indeed, there are so many bananas that the gorilla cannot eat them all, so that, full to the point of indigestion, it has to leave some behind where they become food for the chimpanzees. Chimpanzees are candidate gorillas that didn't get picked. For years afterward, you will find their executives muttering to themselves as they walk down the street, "I coulda been a gorilla, I coulda been a gorilla," but the fact is, they just weren't in the right place at the right time. So they need to give up this form of self-flagellation and get on with their very real market opportunity, which is to play the role of the kinder, gentler gorilla, the one who will return your phone calls and will negotiate on price and deliverables, the one who arguably has the best product features (although never the best whole product) and who actually has enough service people to serve you. We cannot all be the gorilla, but as the saying goes, a rising tide floats all boats, and there is no reason for a chimp not to prosper as well.

And even after these companies have had their privileged time at the banana windfall, there are still leftovers for a host of monkeys. Monkeys represent a completely different breed of primate. They come to the market late, only after the tornado has started, with no sunk cost, no commitment to any architec-

ture, no R&D, and no marketing investment—just an opportunistic frame of mind. Their strategy is simple. Clone the
gorilla product and sell it cheap. All markets appreciate having
a low-cost clone alternative, and as long as demand exceeds
supply, there will be plenty of customers for the monkeys as
well. The booming economies of Japan, Korea, Singapore, and
Taiwan all got their start in this way, and executed properly it is
a phenomenally profitable strategy.

What makes all this revenue share distribution really interesting, however, is when it is complemented with a second pie
chart, indicating *profit share:*

Post-Tornado Market Share by Profits

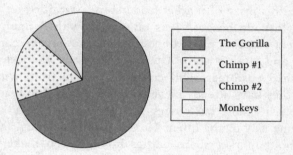

As this chart indicates, by the time the market has stabilized
and tornado growth ceases—once, that is, the market moves to
Main Street—the market leader is earning a dramatically disproportionate share of the total profits. Moreover, because
future revenues and profits are largely a function of selling into
one's installed base, and because the gorilla has by far the
largest installed base, it typically enjoys this advantage *for the
rest of the life of the market!* This reflects the magnitude of the
prize pragmatist customers confer upon the market leader,
which, while not exactly intended, nonetheless acts as a powerful incentive to companies to strive for this status, with the
reward to the customer being order and stability in their marketplace.

The reason the gorilla's profits are so large is that during the
tornado it has the privilege of setting the market's *reference*

price. This is the price that all the chimpanzees and monkeys must discount below in order to compete successfully against the gorilla. How much they have to discount is a function of how much premium the market places on the gorilla's whole product relative to theirs. At the same time, the gorilla has the highest volume of sales, so it has an equally large advantage in operational costs from economies of scale. As we noted earlier, highest price + lowest cost = great margins! Every other company must price lower and have a higher cost structure, still garnering good margins perhaps, but not in the same class. The gorilla's fabulous margins, then, are a function not of brilliant marketing but of how the tornado market's mechanism operates.

Now, this prize of market leadership is awarded only during the tornado because it is only then, with so many new customers entering all at once, that market shares can shift swiftly and dramatically. Once the tornado is over, most established customers will continue to buy from whatever vendor they have already picked, and there are simply too few new or switchable customers to shift market share significantly one way or the other. Thus it is only during a tornado that all-out market share battles in high tech make sense. Winning this battle is the wealth-creation engine for all high-tech fortunes.

The Two Great Tornadoes of the 1980s

In the previous decade there were two great tornadoes that fundamentally changed the balance of power in the computer industry. Each had the remarkable property of having a second tornado extend itself out of the first, so that the ultimate impact of both extended twice the period of a "normal" tornado.

The first of these was the midrange computer tornado. In its first phase, it developed around a minicomputer architecture set by DEC and Oracle, with the former company providing the requisite large-scale infrastructure, and the latter the driving energy. In its second phase, which is still ongoing, Oracle continues to play a key role, but the real action lies in the replacement of the minicomputer's proprietary operating systems with a client/server architecture based on Unix, and it is Hewlett-Packard that is rising to prominence this time around.

The second and even greater tornado is, of course, the PC market. It has grown from a few hundred million dollars in the early 1980s to over $100 billion today. In its first phase IBM provided the requisite large-scale infrastructure while Lotus's 1-2-3 provided much of the initial driving energy. In its second phase, Microsoft and Intel have emerged as the dominant companies, with no hardware single vendor playing a comparable role, although Compaq and, to a lesser extent, Dell have gained new prominence.

Both tornadoes incorporate a myriad of interactions among hundreds of companies operating in multiple sectors of the market over any number of years representing a level of complexity that defies analysis. But stepping back from each we can see the characteristic tornado form—the massive influx of new customers that generates whole new industries overnight and catapults the shareholder value of a very few companies into the stratosphere.

DEC and Oracle

In the case of the DEC VAX, at the outset of its adoption life cycle, the chasm-causing discontinuity was both technical—IT groups were unfamiliar with its operating system and the networking, although it did allow them to leverage their knowledge of COBOL—and organizational—IT groups were centralized, and VAXs were distributed. For the most part, therefore, IT (or MIS—Management Information Systems—as it was then called) simply refused to endorse the DEC paradigm.

But the demand for distributed computing would not let up. IBM had convincingly demonstrated the value of computer data as *management information,* and the divisional managers were getting hammered by corporate staff because the latter had better access to computer information. Before going into any future corporate reviews, therefore, the managers insisted on getting their own reports first—thereby deluging MIS with requests—and thus the MIS backlog was born.

There simply was no way to solve this backlog problem within the centralized paradigm of mainframe computing. IBM, who had invented the concept of management information systems to spur greater demand for its mainframe computers, ended up creating a monster, a vortex of demand so great as to bring on its own downfall. It needed a distributed solution. IBM tried to respond with its 43XX series, but the amount of on-site expertise needed to run it was just too high (its whole product was simply too complex), so in effect, the backlog was still in place.

At the same time, there *was* a distributed computer that increasingly did appear to fit the bill. This was the DEC VAX, and to a greater or lesser extent any number of its competitors, including the HP 3000, Data General's Eclipse, Wang's VS series, and others, eventually including IBM's own AS/400. Originally adopted as an engineering department computer, where it resided without central MIS support, the VAX then migrated to the factory, for MRP (Materials Requirements Planning) and shop-floor control applications, both of which generated a lot of management information. As a result, it began to engender a shadow MIS organization, the first generation of what we have subsequently come to call *departmental computing.* By the early 1980s, the expertise level outside of corporate MIS was high enough for divisions to consider expanding the use of these departmental VAXs to full responsibility for the entire operation. The arrival of the relational database vendors turned up to provide one of the final missing links—an applications development platform and tools sufficiently easy to use that divisional personnel, supplemented by independent software vendors (ISVs) or local VARs, could deliver the necessary programs without a lot of central MIS help.

At this point the tornado started. Probably the trigger event was when Oracle committed to cross-platform portability based on using SQL—IBM's very own standard—as a common application interface. For the first time, central MIS could see a way to maintain a supportable corporate standard and still permit distributed computing, and the last bulwark of resistance buckled.

The Lessons That Oracle Taught

Oracle rode this tornado to market dominance, and in the process demonstrated some of the essential principles of tornado marketing. Among them are:

1. Attack the competition ruthlessly.
2. Expand your distribution channel as fast as possible.
3. Ignore the customer.

While the last of these principles may seem a bit startling, we will see in a moment that it falls directly out of the dynamics of tornado marketing. But let us begin with the first item on our list. Why is it so important to *attack your competitors* during a tornado instead of *serve your customers?* Why, specifically, was Larry Ellison once quoted as saying, citing Genghis Khan, "It is not enough that we win—all others must lose"?

The answer is that the market expects the gorilla company not just to excel but to dominate—indeed, it requires it to do so. If the gorilla shows weakness, if the market wavers in its confidence, if the third parties hedge their allegiances, then the whole point of having a gorilla, which is to set and extend de facto standards as the market moves forward, is undermined. In chaotic situations, the first source of order and security is a centralizing dominating power—that is precisely what the tornado needs and wants from the gorilla. So just as the first job of a newly hatched queen bee is to go kill off all the other nascent queens, so it is the job of gorilla to beat up on the chimps. If it doesn't, then the market will question whether it really is the gorilla, potentially putting that title at risk.

For everyone else in the market who is not the gorilla, focusing on your competitors is still the order of the day. This is because the tornado market is a *zero-sum game*. Every new customer I win is one you lose—*for life*. Going forward, that is, they will be part of my installed base, not yours, so you lose access not just to their current revenue but all future revenue as well. We are setting the boundaries not just for ourselves but for future generations as well. Under such conditions all social institutions generate a pecking order, and the higher you can be in it, the better your results will be. Beating a competitor is the only way to move up in the pecking order. Hence that must be your focus.

It is equally important to note here, however, that the tornado is the *only* time when beating the competition is significant. At no other time, that is, does the market act like a zero-sum game:

- In the early market, competition barely exists, except in the sense that one is competing against the old ways, and when you win, nobody else loses.
- When crossing the chasm and working your way through the bowling alley, your focus is on niches of customers who have been chronically underserved by the existing paradigm. Unwanted before you arrived, they are hardly a great loss when you win them for yourself.
- Finally, once the tornado is over and the market moves on to Main Street, future growth will come primarily from serving your own installed base and not by attacking the base of other companies, it being too disruptive for most customers to switch vendors.

Tornado marketing, in other words, is the *exception condition*. I stress this because all companies promote their winners, and the biggest winners are inevitably those managers who succeed during the tornado stage. These people are typically intensely competitive individuals, and it is their competitive drive that helps bring them and their company victory. It is extremely difficult for such individuals to entertain, much less actually accomplish, a change in style and focus. But if they do not change, if they are unable to tear their eyes away from the competition and focus them back on the customer, which is where the real action shifts once the tornado subsides, then inevitably operating results begin to pale. And thus it is not uncommon to see management turnover at the top coming shortly on the heels of what everyone acknowledges to have been meteoric success.

The Second Rule of Tornado Marketing

The second lesson Oracle taught high-tech marketers about the tornado is the importance of expanding distribution as fast as possible. In a tornado, customer demand is at its most intense, and if you are not there to take the order, then someone else will get it. It is tempting at that point to say, "So what? I'm fully booked." But remember, it is not just a sale you are losing here: it is a customer for life. The tornado is when you set the limits on the size of the installed base you will serve over the next decade. This means you need to be on every possible shelf you can and have exposure in every possible account.

What set Oracle apart from Ingres, its primary competitor, during the minicomputer relational database tornado was that Larry Ellison drove for 100 percent growth while Ingres "accepted" 50 percent growth. To garner that 100 percent growth he simply doubled the size of his sales force every year. He didn't ask for a forecast, he dictated it. To execute on this agenda, each year he hired the brightest, brashest gunslingers he could find—many of them fresh out of MIT or Harvard or Stanford—compensating the winners lavishly, and firing the losers. There was no account development. There was no relationship marketing. It was pillage and plunder: get the sale and get out before the customer looks too closely beneath the covers. For God's sake, don't look back or go back—just go out and sell the next prospect.

To further focus its sales force, Oracle would each year target a competitor to take out. One year it was Cullinet's IDMS/R, another year HP's Image, another Ingres. Salespeople got extra support and extra commissions for replacing the targeted vendor's package. And success was further fueled as word-of-mouth report of wholesale switching to Oracle spread through the competitor's installed base of customers. Oracle, in other words, was using its competitors' own users' groups as word-of-mouth communications channels! And the message these users sent to one another was a simple one: these guys are not nice but they are winners, so we're all better off if we get on this bandwagon now instead of clinging to a loser.

None of this was reflected in Ingres's approach. They *were* the nice guys. They said, we simply cannot grow any faster than 50 percent and still adequately serve our customers. No one can. Look at Oracle. They are promising anything and everything and shipping little or nothing. Everybody knows it. Their customers hate them. They are going to hit the wall. They will implode, just wait and see. We are doing things the right way; we are going to stay our course.

Ingres was confident it was taking the high moral ground and would be rewarded. It turned out it was only half right. In 1991 Oracle did indeed hit the wall, but that was long after the critical market share competition was over. By that time, Ingres was a bewildered company that had lost its sense of direction and sold itself to ASK Computers. It simply could not believe what had happened. It was as if Darth Vader had slain Luke Skywalker, as if Bambi had met Godzilla.

What Ingres—as well as many of the rest of us at the time—did not understand is that, for pragmatist customers, the first freedom in a rapidly shifting market is order and security. That can only come from rallying around a clear market leader. Once the apparent leader-to-be emerges, pragmatists will support that company, virtually regardless of how arrogant, unresponsive, or overpriced it is. Thus the penalty for poor customer satisfaction in a tornado is negligible compared to the rewards for going out and getting the next customer.

And that brings us to the third and final lesson that Oracle taught.

Ignore the Customer

In a tornado, the correct marketing strategy really is to *ignore the customer!* The reason is that, in a tornado, customers are lining up for the hot product. They do not need—or want—to be *courted*—the problem is not to create demand: they need—and want—to be *supplied*. Anything you do to restrict the throughput of the supply process works against this goal. That is why Henry Ford not only could say, but was correct in saying, "You can have any color Model T you want as long as it's black."

To be sure, once the tornado was over, Ford ended up painting its cars in two-toned purple if that's what the customer wanted. But that is not what the market requires or the customer desires *during* the tornado. They just want to get their first car, or their first telephone, or their first PC, or their first laser printer. They want the *commodity*. So your focus must be on getting them that item as quickly, easily, and cheaply as possible. This means becoming intensely internally focused on your delivery capabilities and not letting yourself get distracted by "secondary" factors such as an individual customer's particular needs.

To be scrupulously accurate, we should say, during the tornado ignore the economic buyer and the end user as customers, and focus exclusively on supplying the infrastructure buyer. This buyer has the same motives as you do—rapid deployment of a standard product. By contrast, the economic buyer cares most about return on investment and the end users about impact on their particular application.

Now, in the bowling alley, economic buyers were a key ally, needed to champion the "premature" adoption of your new paradigm with an infrastructure buyer reluctant as yet to change. The motive for their support was dramatically improved performance on a mission-critical application that provided a compelling return on investment (ROI). Now, however, we are talking about a wholesale deployment of a new infrastructure. Such deployment is rarely justifiable by conventional measures of ROI, unless one takes a very long-range view. Since line executives are typically responsible for earning positive returns within a year to eighteen months, they do not make good allies at this time.

In actual fact, all the cost-justification exercises used to gain economic buyers' support for tornado purchases are pure puffery. That is the meaning behind the recurrent articles in *ComputerWorld* about the hidden costs of client/server systems. The only thing "hiding" these costs were the proposals that promised immediate cost savings in the first place. It is the reason why the productivity studies of PCs for years showed little or no returns. Infrastructure investments have a much longer-term impact on revenues. It was not, for example, until the massive downsizing of the early 1990s that *Fortune* 500 corporations actually gained the economic return on their PC infrastructure investment in the 1980s. As this example shows, however, when the impact of a paradigm shift does make itself felt, it packs a wallop. That is why it is not safe to wait too long for transition to the new paradigm. And that, in turn, is why infrastructure investment is ultimately the right strategy.

To sum up, although accelerated deployment of a one-size-fits-all infrastructure during the tornado alienates both the economic buyer and the end user, it does in fact serve the client organization and should be supported. The irony is that to be effective you must ignore the very customers for whom this is all being done. Having said that, however, you do not, despite the example of any number of market leaders, have to take rudeness to a high art. The same strategy can also be executed with good grace and yet with equally devastating impact on the competition. For that example, let us turn to Hewlett-Packard's printer business.

The Lessons That HP Taught

The growth of the PC printer business, both laser and ink-jet, from virtually nothing to a $20 billion industry led by HP, while not one of the two decade-leading tornado stories is still a wonder. This is because it represents an early win by an American business in what was, in large part, a manufacturing competition—something the Japanese were supposed to win. What made the victory so startling was that HP's major competitor, Canon, was not only Japanese but also *owned or shared in the rights to all the core technology!* What made HP so successful during the tornado?

In a tornado HP showed us there are three critical priorities:

1. Just ship.
2. Extend distribution channels.
3. Drive to the next lower price point.

HP brought to the "Just ship" objective a history of leadership in quality improvement processes that allowed it to scale up production, first with its laser printers, and later with its ink-jet printers, with remarkably few hiccups. Thus, as the demand continued to ramp, HP was there with the product. Quality and yield are critical during the tornado. If your engine fails, you lose your place in line. It's like having a mechanical failure in a car race: pit stops hurt.

All this sounds simple enough until you compare HP's performance with IBM's problems with supplying enough of its highly popular ThinkPad notebooks, or Dell's inability to field a suitable notebook at all during that market's critical tornado period, or, to go to the software world, Lotus's, Ashton-Tate's, or Microsoft's inability to ship products within even a year of their announced target dates.

What gives HP its "Just ship" advantage is a property of its corporate culture, which is based on consensus decision-making and trust. The former ensures that the necessary cross-functional communication takes place to ensure stable, scalable processes. The latter keeps consensus processes from paralyzing action because authority is delegated down far enough into the organization that consensus overhead does not become intolerable. (Indeed, HP almost lost its way here during the late 1980s—veering dangerously close to an overly centralized matrix management scheme—but was put back on course by direct intervention from Hewlett and Packard themselves.) The champion of this decentralized, trust-oriented culture within the printer division was Dick Hackborn, who continually made it clear to his managers that they had the responsibility *and* the authority to attack their markets aggressively.

Finally, a key part of the "Just ship" strategy is not to get any returns. Can you imagine, for example, what might happen if a major microprocessor company shipped a flagship product into a tornado and it contained a major bug? The Pentium debacle cost Intel a $500 million write-down. A similar problem also hit Intuit recently when it shipped a version of its TurboTax product with a bug that could cause significant errors in a tax return. Intuit was more graceful than Intel in acknowledging its problem, but it still had to take the hit. Finally, even HP, with all its cultural advantages, is not immune to this problem. In 1993 one of its ink-jet printer divisions incorporated a new type of rubber roller into its paper-handling mechanisms, only to discover in 1994 that this new rubber "bloomed" after about six months, excreting to its surface a slick powder that made it unable to get traction for picking up paper. By this point, 1.1 million units had shipped. What to do? Having discovered the problem in April, the division management at HP convened an 8 A.M. meeting every morning for the remainder of 1994 to stay on top of this problem. Tornado problems require that kind of attention.

The second key tactic in a tornado is to extend channels of distribution to make maximum contact with the customer. At the time that the PC laser printer was introduced, HP had little history of indirect distribution in its computer lines, although it did have some with its popular line of calculators. As long as laser printer price points were above $10,000, this mattered little, but as prices fell—or, rather, as HP drove prices downward to under $5,000, and then under $3,000—it became an increasingly critical success factor, and HP went into the PC dealer channel. And now, as ink-jet printers have taken PC printer prices lower and lower, under $1,000, and then under $500, and most recently under $200, HP has continued to extend its distribution channels, first to computer superstores, then to office superstores, to mail order, and most recently to price clubs and other consumer outlets.

The rule is simple: if you are in a tornado, you simply must not leave any shelf unfilled. Canon, however, did just that. It did not have the experience or relationships with the PC industry to know where and how to get distribution. By the time it figured it out, establishing a strong U.S. sales division in 1992, it was too late to unseat the gorilla. But Canon at least had the excuse that as an offshore company it lacked distribution relationships in the U.S. market. Many U.S. vendors, on the other hand, have voluntarily ruled out some distribution channels, usually as part of a strategy to maintain a premium image and higher price margins. The results of this tactic are now well known:

> **If you refuse or neglect to supply any channel with your product, you leave that flank unprotected.**

To be sure, initially that shelf may be filled with some inferior clone product, but as the market shifts to lower and lower price points, the volume in the "lesser" channels begins to dwarf the "prestige" channels, and it is these same low-end players who now have the advantage. This approach has been the cornerstone of Packard Bell's market development strategy. Packard Bell in recent quarters has risen to the leading supplier of PCs based on units purchased, outpacing Compaq, IBM, and Apple, the industries three traditional leaders.

Companies with prestigious brand names are loath to chase the Packard Bells of this world for fear that it will cheapen their image. This leads them to stay within the safety of high-end distribution channels where customers will appreciate their "brand value." But this ultimately results in an enclave strategy of gradual withdrawal leading inevitably to barbarians at the gate. It is a strategic error based on a misunderstanding of the third key tactic of tornado marketing—price point management.

Managing Price

Prior to the tornado, markets are not very price-elastic. Value propositions are either based on a visionary dream or a niche-market value proposition, and pricing can and should be value-based, to optimize for margins, and not commodity-based, which means optimizing for market share. Once the tornado is over, on the other hand, markets are very price-elastic. This is because, during the tornado, the whole product becomes institutionalized and then commoditized, so that pricing can be commodity-based—all in the service of rapidly expanding markets and market share. The transition from value-based to commodity-based pricing happens during the tornado, and leveraging that transition is key to capturing market share, especially in the tornado's later stages.

This is particularly true in retail markets, where hitting the next retail price point creates a burst of buying from customers who heretofore felt the purchase price was too rich for their blood. In retail, magic price numbers usually end in 99, as in $999, $799, $499, $299, and $99 (although actual numbers vary by product category, not to mention currency). Seymour Merrin of Merrin Information Systems has done the leading work in this field for the PC industry, helping high-tech companies understand how street pricing works and where the next strategic price point might fall. But the pattern also occurs in industrial purchases. When workstations went under $50,000, and then when they went under $10,000, they got huge boosts in sales volumes.

The point is, the vendor who can first hit the next lower strategic price point gets first crack at a whole new customer base aching to enter the market once prices get down to their level. This creates a burst of new volume, thereby expanding the market share and the future installed base of that vendor. If a market leader has already emerged, then the market may wait awhile to see if that leader will accommodate the new price point—but it won't wait forever. And if the leader snubs the new price point, then the market will go with the clone. The lesson is clear: *tornado markets will be served.* It is never a question of *if,* it is only a question of *who.*

This lesson may be clear, but heeding it can be another matter. Fat margins are a habit that is hard to kick. IBM couldn't kick it when Compaq underpriced them, nor could Compaq when Dell underpriced them. Both companies have since reversed their courses, but not before institutionalizing a permanent rival to their core business. HP, by contrast, has ruthlessly pursued the next lower price point, even as it cannibalized its own sales and margins. As Lew Platt, HP's CEO likes to put it, "If we don't eat our own lunch, somebody else will."

When market leaders drive to be first to the next price point, they leave precious little room for any competitor to respond. Basically, they are giving themselves first access to the volume commodity market, thereby reinforcing their hold on market share leadership. Competitors must hope for some glitch in the supply chain or make do with the leftover market. Longer-term, they must plan to pull out of this tornado and reenter the bowling alley with some kind of offering that can start a new market outside the leader's dominance.

The Lessons That Intel and Microsoft Taught

Thus far we have looked at key shifts in strategy needed for tornado marketing in the areas of target customer (ignore the customer—just ship), distribution (expand as aggressively as possible), pricing (be the first to hit the next lowest price point), and competition (attack it directly and ruthlessly). All of these lessons could equally well have been taught by attending to the practices of Intel and Microsoft.

At the end of 1993, if you added up all the profits of the top 150 Silicon Valley high-tech companies, you would have discovered that half were earned by Intel. This would lead you to conclude that it is a margin-flush cash cow, ripe for attack by some aggressive, lean-and-mean low-cost competitor. After all, it has near monopoly positions in each of its microprocessor markets. So why is it slashing its prices 20 and 30 percent *routinely?* The answer is simple: Mr. Grove and company do not need to read a book on tornado marketing—they are writing one. And its motto is, *Only the paranoid survive.*

And the same applies equally as well to Microsoft. American folklore tells us that in the nineteenth century tornadoes were tamed and ridden by a fellow named Pecos Bill. In the twentieth century, Bill has hopped a ride up to Redmond, Washington, where he continues to demonstrate the art— although mercifully he has yet to be celebrated in song.

In addition to exemplifying all the rules noted above, Intel and Microsoft have also taught us how to manage the whole product and partner and allies inside the tornado. The basic principles here are as simple as they are draconian:

1. Recruit partners to create a powerful whole product.
2. Institutionalize this whole product as the market leader.
3. Commoditize the whole product by designing out your partners.

In other words, first you design partners in, then you design them out!

First you design partners in. The key to winning in the bowling alley is to develop niche markets in advance of the general, horizontal market, by delivering whole products to carefully targeted customers. Microsoft in the CD-ROM market, for example, has carefully nurtured partners, initiating its annual conferences as far back as 1985, some seven or eight years before the tornado actually hit. Intel is doing the same thing today with PCMCIA card vendors, parallel computer designers, and video-on-demand entrepreneurs.

Institutionalize this whole product as the market leader. If and when any of these offerings get swept toward a tornado, the goal then is to institutionalize your chosen partners and yourself as the core set of market leaders providing the "essential" solution set. In the case of the DOS tornado, the essential set was Intel's 286, and later its 386 microprocessors, Microsoft's DOS operating system, Lotus's 1-2-3 spreadsheet, MicroPro's WordStar word processor, Ashton Tate's dBase database, Seagate's or Conner's hard disk drive, HP's printer, and, to share files and devices, Novell's Netware network operating system. All of these companies did very, very well during the DOS tornado.

Commoditize the whole product by designing out your partners. Once you have won the tornado gorilla position, however, then you design these same partners out. Thus, as the industry shifted to support the Windows tornado in 1991, there was a noticeable shift in Microsoft's strategy. In the new pecking order, Intel is still in the middle of the game with its 486 and Pentium microprocessors, as are Seagate and Conner with their disk drives, and HP with its printers. Lotus 1-2-3 and WordPerfect (who displaced MicroPro during the DOS tornado—more on this later), however, have been designed out by Microsoft.

Initially this happened because Lotus and WordPerfect let Excel and Word have the Windows market to themselves for virtually two years, for reasons we will discuss later in this chapter. Now, as Lotus and WordPerfect are trying to challenge these products with stand-alone alternatives, Microsoft has shifted the playing field to office automation suites, in which all the leading applications—word processing, spreadsheet, presentation software, e-mail, and database—are bundled into a single purchase. Customers making this purchase will inevitably favor the market-leading word processor and spread-sheet—advantage Microsoft, with Excel and Word—which will also have the effect of institutionalizing all the other Microsoft applications included in the suite, which are not established market leaders today, but by these dynamics soon will be: Pow-erPoint for presentations, Microsoft Mail for e-mail, and Access for database. These suites, then, not only design out, they lock out competition. This is tornado warfare at its most cutthroat.

The rationale for designing out partners is not just gorilla greed. It is an essential part of the natural commoditization of the whole product. In tornado markets, commoditization always follows institutionalization, fusing together in an inte-grated whole what the market has already come to endorse as the standard set of component parts. The market's goal is to serve the broadest number of customers possible by reducing cost and eliminating distribution friction. The fewer the number of component parts, the fewer the number of suppliers who need to get margins, the lower the whole product can be priced, the more reliably it can be distributed, and the more easily it can be serviced. This commoditization of the whole product is a fundamental force in mass markets: it *will* happen—the only question is how you will align your strategy with it.

Now, as Microsoft moves toward its next OS tornado—Win-dows 95 on the client side and the next release of Windows NT on the server side—it already has its eyes set on designing out

Novell. Why do you need a network operating system if you can build all its functionality into both ends of a client/server standard? In similar, albeit longer-term fashion, Microsoft has its eyes on designing out HP's added value with printers via a technology called Microsoft At Work, designing out Lotus Notes (which arguably is just now getting designed in) via a technology called Microsoft Exchange, and designing out Oracle's database with a suite of products called Back Office. In each case, however, *in the short term*, Microsoft is partnering with every one of these same vendors, and these companies are willingly partnering with Microsoft. Why?

It's the money. Partnering with Microsoft has made a lot of companies rich; the pervasiveness of its platforms creates an invaluable de facto standard for huge chunks of infrastructure. Moreover, companies the size of those mentioned also have plans for designing Microsoft out of the equation—and undoubtedly there will be successes on both sides.

It is a little more dicey, on the other hand, when you are a much smaller partner adding value to core systems in areas the gorilla has not yet seen fit to address. Jean Louis Gassée, late of Apple, used to call this strategy "picking up dimes in front of steamrollers." In our present context it might be called *hitching a ride in someone else's tornado*.

Few companies have the clout to create a tornado. Those that do should optimize that clout, as Intel and Microsoft do, by the designing-out strategy just described. The rest of us should take that strategy as a fact of life and do our best to get rich on the periphery. That is the attitude that Stac Electronics took when, after successfully suing Microsoft for pirating their disk-space optimization software, they then immediately entered into a partnership with them. As the gangster who was caught in an assassination plot in *The Godfather* said, "Tell Michael it was nothing personal—it was just business."

Tornado Mistakes

Having seen how some of the most successful companies in high tech have won during the tornado, we should also take a look at how companies can lose as well. With all the wealth in play during a tornado, there is nothing more tragic than to snatch defeat from the jaws of victory, but it has been done, and more than once. In defense of the companies cited below, most of their "mistakes" looked a lot more like "good business tactics" at the time. So it is not so much shame on them for making these mistakes the first time, but rather shame on us if we repeat them.

1. *Tornado forces are bigger than any one company's ability to control, so don't try.*

   With VCRs being so ubiquitous today, it is hard to recall that a mere fifteen years ago they were a novelty. By the time the VCR tornado got going, the market leader was Sony, and the dominant technology was Betamax. Today, however, there are no Betamax recorders. All consumer VCRs are VHS. How could this have happened?

   Sony tried to control the tornado. It refused to license its technology to other vendors, which meant not only that other VCR manufacturers were excluded from the market, but also that movie distributors had only one portal through which to pass to their customers. Sony's reasoning was that this was their technology, they had invested in all the work to get the market to this point, so why should they share? The answer, as we now know is: The tornado must be served.

   When tornado demand hits, it far exceeds the initial supply. When a vendor acts in any way to further restrict supply, it is fighting the tornado, and the market will try to go around it, isolate it, and spit it out. That is what the other VCR manufacturers and the movie distributors did to Sony—albeit after some precarious years when video rental stores carried two types of recorder for rent and had two sections—Beta and VHS—for tapes. During this time, Sony might have pulled itself back from the brink through licensing. That would not have gotten VHS out of the game, but it would have kept Sony in it. But Sony did not choose to do that.

This same pattern played itself out in the PC industry when IBM tried to retake control of the PC tornado by introducing a proprietary 32-bit bus in the form of a licensable MicroChannel architecture. Compaq led a secession movement of the other PC vendors, proposing EISA architecture as a counter-standard. At the end of the day, neither standard won—the pragmatists just stayed on the old 16-bit ISA bus—but because Compaq was able to face IBM down, it emerged as the new market leader, costing IBM severely in prestige. Prior to this debacle, PCs were labeled IBM-compatible; forever after, they have been known as DOS or Windows compatible.

This same temptation to try to control the tornado force also all but overcame Adobe Systems. They were licensing their PostScript font technology to third parties like Phoenix but only to a certain level. That is, there were three "levels" to their implementation of PostScript, and they were only licensing the first two. As more and more vendors became dependent on having a fully commoditized font standard, and as Adobe sought to hold back the final portion of its standard for proprietary advantage, the industry struck back through two rival font technology efforts, Truetype and Royal. Threatened on two fronts, Adobe backed away from its initial hardball stance, but not before some permanent damage was done to its market prestige. Most important, it was Adobe's inability to respond to the PC industry's demand for commoditization, its unwillingness to cooperate to find ways to eliminate the bottlenecks that it itself was creating, that caused the threat in the first place. Again, the key lesson here, as with all things in the tornado, is: Don't take it personally. These are simply tornado market forces acting themselves out.

Since the tornado *will* be served, correct strategy is to proactively serve it first. This is what the initial IBM PC strategy did so well. It created a clone market that institutionalized and then commoditized IBM architecture, creating massive wealth for IBM but also for many other companies. In such a situation the entire industry has a stake in maintaining the status quo, including keeping the market leader in place. Unfortunately, IBM was not able to play out the later moves in this strategy as effectively as Microsoft and Intel were. In retrospect, it appears IBM got spooked by the low margins. The lesson, which HP has taken to heart in its printer business, is that low prices and margins come with the territory, and the right way to serve the tornado is to drive them even lower.

2. *Don't introduce discontinuity during a tornado.*

Whatever product architecture you take into a tornado you must stick with for the duration, regardless of its limitations. The fate of WordStar demonstrates the consequences.

When the PC tornado hit, three software products were immediately institutionalized as the market leaders: Lotus's 1-2-3 spreadsheet, Ashton-Tate's dBase database, and MicroPro's WordStar word processor. All three had greater than 50 percent market share in the early DOS market. Yet a few years later, with no paradigm shift in the market to account for it, WordPerfect swept past WordStar, taking the leadership mantle away from it forever.

Given the phenomenal set of advantages that mainstream markets afford to market leaders, one's first reaction is to say, *that's impossible*. Here's what happened. At the outset of the tornado, once MicroPro saw that it had the market-leading position in word processors, it immediately focused all of its research and development energies elsewhere. Why? Because the conventional wisdom at the time said that you could not be a one-product company. Lotus and Ashton-Tate, by the way, were doing the same thing. All three companies spent millions and millions of dollars chasing any business opportunity other than the one they were really good at.

The difference between MicroPro and its companions, however, is that when WordStar was challenged by a strong new product entry, it blinked. Instead of "upgrading" its existing product, the path taken by Lotus and Ashton-Tate, it chose to purchase a code base from another vendor and bring out a wholly new product called WordStar 2000, far superior to anything it had in-house. In addition to the many virtues of this new product, however, it had one fatal flaw: its file format was incompatible with the WordStar installed base.

As a result, MicroPro customers were forced to confront yet another *discontinuous innovation*—basically, a new adoption life cycle. Sticking with their market leader conferred no advantage, for switching costs were going to be imposed regardless. This meant that all previous bets were off, and while WordStar 2000 wasn't ruled out as an alternative, it wasn't automatically ruled in. Moreover, WordPerfect had been developing momentum, so it looked increasingly like the better choice. With a tornado in progress that required virtually every PC owner to have a word processor, people made their buying decisions quickly, and when they went to WordPerfect, there was no time and no way for MicroPro to recover.

We now know that the correct strategy for this situation is to stay the course with the old product architecture, regardless of how antiquated it might look and feel, at least to the extent of maintaining backward compatibility with the installed base. This is what Windows has done for DOS, it is what IBM's AS/400 did during its tornado for the System 38 and—painfully—for the System 36 as well, and it is what Intel did with the 386 microprocessor for the 286, albeit through some rather bizarre architectural contortions.

The fundamental principle here is that continuous innovation favors market leaders, while discontinuous innovation favors market challengers. If you are in a tornado and winning, you want the market to stay continuous. Even if you are not in the gorilla position, if you are still profiting, you probably want it to stay continuous. Only if you are not winning, and think you can win a *future* tornado, should you opt for discontinuity.

3. *Tornadoes design service out, not in.*

Perhaps the biggest casualty in the ongoing PC industry tornado has been the PC dealer channel, including such once high-flying companies as Computerland and Businessland. Each year of tornado volume further commoditized the PC solution set, designing out the need for the very expertise that these companies had made the mainstay of their businesses. The ability for this channel to earn the margins it needed from the services it knew how to provide had been fatally undermined.

Near the end of its viability, Businessland made a strong pitch for converting itself into a service provider to business. The strategy was to break even on the product sales and make the margins in services. This is not an uncommon response to late tornado or Main Street situations where commoditization has eroded margins—witness the strategies of any number of mainframe and minicomputer companies converting themselves into systems integrators. Unfortunately, it just doesn't work very well. The whole point of commoditization is to enable new market price points, and the market is very reluctant to give back those hard-earned dollars to any kind of service.

In any event, Businessland's strategy failed, as did that of many a PC dealer. The market now supports basically three kinds of customer-contact institutions: *superstores*, which win the commoditization game; *boutique VARs*, which win the high value-added service game by finding solutions for niche needs that have not yet succumbed to commoditization; and the *traditional PC dealers*, which have converted from inbound retail storefronts to outbound sales to business. All three are sustainable tornado positions. The one unsustainable position is to be an "integrator" of things that are perceived to have been already integrated. That is the strategy that fights the tornado.

4. *Don't bet on preventing a tornado.*

In the latter part of the 1980s the PC market was going through a crisis because for the first time the operating system standard was in jeopardy. Initially everyone was sure the new standard was going to be OS/2. Later it became increasingly likely it would be Windows. Having to develop for not one but two immature operating systems was putting enormous strains on the resources of the independent software vendors (ISVs), and many, including Lotus and WordPerfect, opted to support OS/2 only.

For a while, this was sound strategy, but as Windows's stature in the marketplace increased, neither company responded by shifting its development efforts. Ultimately this led to giving Microsoft a two-year advantage in the Windows application market for word processors and spreadsheets. This proved more than enough time for the company to snatch the gorilla status away in both categories, leaving WordPerfect helpless (hence its acquisition by Novell) and Lotus badly wounded. How could these two companies have let this happen?

Both companies fell victim to denying the tornado. The logic behind their strategy was simple. If we port the leading word processor and spreadsheet to Windows, it will cost us a great deal more development work, and we will come in behind Microsoft. If we don't port our software to Windows, if we insist OS/2 is the correct standard instead, then Windows will be incomplete as a whole product, and the market will force Microsoft to OS/2, where we will have the lead on it.

This strategy worked well for a while. In particular, Windows 2.2 failed in the marketplace because OS/2 1.1 represented at least as good a whole product, and because Windows was not supported by Lotus or WordPerfect. With two such strong alternative candidates vying to be the one standard, pragmatist customers were unsure which one would win. So they did what all good pragmatists do in that situation—they waited.

But by the time Windows 3.0 came around it had been clear for some time that the vast majority of independent software vendors were going to rally around it, not OS/2, and that Microsoft was providing very strong products in the word-processing and spreadsheet categories. At this point Lotus and WordPerfect clung to their strategy with vain hope. They denied the tornado because they didn't want it to happen. Denial strategies, psychologists tell us, can never win and in losing exact a painful price.

The winning strategy, assuming you have big-company resources, is to distribute your bets at the beginning of any open systems contest and then over time shift them away from the losers toward the emerging winner. That is, as soon as you see one alternative lagging, kill it immediately, and reinvest that resource in one that is gaining. This strategy works because it is a lot easier in a tornado to see the losers than to pick the winner. You just continue this process of subtraction until there is only one project left. But at no time let yourself fall prey to wishing. Do not *gamble*. Just place your bets, take your losses (and your winnings), and move on.

Finally, if you do not have this kind of resource, if you cannot afford to back many horses at the same time, then this whole business is likely to be a non-issue. To be sure, by betting wrong, you will miss the tornado platform, but given your size going in, you were not likely to come out the gorilla anyway. Missing the tornado, therefore, is not a catastrophe for you. Indeed, it might be a benefit in disguise, since in a smaller pond, you may yet emerge a market leader.

Was Apple's Macintosh Strategy a Tornado Mistake?

One of the favorite parlor games in Silicon Valley has been to second-guess Apple's Macintosh strategy, virtually from the time it was initiated. Many people would argue that indeed it has been a succession of tornado mistakes. I would like to close this whole discussion of tornado strategy by arguing the opposite side of the case.

First, let us be clear about what Apple's strategy has been. Apple chose not to try to prevent the PC tornado from going forward—not to get in its way—but at the same time not to participate directly in it. Instead it became the only significant vendor in the market to decide not to be IBM-compatible. Moreover, although it considered doing so multiple times, it never licensed its operating system software, not until 1994 when the tornado was long past. Instead, it decided to take the higher-value-added approach to market development.

What are the consequences of such a strategy in a tornado? Here is what the model predicts:

- You will sell out everything you can make. This is true of every vendor in the tornado, so it should be true of you as well.
- You will get fabulous margins because not only are you selling in the hot product category, you are adding value on top of that.
- You will lose the tornado battle to someone who is adopting the low-road marketing strategy: commoditize and just ship.
- As this market share battle becomes visible, with the other company winning, you will get kicked out of the tornado and be tagged as a niche or high-end player.

This, in retrospect, appears to be what happened to Apple during the PC revolution. Apple was first into the PC market as a product category but not as a market category, at least not for the business sector. Why wasn't it able to become the business gorilla?

At the time, only one company had market permission to start a business customer tornado and be the leader, and that was IBM. That is, no one in the early 1980s could imagine a major computer market that would not be led and dominated by IBM, so everyone was waiting for their PC. Eventually IBM did enter the market, and from the outset it left Apple in the dust. But there was nothing that Apple could have done about it, so the company—wisely, in my view—pulled out of that tornado and established itself instead as a strong niche leader in the graphics, business presentation, home, and education markets. Thus, while IBM compatibles could claim more than 80 percent of the total PC market, Apple Macs could claim a correspondingly dominant market share in their niche markets.

The question is, by so doing, did Apple win or lose? I would argue it played the game correctly, given the hand it was dealt. And I would argue the same for its actions during the next round of the competition, when the market actually moved toward Apple by embracing its Macintosh GUI (Graphical User Interface) standard. At this point Apple had, at least in theory, the opportunity to head off Windows, or at least blunt its impact by broadly licensing its Mac OS software. If it had done so, many analysts contend, it would have created a much larger installed base of Macintosh-compatible systems and thereby given ISVs, who have always had a special feeling for the Mac anyway, more reason to develop for that platform.

While many armchair quarterbacks today chide Apple for not making this move, tornado theory would predict it could not have had the desired effect. Microsoft, as the market leader in DOS systems, could never be dethroned as long as in its move toward GUI it sustained backward compatibility with its installed base's product architecture—as long, that is, as it did not force switching costs on its current customers. Apple could not promise anything comparable because unlike Microsoft it could never control the DOS standard.

Apple's effort, more likely, would have ended up like the market consortia that RISC microprocessor vendors like Sun and HP tried to build around their architectures. Solbourne Computer, the best-known licenser of Sun's operating system, is now defunct as a computer manufacturer, and the two major licensees of HP's PA RISC chip, Samsung and Hitachi, have yet to bring a significant product to market. In the meantime, these efforts have consumed an enormous amount of marketing resource to little avail. Given that, Apple's best move probably was its lawsuit attempt, but when that failed, Apple was penned even more tightly into its niche status.

A third opportunity now stands on Apple's horizon, a third tornado coming into view, this time from a market that Apple more than any other company has helped create: the home computer market. Can the company play the game any differently this time around? With each successive version of Windows, Apple's advantage in GUI fades further, but it still has a significant advantage in plug-and-play integration because it has a proprietary system architecture that it controls. This should confer a major competitive advantage in the fight for consumer satisfaction in the home. Moreover, its marketing has always had a more of a consumer feel to it than its competitors'. Can the company make something sustainable from these advantages?

It is not easy for me to see how. Independent software vendors are too deeply committed to the Microsoft architecture to give Apple the support it needs. ISV loyalty to Microsoft is not out of love necessarily but out of installed base commitments, distribution channel expectations, and sheer available market size. Without the allegiance of these software vendors, no hardware vendor can prosper. Apple has succeeded to date because it has inspired ISVs by consistently out-innovating the Microsoft/IBM/Compaq alliance and because, to this day, it is the only major personal computer company that has ever demonstrated even a modest appreciation for esthetics. These are major strengths that should not be underestimated as competitive forces, particularly in the home market. But now its competitors are learning these lessons, and Apple's position has increasingly been compromised by having had to give ground in market share battles overall. It always seems to find itself fighting a retreating action. This is the painful price of not winning the tornado battle. The lesson here is that once a gorilla cartel like Microsoft or Intel gets established, it gets harder and harder to be a chimpanzee.

The victory scenario for Apple would play out a lot like England's strategy in World War II. Having refused to collaborate with the dark forces, it now needs to recruit an ally bigger than its opponents, someone fresher and more resourceful, which it can then guide into the home computer fray. That ally cannot come from the computer industry, but it could come from telecommunications, entertainment, publishing, or photography. Today, despite all kinds of statements of direction, all four of these areas have produced more smoke than fire, but with Apple leading that might change. At any rate, their entry would at least create a game whose outcome is not predetermined. It has been some time since Apple has seen such an opportunity.

Recap: The Tornado *vs.* the Bowling Alley

The most important lesson of this chapter is that the critical success factors for tornado strategy are diametrically opposed to those for the bowling alley. As a consequence, companies who have won great victories in the bowling alley and persist in their to-date successful mode of operation doom themselves to become second-tier players in the tornado and play increasingly marginalized roles as the market goes forward.

Here is a recap of the key contrasts:

Bowling Alley	Tornado
Focus on the economic buyer and the end user; approach the infrastructure buyer late in the sales cycle.	Ignore the economic buyer and the end user; focus exclusively on the infrastructure buyer.
Emphasize return on investment as the compelling reason to buy.	Ignore return on investment. Focus on timely deployment of reliable infrastructure.
Differentiate your whole product for a single application.	Commoditize your whole product for general-purpose use.
Partner with a value-added distribution channel to ensure customized solution delivery.	Distribute through low-cost, high-volume channels to ensure maximum market exposure.
Use value-based pricing to maximize profit margins.	Use competition-based pricing to maximize market share.
Avoid competition to gain niche market share.	Attack competition to gain mass market share.
Position your products within vertical market segments.	Position your products horizontally as global infrastructure.

What comparisons like this make clear—and we will see a similar set at the end of the next chapter between the tornado and Main Street—is that it is absolutely critical to gain management consensus on where the market is in the Technology Adoption Life Cycle. Without such agreement, departments and work groups march forward under opposing banners, canceling out each other's work, creating confusion everywhere, and making market feedback impossible to interpret. By contrast, a common effort in *any* direction—even the wrong one—quickly generates positive results, either in the form of an immediate victory or a course correction leading to subsequent success.

It behooves us, then, to have a good mechanism for gaining that consensus, and this book will offer one. Before we turn to it, however, we need to incorporate the third and final inflection point in the Technology Adoption Life Cycle, the transition from the tornado to Main Street.

CHAPTER 5

ON MAIN STREET

When Dorothy steps out of the tornado into the land of Oz, she is remarkably accepting of her new fate, and after a brief interlude for adjustment, sets right off down the Yellow Brick Road. How admirably resourceful! If only our high-tech companies could show such pluck!

Unfortunately, when they exit the tornado, they are in denial. And no wonder. The typical transition to Main Street begins catastrophically, displaying one or more of the following characteristics:

- Dramatic shortfalls in projected revenues and profits
- Restatements of earnings that go back one or two years
- Massive exodus of the executives responsible
- Drastic downturns in stock price
- A shareholder lawsuit, to be settled out of court, which further drains an already abused stock of capital

Welcome to Main Street. Your customers hate you; your employees are burned out and demoralized; your management team's greatest expertise is political infighting; Wall Street hasn't a clue; and your banker is on Line 1. *And you were the winner!*

Why So Calamitous?

Let's get one thing straight right off. Tornadoes do not end any faster than they start. There are always plenty of warnings. The problem is that we ignore them all. We just keep the pedal to the metal, and the results are, well, bloody.

Why do we do this? As with many ill-considered actions, it's because it seems like the right thing to do at the time. Consider the context. For the past four years or so, we have been part of an organization that has been growing at 100 percent or more per year. Without any additional stimulation effort on our part, market demand is screaming, and we in turn are whipping ourselves to outsell and outship the competition.

Everyone is running on adrenaline, and macho management is the winning tactic. If you say you can sell 200 percent of quota, I say I can sell 300 percent—bet you a thousand dollars and meet you at the President's Club in Kuala Lumpur. It's a competitive spirit, and it's like a drug, or more probably a hormone. It gets in your blood, and you can't see straight. So when the first signs of a slowdown begin to emerge, you bash right through them. Only the strong survive. Make it happen. No fear. Just do it. Just win, baby.

For a while this approach works a lot better than one might expect. There is normally enough slack in any market to reward a do-or-die effort once or even twice. But then the signals start getting stronger, to the point where even *we* can see them. But how do we get off this carousel? And who is going to blink first? The problem now, with all our macho slogans still ringing in our ears, is that there is no way we can retreat and save face. So, since saving face is more important than winning (this being the fundamental vulnerability of all macho strategies), we blast ahead anyway.

This is bad enough, but it gets worse. As we start getting close to the end of quarters or fiscal years, we begin to get more "aggressive" about bookings. Year-end sales get booked on December 38th. Future commitments get scored as current revenues. Sales into indirect channels, which are still subject to returns, get booked as if they were already sold through. *Questionable accounting practices* is what this is sometimes called. And now, of course, we are not just trying to save face with our colleagues. We are trying to save stock price on Wall Street, which of course is a losing battle. Wall Street has pegged us as a hypergrowth stock, which has shot our valuation way up. Now hypergrowth is stopping. The tornado is ending. There is nothing we can do about that. So of course our valuation must go down. Trying to keep it up artificially is a losing game—the best you can do is postpone the inevitable, each time at the cost of making the eventual crash that much more catastrophic.

Sooner or later, then, all this catches up with us. And when it does, resignations must and do follow, in Watergate fashion, with everyone trying to stonewall along the way. Eventually, to be sure, the bloodshed stops. Eventually people start picking up the pieces, and the high-tech enterprise is able to wean itself from the drug of hypergrowth, substituting instead the sort of business disciplines that are routine in other industries. But it does so with its head cast down, and at the first sign of a new tornado, it is off and running again.

In other words, we never learn. And that is the remarkable news from Silicon Valley regarding Main Street—not that we have lessons to teach but rather that, unlike other business sectors, we have been unable to prosper in this location. The reason why is that Main Street's normal dynamics are undermined by rapid change, the very essence of high tech, making its economics far less attractive than normal. That in turn has led to a whole generation of executives taking an anti–Main Street approach to their business planning, substituting instead a vision of perpetual tornadoes. That vision, it will come as no surprise, is flawed, and in the end, technology-based companies must make their peace with Main Street if they are ever to sustain prosperity. It is the goal of this chapter to facilitate that process. But before we set about correcting the errors of our ways, we need to appreciate why we made them in the first place.

Main Street Undermined

The fundamentally defining element of high tech is that all its products rest atop an ever-escalating price/performance engine known as the semiconductor integrated circuit. As we noted in the opening chapter, in the 1970s this technology increased in price/performance an order of magnitude or power of ten every ten years. In the 1980s, the rate of price/performance improvement sped up to an order of magnitude every seven years. In the 1990s it has become every 3.5 years and is still compressing. Ten times the power for the same price, three times in a single decade! Applied to your new car, it would mean it could cruise at 55,000 miles per hour and drive for 350,000 miles on a single tank of gas—meaning, among other things, you would never need to buy gasoline.

The semiconductor chip is the genie inside high-tech's lamp. It seems to have granted our every wish—or will at least in the next release. But here we should heed Goethe's famous warning: "Beware what you wish for in youth—it may be granted in middle age." If infinite price-performance improvements coming faster and faster seems like a dream come true, it can also be a nightmare. Here's why.

As we also noted earlier, price/performance escalation stimulates an unstoppable series of paradigm shifts. Each time the underlying constraints that shape the current paradigm are removed, the design trade-offs that characterize its strategy become obsolete, and a new generation of capabilities are enabled. Vendors, regardless of how secure their position was under the old paradigm, must switch to the new or leave themselves open to the new crop of competitors. There is no time to settle down and prosper on Main Street. Instead, we find ourselves living in "Tornado Alley."

As a result, the same semiconductor engine that makes the high-tech sector as a whole a vibrant and stable economic institution actually undermines the individual companies that comprise it. You simply cannot build long-term Main Street franchises if tornadoes keep tearing through the town. No wonder the high-tech marketplace is continually revamping its power structures. With hot new companies entering on the wave of each new ripple in the price-performance curve, the market must rewrite the rules that it put in place seemingly only moments before.

All this has led some high-tech leaders to embrace a philosophy about market development that eschews Main Street altogether, along the lines that follow.

Stairway to Heaven?

The underpinning of this philosophy, not surprisingly, is the Technology Adoption Life Cycle, but visualized as an **S**-curve instead of a bell curve. As such, it describes market growth in terms of its accumulated revenues instead of its current ones. But it is pointing at exactly the same phenomena. Looking not unlike an integral sign from calculus, its curl at the bottom equates to the early market, the chasm, and the bowling alley, when revenues accumulate slowly; its steep rising stem to the tornado, when they accelerate rapidly; and its curving at the top to the transition to Main Street, when the rate of new revenue accumulation subsides.

High-Tech Sector Growth Model

This model has a tendency to underestimate both pre-tornado period risks and post-tornado period rewards, but it has no problem drawing attention to the essence of the tornado. And for as long as I can recall, technology marketing has assumed that, as one reaches the top of one **S**-curve, one should be looking to transition into the bottom of the next one.

Some might call this building a staircase out of seahorses. I would call it *scheduling tornadoes*. It is not only presumptuous—it just doesn't work. Or rather, it works for the high-tech sector as a whole, and even for a few highly blessed companies at its core, but is inoperable as a company-specific strategy for any but these chosen few. Let's see why.

The companies that have in fact been able to accomplish this miracle on a consistent basis are well-known fixtures in the industry. Intel has been able to institutionalize a staircase of **S**-curves with its 8086 architecture series, and Microsoft too has been able to jump tornadoes with its transition from DOS to Windows. Apple was able to go from the Apple II to the Macintosh, IBM extended itself beyond mainframes to launch both the PC revolution and an extremely successful AS/400 line, DEC shifted from the PDP to the VAX line, Lotus appears to be transitioning successfully from 1-2-3 to Notes (albeit with some shaky ground in between), and Hewlett-Packard has done it in two very different domains—from the proprietary 3000 to the open systems 9000 in minicomputers, and from the LaserJet to DeskJet transition in PC printers.

But when we survey the totality of companies who have had one—and only one—great success in high tech, we are painfully reminded of how many companies have been unable to capitalize on the next paradigm shift—not Four-Phase, Data General, Prime, nor Wang; not Cullinet, MSA, McCormack & Dodge, nor Ross Systems; not Tandem, Britton Lee, Teradata, nor Cray; not Borland, Ashton-Tate, WordPerfect, nor Software Publishing Corporation; not Osborne, Atari, Coleco, nor Commodore; or to look at some very powerful companies today, not—or at least not yet—Sun, Novell, Sybase, or Dell.

When a game generates so few real winners and so many potential losers, and when the losers are of such a high caliber, it simply means it's a bad game to play. No one company, I would argue, can expect to get all these transitions lined up to its advantage. It would be like building a business plan based on getting funding from lottery jackpot winnings—*repeatedly!* Sooner or later we will get left out in the lurch, get out of phase with the shift, and be tossed aside. There simply has to be a more secure underpinning to our businesses.

Main Street market development is at least a partial solution to this problem. Over the last two decades, high-tech marketing has left an enormous amount of money on the table by racing away from Main Street well in advance of the next tornado's arrival. In part that practice has been based on the mistaken notion that Main Street equates to low-profit commodity markets, a notion that this chapter will dispel. In part it has been based on the post-tornado organization's immaturity, its inability to accept less-than-meteoric growth going forward.

What these high-flying organizations must understand instead is that Main Street is as natural and appropriate a part of the life cycle as any other phase, and falling into denial here is just as costly as it is elsewhere. When markets give you Main Street opportunities and you do not capitalize on them, you lose your best source of funding for recycling back into the next tornado.

At the same time, what analysts outside the technology sector must appreciate, is that there can be no long-term stable Main Street markets until the price-performance escalation of semiconductors ceases. As of this writing, such an endpoint cannot be forecast. So the notion of settling down on Main Street must also be dispelled.

What we need is a rational model for making the transition, extending the franchise, while keeping our eye out for the next wave. Nothing like this has been needed before, not at this level of speed and intensity, so it is here after all that Silicon Valley does have some unique lessons to teach—after we learn them ourselves.

The Fundamentals of Main Street

Main Street markets begin when the waves of frantic infrastructure replacement begin to subside, the new paradigm begins to settle in. Consumption of the core commodity continues at a prodigious rate, but now supply has once again got ahead of demand. Indeed, it has *accelerated* ahead of demand, since as long as markets are undersupplied, the industry *ramps* capacity aggressively, creating painful overshoots that contribute to the chaos and carnage we have already chronicled.

With supply exceeding demand, buying power returns to the customer, and vendors must once again compete for their business. This competition takes on two forms—a price-based competition, focused on the infrastructure buyer, and a value-based competition focused on niches of end users. Main Street, in other words, has two sides, as illustrated by the following diagram:

Main Street Market Opportunities

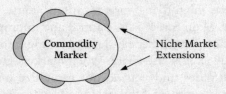

On the commodity side, unit volume continues to grow but price erosion makes net revenues flat. Even products with advanced technology are subject to this flattening, as the technical workstation industry all too readily will testify, with unit growth in 1993 and 1994 in the 30 to 40 percent range, but revenue growth in the 8 to 15 percent range. Every year this industry must run faster and faster just to stay in the same place.

The commodity side of Main Street has most appeal to two constituencies—conservative economic buyers and purchasing agents. The latter are compensated for securing commodities at the lowest price. Main Street for them begins whenever the product category in question is sufficiently standardized that it can be let out for lowest bid. Conservative economic buyers also seek low prices, but for a different reason. They do not think the product can be worth very much to them, not because it is a bad product, but because they have trouble getting value from anything technical.

To serve these customers, vendors must develop a whole series of low-cost disciplines, which will have the following salutary effects:

- It will expand their unit market share, creating more "customers for life."
- It will increase their profitability on higher margin sales.

That being said, vendors also need to get margin relief from some form of value-based pricing. This in turn means gaining sponsorship for value from someone in the buying organization. We should note that, as we move on to Main Street, our two previous sponsors for value-based pricing have both withdrawn their interest. The pragmatist economic buyers who sponsored us in our bowling alley days have long since directed their attentions elsewhere because the infrastructure roll-out has resolved their problems. And the IT community, which sponsored value-based pricing during the tornado to ensure quality underpinnings to the infrastructure it was anxious to deploy, finally has things back under control and is focused elsewhere. Now that these two groups have removed themselves from the field, we must find a new sponsor, someone else who will assign value to our differentiation. It is in this context that we focus our attention, really for the first time, on the end user. They are the ones who define the lucrative niche markets on Main Street, the added-value extensions that live at the periphery of the core commodity infrastructure.

Focusing on the End User

Prior to Main Street, end users have only a secondary voice in high-tech purchase decisions, the special issues of the economic buyer and the infrastructure buyer taking precedence. But now that those issues have been resolved, end users can come into prominence. What they want is personal satisfaction from using the product, be it in the form of greater productivity, enhanced enjoyment, or reduced pain. This holds true regardless of whether the product is a business or a consumer purchase, the question being in the latter case whether they can afford it, in the former case, whether they can get their boss to pay for it.

In either case, this desire for personal satisfaction, from a vendor perspective, creates the ground for a value-based competition based on differentiated offerings. Such ground is critical to stake out and develop if the vendor is to get any relief from the margin pressure of low-cost commodity procurements. The goal of end-user marketing, then, is to leverage their preferences into higher margin returns.

Now the amount of leverage end users have, particularly in business, is limited, and so the amount of additional margin one can gain is modest. This means that the investment in differentiation one makes to secure that margin must also be limited. One cannot, for example, redesign the whole product just to get a few more dollars per unit. Instead, one must leverage the whole product that already exists, making what are from a technical point of view minor modifications to it, but what to an end user add differentiating value.

This is the strategy of *mass customization*. It is hardly news anywhere outside of high tech, being the fundamental basis of much consumer packaged-goods marketing. But it is having a startling impact inside high tech. Ours is an industry founded by and run by engineers. On Main Street, for the first time, the power of the R&D function comes under challenge. It no longer holds the key to going forward. Mass customization does not require technology breakthroughs but rather perceptive design alterations. This is the province of marketing—or should be. But ceding control to marketing represents such a huge culture change that many high-tech enterprises simply cannot execute it. Instead they continue to force new R&D on a market that has lost its appetite for it, generating unnecessarily high costs and low incremental returns, which then sours them on Main Street and pushes them back to the staircase of **S**-curves, desperately seeking another tornado.

The fundamental lesson of Main Street, the one which we deny, is that it does not need *more advanced* high-tech solutions, it needs *more accommodating* ones. This, in turn, implies a whole new set of disciplines with which our sector is unfamiliar. These disciplines, well known from other industries, must be redefined for use in high tech, a task our industry is just now undertaking.

The Money Is Already There

The defining characteristic of Main Street is that continued profitable market growth can no longer come from selling the basic commodity to *new customers* and must come instead from developing niche-specific extensions to the base platform for *existing customers*. The end users want these extensions, but how are they going to pay for them? It turns out they don't have to—*they're free!*

Okay, maybe not exactly free, but they certainly seem to be, for as the price performance of high tech continues to improve, the product customers purchased two or three years ago now costs much less when bought today. But customers still build their budgets on the assumption that product prices are going to stay the same, or perhaps increase a little. As a result, whether as a business customer or as a consumer, they have allocated more funds to the next purchase than are required and are pleasantly surprised to find some left over. Now the job of purchasing agents is to get those leftover funds back, and, left to their own devices, they will. But the job of vendors is to attract end users into spending those "free" dollars instead on added-value extensions that appeal to them.

To do that, we need to give them the right kind of offer, what we have ended up calling the *whole product + 1*.

The Whole Product + 1

The idea behind +1 extensions to the whole product is to leverage the commoditized whole product created in the tornado, creating differentiation through secondary characteristics rather than through driving up its primary performance vectors. The latter is happening too, of course, but increasingly it is being taken for granted and is unable to generate the needed profit margins. These secondary characteristics, on the other hand, are rooted as much in the subjective experience of the end user as they are in any objective change to the product itself, and represent an unexploited opportunity to create perceived added value.

Hewlett-Packard, for example, targets home office users at the commodity level with very low-cost 500 series ink-jet printers. At the same time, however, they also conduct target niche campaigns to go after:

- those who are *space-constrained*, offering them a compact portable printer from their 300 series, or
- those who *do not yet own a fax*, with their *OfficeJet* printer-fax, or
- those who *create commercial flyers*, with a higher performance color printer such as their 1200 or new 850 series.

Or take the example of Intuit, which has made home finance computing so accessible through a host of low-cost promotions of its core product, Quicken. Now they are using value-added extensions to go after:

- their installed base, with an upgrade called Quicken Deluxe,
- those who are just starting a small business, with a bundle called QuickBooks With QuickPay,
- those who use credit cards frequently, with a Quicken Visa card that offers a register of charges downloadable into Quicken format.

These are all whole product +1 offers. They leverage the existing commodity infrastructure by adding one differentiating element on top of it. The goal is to win the sponsorship of a specific category of end users, justifying a higher price based not on a higher cost but rather on a higher value received.

Well, so what? After all, this same concept has been the

underpinning of consumer packaged-goods marketing for the better part of a century. Breakfast cereals have their +1 extensions (two scoops of raisins, alphabet shapes, frosted flakes), as do beers (light, cold-filtered, dry, iced), and shampoos (conditioning, coloring, dandruff-reducing). In each case the vendor has been able to isolate a new target segment who will pay a premium for, or base their product selection on, the +1 factor. And their advertising and promotion has successfully focused end-user attention on this one factor as a way of differentiating what is, from a purely utilitarian point of view, a highly *undifferentiated* core product.

So? So the big deal is that this set of tactics is so foreign to engineering mentality as to be virtually paralyzing to high-tech companies.

Overcoming Fear of +1 Marketing

+1 marketing violates a fundamental assumption at the heart of the engineering world, that the value of anything is a function of its objective utility. The notion of a purely subjective value—of just liking something because it has a nice shape or a pretty color—is not really understood by engineers. They know it happens, they know it happens to them, they know it can affect purchase decisions, they even know it affects their own purchase decisions—but it just does not make sense. Therefore they try to distance themselves from it. And they do this by assigning it to marketing.

Marketing, in the engineering universe, is that place where the laws of utility are suspended. They are of two minds about this. On the one hand, if painting the product red sells more product, by all means paint it red. On the other hand, since there is no rational cause operating here, you cannot trust marketing, as anyone can see for themselves, since sometimes when they paint it red, it does not sell more. So marketing is essentially voodoo. It is for flakes. It is not a real discipline. It is a con job.

And that is when engineering is being nice. Now, this has been the source of much high-tech humor and joshing back and forth between the two groups, but in fact it represents a life-threatening disability when it comes to Main Street success. Because on Main Street continued high-profit margins can only come from end users sponsoring our product over the low-cost clone, and the only thing that will get them to do that is to deliver them subjective experiences of the product that fulfill their needs. That means engineering must learn to authentically empower marketing.

The problem is, engineers will not turn over the reins to any institution until they can understand its underlying mechanisms, how and why it works. They can't. It would be like walking out on air. And that is what is so paralyzing about Main Street's imperatives, why Main Street denial is so prevalent throughout high tech.

To go forward from here it helps engineering considerably if it can conceptualize marketing as a *systems discipline.* In this frame of reference, markets are economic systems, and the role of marketing is to facilitate the transfer of money from the market into the company by ensuring that the company is delivering value out to the market. It is a systems-level exchange that obeys the laws of equilibrium. If either side of the system lacks what the other needs, the exchange does not happen. But when the right pairings meet up, it does. Defining who our right customers might be, and what value they might want, and what whole product or whole product + 1 we can provide that delivers that value—all this is the new meaning of marketing.

The goal here is to permit R&D to let go of controlling the company's invention process—not everywhere in the life cycle, to be sure, but when on Main Street. If we really can get the ball served into marketing's court, then it can be marketing, rooting its processes in customer interaction and communication, that can come to R&D with product ideas, not the other way around. That is how it works in consumer packaged-goods companies—"We've found a niche of people who would like a raspberry room deodorizer, can you make one?"—and how it must be done on Main Street in high tech.

A company like Intuit has captured the attention of our

industry precisely because of its ability to do just this. In part as a legacy of its chairman Scott Cook's stint at Procter & Gamble, Intuit has repeatedly demonstrated the kind of customer-focused market learning, experimentation, and research necessary to drive this kind of innovation. Now it's time for the rest of the industry to catch up. To do that we need some new tools, the most important of which will help us rediscover just who end users really are and what they really want.

Rediscovering the Customer

To win high margins on Main Street, we have stated repeatedly, otherwise commoditized offerings differentiate themselves by providing just the right +1 factor to a target niche of end users. So what do these end users want? It turns out that answering this question is quite a challenge for any post-tornado organization. Here's why.

During its hypergrowth, it quite correctly has ignored the customer, focusing instead on its supply chains and distribution channel relationships, driving toward increasingly indirect forms of distribution in order to lower costs and expand coverage. These same channels are not anxious to share their own customer information with vendors, for fear that the vendors will go around them and sell direct, say, by mail order. At the same time, truth be known, these channels are often as customer-ignorant as the vendors themselves, lacking anything like the information systems they would need to track down niche opportunities. And so, like an audience coming out of a matinee movie, vendors and channels alike exit the tornado blinking and befuddled, saying—*"We have to get closer to the customer!"* Okay, but how?

The key here is to leverage your number one asset, the fact that people are still buying your commodity product. By experimentally promoting or bundling this product with a specific "added-value" offer, you can create communications to attract whatever type of target customer you might be interested in. Then by tracking down and interviewing the customers who actually respond to this offer, you can learn more about their relationship to your product, how you can improve future offers to them, and gain more of their purchase dollars.

In short, the basic discipline for Main Street marketing is:

- Make an offer.
- Learn from it.
- Correct your mistakes.
- Make another offer.

This is the opposite of the deliberate, careful approach used in the bowling alley, where an "offer" involves coordinating a substantial amount of investment, including a series of partnership relationships, and risking one's reputation in the process. On Main Street, offers are much *lighter*. They can be pulled together faster, they typically involve no more than one partner, and if they fail, the market normally just ignores them. So one can use offers much more aggressively, and many companies do.

The Offer as the Research Instrument

Where companies fall down, in many cases, is that they neglect to think of this activity as a research mode, as *test marketing*. Instead, they think of it as a product-moving promotion, and thus fail to build *learning* into the offer mechanism. This is close to criminal. Most high-tech offers, particularly in the retail end of the business, require some additional processing to fulfill them. Once the customer has entered this process, but before the offer has been fulfilled, there is a window of data collection opportunity. This is the time and place to learn about niches.

During the fulfillment portion of the purchase process, in other words, you have a "live customer" on the other end of the line. No other research point can so reliably qualify a respondent. If you make contact before this moment, you are never sure you are listening to a true buyer. And if you wait until after the offer is fulfilled, there is always a chance you are getting a biased sample—say, people who respond to surveys of their own free will or people who file customer registration cards (which, incidentally, typically eliminates most *Fortune* 500 customers). But if you collect data *during the purchase*, then you have your hands on something special.

Some of this data will inevitably fall out of the order configuration process—what type of computer do you have, do you want the single or multi-user license, etc. To really get into the subtleties of a customer's reason to buy—their niche needs and the demographics and psychographics that go along with it—requires a carefully scripted additional effort. If you realize, however, that this data's value may well exceed the value of the profit margin on the product being sold, you will plan to offer your customer a special reward for giving it to you ("If you can take the time to answer a few additional questions, we'd like to send you this valuable [free offer]").

Such are the underlying mechanics behind what is sometimes called the "Ready, Fire, Aim" approach to niche identification. The point of going into these kinds of tactics is to make one point absolutely clear:

> **Ignorance of target customer niches is no excuse for not immediately pursuing a niche-based marketing program on Main Street.**

If you don't have a clear target customer in mind, make one up! Put something out there and see what happens. Get your organization moving. Gain the core competence of iteratively probing, learning, and responding. Neither the risks nor the resources required are sufficient to deter you from diving directly into the marketplace, and the reward of finding a profitable niche is more than adequate recompense for the temporary setback and embarrassment of having a first offer resoundingly rejected.

A word of warning, however: if the foregoing seems like a pretty straightforward idea, it is not. Most companies simply cannot execute this program, despite acknowledging its attractiveness. Success based on persisting through learning requires an iterative approach, which in turn requires procedures and organizations that can "turn the crank" quickly on marginal ideas. Unfortunately, successful companies normally purge their companies of this capability during the tornado, replacing it with procedures that intentionally make pursuing anything less than a multimillion-dollar home run opportunity not worth the trouble. Such an anti-niche approach was good strategy then, when friction was the enemy, but it is bad strategy on Main Street, where niches are the prime source of nutrients. It's just one more thing you have to reverse as you make this life cycle transition.

Finding Your +1 Opportunities

In the old dysfunctional relationship between engineering and marketing, the former had responsibility for the whole product, the latter for the +1 factors. Since neither really understood what the other was doing, the relationship between whole product and +1 factors was arbitrary and often forced. You could see this most easily in the advertising campaigns, where the subjective representation of the product had nothing much to do with its reality and a whole lot more to do with whatever style or image was currently in vogue in the marketing department.

This is a losing strategy. The right way to proceed is to take a systems view of the market and ask ourselves, what do we have to offer at little or no incremental cost to ourselves that the market would pay us more money for? If we look outside high tech, one answer to this can be a *compelling fantasy*. Nike shoes, Mont Blanc pens, Harley Davidson motorcycles, the Vermont Teddy Bear Company teddy bears, and Ben and Jerry's ice cream all get extraordinarily high premium prices for their products by virtue of marketing communications that shape the consumer's experience in desirable ways. This is the realm of mystique advertising, something that meets our criteria of adding little incremental cost to the product while delivering added value to the end user.

That being said, however, let us recognize first that such wins are rare, and second, that nerds are not good at mystique. If we are going to have a better than even chance of winning the game, we need to play by a different set of rules. So let us ask the question again: *What do we have to offer at little or no incremental cost to ourselves that the market would pay us more money for?* That answer is, a ton of stuff—and it's already in the product!

Consider all the menu items on your favorite software program, all the buttons on the remote control for your TV, or the ones on the front of your telephone. Do you know what every one of them does? Okay, maybe you do, but nobody else does. So what does that mean? It means that R&D dollars have been put into these products that customers have never gotten out. In short, hidden inside every successful high-tech product is a wealth of untapped R&D investment. The easiest way to create and leverage +1 marketing programs, therefore, is simply to focus them on the heretofore unused portions of these feature sets, to call out these features one by one, match them up with the niche of customers that would most benefit from them, and celebrate them in marketing communications campaigns.

The key point here is a simple one: Until a product's feature is used, it has no value. What Main Street marketing allows customers to do is to catch up to the value latent in the high-tech product line but had to be suppressed in order not to confuse people during the rush to deploy the new infrastructure. Now that things have settled down, they can have a chance to experience this value, but only if we teach them to. That is the function of +1 marketing. It focuses on one or more of these features, finds out who might really like it, and figures out why it is not being used today. Then it invests whatever +1 R&D is needed to remove the obstacles and repackages the offering, targeted at a specific niche of customers, touting the new +1 capability. By so doing, everyone wins—everyone, that is, except the purchasing agent. The end user gets more value, the economic buyer does not go over budget, the technical buyer still gets standard reliable infrastructure, and the vendor gets higher margins.

+1 market research, then, is a joint enterprise between R&D and marketing, the former helping to surface the latent potential still unreleased in the product, the latter seeking out niches of people who might value that potential if it were repackaged to be more accessible to them. Once a good match has been found, then the goal is to deliver to that niche.

With all this focus on niches, it may seem like we are back in the bowling alley, but when it comes to the actual delivery mechanisms, Main Street and the bowling alley are miles apart.

Delivering +1 Programs to the Marketplace

Although niche marketing is the guiding principle behind both bowling alley and Main Street marketing, the critical success factors for delivering value to the customer differ considerably. In the bowling alley, there is no existing infrastructure in place to support your whole product. The key to serving niches here is to bring all the necessary support along with you. It's a bit like going backpacking—the goal is not to leave out anything critical. To accomplish this goal you rely heavily on a value-adding channel of distribution, which in turn implies scarce expertise and added cost, but as there is plenty of profit margin there to pay for it, it is not a concern. On Main Street, by contrast, you can take a supporting infrastructure for granted, which means you are not dependent on recruiting partners and allies. This is a good thing, because now there are no profit margins to pay for them. Instead, you must deliver +1 value within the constraints of the high-volume, low-cost distribution system that was brought into being by the tornado.

In terms of partnering, on Main Street at most you can partner with one other company (beyond whatever the market has standardized for the commoditized whole product), and you would only do that if the company were critical to the +1 factor. Bundling is a typical tactic in such an instance. In so doing you should realize that there is only enough added profit margin to suffice for one company—either you or the bundle supplier— with the other company getting some other type of reward. For example, the reward for the "other" partner might be an expansion of its installed base, with its costs covered, with the goal of making money later on in an aftermarket. Typically this means it will get the names and contact information of all the +1 customers, a motive which is putting more and more emphasis on transaction-time data capture for database marketing systems.

Customers will expect to buy +1 offers from the same channels of distribution that they learned to use during the tornado phase of the market. That is, once you have taught the customer how to go to a low-cost channel to get their needs met, you cannot ask them to now abandon that channel and go back to a higher cost alternative. This means that the +1 offer must not require more services than the tornado distribution channel can provide. In the case of retail channels, this normally means no channel-provided services at all. Instead, what the channel will provide is additional shelf space (a very precious commodity) in return for higher margin sales.

Since shelf space is so precious, and since the retail channel adds little or no value during the sale, many +1 programs have migrated to mail-order, catalog-based selling. Catalogs are an ideal venue for presenting +1 offers because you can make sure the message gets given correctly and you can use database marketing techniques to increasingly refine your target customer mailing lists. Additionally, mail order or telesales is an optimal fulfillment channel when the offer has no service component, as it incurs no costs that do not add value to the customer.

Competing on Main Street

Nothing is less understood by a successful tornado organization than how to compete effectively on Main Street. Recall that in the tornado you play a zero-sum game, fighting other companies to win the maximum number of new customers-for-life. On Main Street that fight is over—the market-share boundaries have been set—and all that's left to fight over are the latecomers and a handful of "switchable" customers who, if they were once disloyal, cannot be counted on as customers-for-life anyway. But try telling that to successful tornado managers. They know only one path to their goal—straight through the competition—and so, like veterans of a long-ago war, they simply keep fighting.

In so doing, they miss the true competition that differentiates Main Street winners from losers, which is more against the purchasing agent than against another vendor. The goal on Main Street is to maximize the financial yield from your installed base. You have captured your territory, now it is time to till it, and the company with the highest yield per acre is the victor. We want farmers, not soldiers, to win this competition that is more about squeezing value out of your own earth than annexing someone else's.

Working against us are purchasing agents who continue to foster competitive warfare to serve their interest in driving bids lower. In their view, the reference competitor is not the market leader's product but the clone. For example, when PCs were in the tornado, first IBM and then Compaq set the reference price. Everyone else had to discount below them in order to get sales. But once PCs moved on to Main Street, it was Dell and Gateway and Zeos that were setting the reference price, and IBM and Compaq were put on the defensive to justify their higher prices. As the risk of getting an incompatible system declines, the value the market assigns to the market leader decreases. The de facto standard is in place, so getting some "off brand" is not as big a risk, and hence the clone requires less of a discount to get the sale. There is still some value in a leading brand, but it is much decreased. Now instead you must earn margins by showing how your +1 programs add value above the commodity.

In terms of competition, then, +1 programs do not compete against other +1 programs as much as they do against the low-cost core commodity. The goal is to distinguish an otherwise undifferentiated offering, garnering a modest premium for niche-specific added value. At the same time, one can also win some additional fence-sitting customers who would otherwise have not purchased the commodity at all, the +1 offer pushing them over the top.

This approach to competition, in turn, implies a light touch with positioning. The +1 rewards are normally not great enough to warrant massive communications campaigns. Instead they are designed to capitalize on a purchase process that is already well oiled. This means more and more of the communications should be targeted closer and closer to the moment of purchase, where the process can be redirected at the last moment to a more profitable end. Merchandising, therefore, normally takes precedence over advertising, and where salespeople are present, training should focus not on how to educate the customer but on how to sell up from the established, low-cost solution (or down from the high-priced premium offer).

Line Extensions: A Late Tornado Tactic, Not Yet +1

Between the "Just ship" strategy of tornado marketing and the Main Street strategy of +1 marketing lies an intermediate step called *line extension*. This is a late tornado tactic, well established in consumer markets, which has been relatively straightforward for high-tech companies to adopt. The goal is to increase market penetration by starting to differentiate separable value propositions while at the same time continuing to focus on high-volume-only sectors to maintain tornado-level volumes.

By differentiating lines of products, one increases the number of *classes of customer* one can engage, thereby moving past an initial saturation point to continued significant volume. Desktop personal computers in business, for example, hit an initial saturation point in 1984, but out of that came line extensions for two new classes of PC computing, servers and laptops. In the 1990s we have seen another saturation point hit, this time encompassing pretty much the whole of the business sector, driving a second set of line extensions into home computing, led by the multimedia PC.

Compaq has been particularly successful with line extension. With the introduction of its Presario line, it moved strongly to compete in the core commodity market for SOHO (small office/home office) computing, taking back market share from companies like Dell and Gateway who had successfully exploited their lower cost distribution strategies to undercut Compaq's high-end position. This required Compaq to target low-end customers for the first time, something it had been loath to do until it changed top executives, because to do so it would have to "compromise" engineering standards. What it discovered, to its chagrin, is that the whole product in PCs had become sufficiently commoditized that these so-called compromises were in fact nothing of the sort—that indeed a low-cost PC with Compaq quality was very much within their grasp.

Other examples of successful line extensions from Compaq include its earlier moves into laptops, targeted at affluent executives and sales force automation applications, and its introduction of a multiprocessor SystemPro server line for downsizing, or upsizing, to an Intel-based platform. All these moves, in and of themselves, represent late tornado marketing, bridging the gap between early tornado line development (hitting a series of price/performance points with essentially the same category of product) and +1 marketing, which targets niches based on no significant additional engineering. Line extension represents a midpoint between the two, often requiring significant engineering (witness Dell's inability to field a decent laptop during this critical period), with the payback of higher volumes than a niche marketing approach could yield.

One key lesson here is that it can be a mistake to go to +1 marketing too soon. The goal instead should be to capture as much territory as possible in tornado mode, treating line extension as a late tornado territory capture technique, and *then* go back and settle that territory with +1 programs after the expansion is over.

Finally, as all of the above has implied, Main Street is not only conducive to the strategies of consumer marketing, it is also the natural habitat of consumer markets themselves. By this point in the life cycle the basic utility of the purchase is delivered by virtually all the solutions offered, and the technology risk has been completely absorbed, so buying decisions can be safely given over to gratifying personal values.

The part of the industry that has already benefited the most from Main Street is PC software vendors. Now with the advent of CD-ROM-enabled PCs in the home, we are seeing the beginning of what promises to be an explosion of titles that will compete for our "edutainment" dollars. Parents of bright children will surely invest heavily here, as heralded by the expansion of retail floor space the superstores are giving over and the emergence of new dedicated edutainment stores like LearningSmith.

So there is much to be excited about in the Main Street world. And the primary goal of high-tech companies should be to convert their approach to marketing in order to leverage these rewards. But all of this must still be advocated with the caveat that the underlying dynamics of high tech do not allow you to settle down on Main Street ever. To reinforce this point, we will close by looking at high-tech companies outside Silicon Valley that have tried to deny this fundamental point.

Trapping Yourself on Main Street

As we have noted repeatedly, the primary threat to Main Street marketing is the underlying price-performance escalation in integrated circuits. This inevitably forces paradigm shifts far earlier than is optimal for profitability. These shifts can be particularly shocking to markets where the tornado has *not* commoditized the whole product, and thus profit margins have stayed very high, as in the proprietary mainframe and minicomputer markets. Market leaders there have found themselves trapped in a velvet cage.

When whole products do not commoditize, markets stay relatively centralized, the number of customers stays relatively small, the number of service providers stabilizes, and profit margins for both products and services can be kept high. It is as if you are still back in the bowling alley, except that you have passed through a tornado, when demand far exceeded supply, which has allowed you to grow your company to *Fortune* 500 status.

At first glance, this looks a lot like heaven, and it would be were it not for those pesky integrated circuits underneath us all. Because regardless of how sophisticated your systems are today, regardless of how high the barriers to entry surrounding your Garden of Eden, if the weeds outside are growing at the rate of an order of magnitude every 3.5 years, they will invade and take over sooner or later. The question is, what are you going to do about it?

The only right answer here is to become a weed too and take over your own garden. Needless to say, however, that was not the first thought proprietary mainframe and minicomputer companies came up with, and for a long time they successfully held off the ever-encroaching jungle with machetes. Account teams would do everything they could to keep the commoditized solutions away from their customer base, including—indeed, especially focusing on—not selling their own company's low-end products.

There is a classic story told of IBM in this regard about a customer who asked the IBM account team for a Unix platform for a client-server application. The team studied the application and came back with a recommendation for upgrading the mainframe. The customer said no, maybe we weren't clear—we *want* a Unix solution, please propose us a *Unix* solution. So the team studied the problem some more and came back with a new proposal, this time for an AS/400. No, said the customer, we do not want a *proprietary* platform, thank you, we want an *open* one, like the IBM RS/6000—please propose a solution on that platform. So the team studied the problem again—not knowing that by this time the customer had invited Hewlett-Packard to propose a Unix solution—and came back with a third proposal, this one based on PS/2's running OS/2. No thank you, said the customer, we've decided to go with Hewlett-Packard. *Then* the IBM team proposed an RS/6000 solution, but would you believe it, the customer turned them down!

This behavior is reenacted constantly among account teams responsible for the installed bases of IBM, DEC, Unisys, Fujitsu, Hitachi, and NEC. The sales channel is in the hands of people whose interest is overwhelmingly to preserve the status quo. As such, it should come as no surprise that not one of these vendors has had an ounce of success with Unix-based systems. Hewlett-Packard, Sun, Sequent, and ATT GIS, on the other hand, are having a field day at these other companies' expense. The balance of power has already shifted, and *still* these companies are unable to respond. This *is* the curse of the velvet cage. The only way to break out is to create a second sales force and put it in direct competition with the first one. Otherwise, your low-end solutions will never find their way to market.

Beyond Main Street

Finally, what happens to products that age beyond Main Street's ability to renew and sustain? What happens to all the casualties of high tech's seemingly endless succession of torna-does? Where are all the CP/M PCs now? Where are the DEC PDPs, the HP pen plotters, the NBI word processors? And what about companies who today are running mission-critical applications that require the use of Cullinet's IDMS, Cincom's Total, Software AG's Adabas, or ADR's Datacom/DB? What is going to happen in the next decade to the mainframes of IBM, Unisys, and others, or to proprietary minicomputers like the HP 3000, IBM's AS/400, and DEC's VAX?

Once they get beyond Main Street, *product-based markets collapse back into service businesses.* At the very low end, these are nonprofit clubs of people who still stay in touch, sharing CP/M software now in the way that Amiga owners will five years from now. At the high end, service bureaus buy up the old platforms, keeping them running by cannibalizing parts from scrap, and selling time to companies who have mission-critical software they do not want to—or sometimes have lost the knowledge necessary to—convert to the newer platforms. For others the road forward will be a conversion, giving business to contract programmers with specialized tools and skills. And for many this road will also lead to the doors of one of the most remarkable companies in the industry—Computer Associates.

Computer Associates appears to be a product company, but in fact it is in a service business. It buys up distressed software companies who have gone beyond Main Street, strips away and discards all their development activity, focuses solely on their maintenance contracts with their installed bases, and imposes exacting financial disciplines to convert them into highly prof-

itable cash cows. In so doing it has earned the enmity of virtually everyone else in high tech. The distressed companies hate
CA because the rock-bottom prices they pay make them
acknowledge how far they have fallen from their original state.
The employees of these companies hate them because within
days of acquisition all but the requisite few have been fired.
Developers hate them because they do not invest in developing
new capabilities for their acquired products. Their customers
hate them because they squeeze premium maintenance fees
from companies who have painfully few alternatives other than
to pay them.

The truth is, however, every ecosystem needs a scavenger
service, and CA plays this absolutely vital role in ours. Oh, to be
sure, in my romantic moments, I turn to Dylan Thomas and
call out to the people late of ASK and Ingres who now sport CA
badges as they walk along their once-bustling, now-bare plaza
in Alameda, saying

> *Do not go gentle unto that good night!*
> *Rage, rage against the dying of the light!*

But who am I kidding? If we did not have a CA, we would
have to invent one. Its function is to be mercilessly cold-
blooded and analytical about what has retained value and what
has not, and it has been awesome in its ability to stay focused
on this proposition.

Other service businesses also grow out of the conditions
beyond Main Street. Collapsed mainframe and minicomputer
hardware and software companies, as well as imploding
ex-monopoly telecommunications organizations, find themselves with a surfeit of highly experienced staff. For years they
carried these people in cost centers dedicated to customer service, borne along by the rich margins their products gained in
their heyday. Now these companies are trying to transform this
resource into a profit center, converting themselves from product companies into *systems integrators*.

To date this has had mixed results. IBM, DEC, and Unisys
all have fielded successful professional service organizations.

But even these companies are walking a tightrope trying to revitalize a work force that has gotten painfully behind the power curve. They still have some strong trump cards, most notably a privileged access to big projects growing out of their long-term relationships with their installed base, but they must aggressively capitalize on this diminishing asset, using the projects they gain to train the next generation of staff, or else let younger and less burdened service firms like Cambridge Technology Partners or Houston-based BSG pass them by.

Finally, one of the more imaginative transformations from product to service orientation is currently under way at Cincom. Famed for products like Total, Supra, and Mantis, all legacies of the 1970s and 1980s, they found themselves in the mid-1990s unable to compete head on with the Oracles and Sybases of the world. Instead of converting themselves into yet another systems integration firm—a category they believe has become increasingly crowded and due for a shakeout soon—they are seeking to become the worldwide sales and support channel of choice for a new generation of software developers who have great products for large business and government, but who haven't a clue as to how to approach mainstream MIS organizations. Cincom, thus, is seeking to convert its relationship equity into a new round of product equity, acquiring the rights to R&D conducted outside its organization. This is the reverse of outsourcing—one might call it insourcing—but it makes sense after you do a post-Main Street situation analysis.

Recap

The key point in this chapter is that high-tech companies should welcome, not resist, the transition to Main Street, seeing it as an opportunity to settle into some profitable niche marketing—at least until the next tornado comes along. Unfortunately, the requisite behaviors to succeed in this program run directly counter to the skills honed during the tornado, as the following table summarizes:

Tornado	Main Street
Sell to the infrastructure buyer.	Sell to the end user.
Focus on need for timely deployment of reliable infrastructure.	Focus on the end user's experience of the product, seeking to gratify their individual needs.
Commoditize your whole product for universal deployment.	Differentiate the commoditized whole product with +1 campaigns targeted at specific niches.
Distribute through low-cost, high-volume channels and advertise heavily to ensure maximum market exposure.	Continue to distribute through the same channels, but now focus on merchandising to communicate +1 marketing messages.
Drive price points ever lower to maximize market share.	Celebrate +1 value propositions to gain margins above the low-cost clone.
Attack other competitors to gain market share.	Compete against your own low-cost offering to gain *margin* share.
Position yourself horizontally as standard global infrastructure.	Position yourself in niche markets, based on the individual preferences of end users.

As you can see, Main Street success factors run counter to the lessons of the tornado, much as the key success factors for the tornado ran counter to the lessons of the bowling alley. Disturbing as this is, there is simply nothing we can do to change it.

What we can do, however, is recognize that all this switching among contradictory states is bound to cause some confusion. In particular, it will be easy for some people to think we are in one stage of the market, while others think we are in another. If this is allowed to persist, people will be working at cross purposes—violently.

Therefore, as noted at the close of the previous chapter, it is critical that teams responsible for charting marketing strategy agree on where they are in the Technology Adoption Life Cycle before they set about formulating any plan of action. How to go about establishing that agreement is the subject of the next chapter.

CHAPTER 6

FINDING YOUR PLACE

The argument of this book is that marketing strategy changes dramatically—indeed, reverses itself—at every major inflection point in the Technology Adoption Life Cycle. By way of illustration, simply ask yourself, having read this far, what role does segmentation play in a successful marketing strategy?

The answers are:

- In the early market, you *must not* segment. Simply follow visionaries wherever they lead you.
- To cross the chasm and negotiate the bowling alley, you *must* segment. This is the basis for your whole product strategy.
- Once inside the tornado you *must not* segment. Ship standard infrastructure to gain as many new customers-for-life as you can during the paradigm shift.
- On Main Street you *must* segment—but not the way you segmented in the bowling alley. Now segmentation is the basis of your +1 strategy.

Since segmentation drives all other elements in a market-focused business plan, this means that successful strategies will reverse themselves several times during the life cycle of a single technology.

If that is not confusing enough, consider the following ways complexity can further increase:

1. Most companies field multiple products at the same time, in different places on their respective life cycles. Thus Lotus, for example, has 1-2-3 approaching end of life, ccMail on Main Street, and Notes just entering the tornado.

2. Different segments within the same market can be at different points on the life cycle. For example, in the United States the Internet is on Main Street among the Unix technical community, in the tornado among college students, in the bowling alley for market researchers, in the chasm for marketing information dissemination, and in the early market for commercial transactions.

3. The life cycle model is recursive. That is, within any given niche segment in the bowling alley, you can have a mini-tornado—a time when for that segment demand greatly exceeds supply—so you may have to mix strategy modes even within a single stage. This is what happened to Mentor Graphics in the CAD market and is happening right now to Silicon Graphics in the animation market.

4. Finally, since markets at different points in the life cycle interact with each other, such as today when Main Street financial applications are porting to tornado client-server platforms using bowling alley development tools, sometimes it is hard to know what phase anybody is at, or even whether or not there *is* a tornado under way, and if so, whose is it?

Faced then with three market development protocols—the bowling alley, the tornado, and Main Street—each coherent in itself but contradictory to the other two, how exactly should you proceed? Finding your bearings in such circumstances can be challenging indeed, but here are some key principles to help you along.

It's the Category, Not the Product

The first step to establishing your place in the life cycle is to realize that it is not your product per se but rather the category of product as a whole that the market positions. Let's take the example of Hewlett-Packard's 200LX, a pocket-sized palmtop PC that comes with Lotus 1-2-3, several calculators, a complete suite of Personal Information Management (PIM) software, and clever interfaces to e-mail, including a fully portable RadioMail unit. Where is that on the life cycle?

Well, the first question we must answer is, what *is* the 200LX? If it is a Portable Digital Assistant or PDA, it is in the chasm—obvious enough if you are Apple, Sony, or Motorola and have shipped few of your still awkwardly performing pen-based units, but not so obvious if you are HP and have shipped three generations of product at reasonable volumes with no pen involved. But that is where the category is, and therefore that is where every member of the category must be.

On the other hand, if we take a different category of product as a reference point, say electronic organizers, which are clearly on Main Street as the millions of units that Sharp and Casio have shipped prove—then the HP product isn't a pen-lacking PDA caught in the chasm but rather an overpriced electronic organizer languishing on Main Street. That's where it would be if it is in that category, despite all its whizzy new-tech features.

But wait, says someone else, it's both! To which the only answer is: No, it is not. Not ever. *Both* equals *nothing*, nonexistence, banishment. You cannot market something that violates the categorical scheme of the marketplace that must support it. Stores won't know in what department to sell it, and consumers won't know where to go to buy it, and no one will know with which products to compare it to determine if it has a fair price.

In 1994 HP chose to be in the PDA market, which I think was a good choice, since that market has a future, has no established leaders, and is more consistent with the 200LX's underlying technological strengths. However, the 200LX's shipment rates confused HP into thinking that the 200LX was closer to the tornado than it really was. Advertising for the product was tornado-oriented, positioning it as a product for a general mass of people who call themselves "road warriors." This was too big a jump too soon, something easy to see if you say we are in the chasm, not so easy if you think you are already in the bowling alley, which of course was HP's view.

The point in all this is that significant marketing expenditure and risk ultimately hinge on a choice about where the product is in the Technology Adoption Life Cycle. There are plenty of companies facing this choice right now:

- Where is Lotus Notes? Is it in the bowling alley, in which case Lotus should be focusing more tightly on vertical markets, or in the tornado, in which case it should be working harder to commoditize the whole product?
- Where are object-oriented databases? Are they still in the early market, in which case companies should be aggressively seeking additional special deals with visionaries, or are they in the chasm, in which case they should be tightly focusing on a single beachhead?
- Where are phone services like store-and-forward fax, conferencing, call forwarding, and caller ID, not to mention underlying enabling technologies like ISDN?
- How about color printing, portable printing, or printing and faxing from the same unit? Where are they?

In most tough calls, the ambiguity comes from a mixing of a Main Street category with some element of discontinuous innovation, the question being how much total discontinuity will be experienced in the marketplace, and thus where will this fit on the life cycle. To help put this issue in perspective, we need to look at the model that follows.

Discontinuity and the Life Cycle

There are two kinds of discontinuity that shape the Technology Adoption Life Cycle. The first is *paradigm shock*, whether experienced by end users or the infrastructure that supports them. An electric car, for example, will give both constituencies a bad time, since mechanics, gas stations, owners, and even the corporations that employ these owners, will all have to learn new ideas, make new investments, and adopt new behaviors. Electric cars, then, represent a high level of paradigm shock.

Notebook computers, on the other hand, represent a fairly low level. One does have to learn more about batteries than one ever wanted to know, and this may well entail an additional investment in a portable battery recharger. And if one gets into the business of sending faxes from one's hotel room, the paradigm shock meter can jump quite a bit. But if all you want to do is write on airplanes, then using a notebook is pretty close to using a desktop. You probably will have to master a track ball as opposed to a mouse, since there is no room for a mouse on the tray table in front of you, but other than that, it is the same software, same keyboard, same deal.

The other dimension of discontinuity is *application* breakthrough, the result of dramatic changes in end-user roles enabled by the new technology, which in turn spur equally dramatic returns on investment. When Voice Recognition Units (VRUs) supplant customer service operators, there is a paradigm shock for the callers but a phenomenal savings to organizations like newspapers, movie theaters, and airlines, all of whom have high volumes of routine calls to process. Faxes have had a similar impact on many of our daily chores, with delis letting you fax lunch orders and building suppliers faxing their remodeling bids to your home. The Internet is actually bringing back a renaissance in writing, as college freshmen discover they can stay in touch with high school buddies at other universities. Writing letters implies delayed gratification, but with e-mail you can often get a reply in the same day, or the same hour if you are in "chat" mode. Even Mom and Dad are getting into the act, as our youngest child, Anna, can testify.

Dramatic improvements in end-user capabilities, then, are the accelerator that drives technology adoption, just as paradigm shock is the brake. Putting these two together as the *x/y* axes of a single model creates the following relationship to the life cycle:

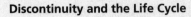

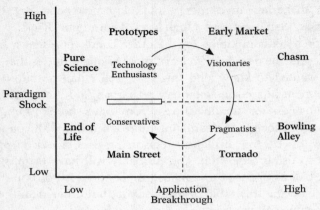

Discontinuity and the Life Cycle

The diagram is simply another way of looking at the Technology Adoption Life Cycle and reads as follows:

- Life cycles start in the upper left-hand quadrant, where paradigm shock is high and the benefit is low, typically because the applications for the new technology have yet to be fielded. It is the realm of pure science and prototypes. At this stage, only technology enthusiasts are interested. Superconductivity is still in this quadrant for most applications, although in some medical equipment it has moved on to the next one.

- In the second quadrant we see the emergence of the early market, built up around one or more visionaries seeing the benefit potential for the new technology and funding the first application breakthroughs. These generate the dramatic competitive advantage that visionaries seek, thereby warranting the pain of displacing the paradigm shock.

Pragmatists look at these application breakthroughs and say, yes, we would like to incorporate that sort of advantage into our work flows too, but not at the price of the paradigm shock currently required. This holding back of the pragmatists is what creates the chasm.

- To speed entry into the third quadrant, companies must single out the issues of a specific beachhead segment, reducing paradigm shock by implementing a limited niche-specific solution prior to supporting all the variations of a general solution set. This is the bowling alley phase, where clever marketing can accelerate what otherwise will be a prolonged period in the chasm.

  As bowling pin segments proliferate, the conditions for a general-purpose infrastructure solution emerge, which at some point the pragmatist majority moves to adopt. Since these people move as a herd, this creates the de facto standards and stimulates the broad base of supplier support needed to obliterate paradigm shock altogether, while still delivering on the application breakthroughs. This is the dynamic that drives the tornado.

- As the tornado subsides, conservatives are able to buy in to the market for the first time, the paradigm shock has been fully absorbed, and the application breakthroughs having become standard operating procedure. The market now moves to Main Street, with further innovation focused on secondary value propositions, or what we have been calling whole products + 1.

  If customers cling too long to the comforts of a familiar paradigm, however, they will eventually fall prey to *increasing* paradigm shock, as the global infrastructure moves on to the new standards and support for the old begins to be withdrawn. Witness the plight today of a CP/M or Apple II user, and see the rapidly approaching fate of current DOS users.

- Finally, the model makes one other statement, communicated by a wall that exists between the upper left and lower left quadrants. It says you cannot move from the one to the other without going through the right-hand side of the diagram. That is, if you come up with a discontinuous technology whose sole benefit is to lower cost and improve productivity within a well-worn application arena, you have an essentially unmarketable opportunity.

The reason is that conservatives simply will not tolerate paradigm shock, nor will they invest in helping vendors reduce that shock over time. They only buy in to new technology after it has been vetted by the pragmatists, who in turn only buy new technology when it can give significant breakthrough to work flows, which in turn means getting visionaries to sponsor the early demonstrations of those breakthroughs. In order to go forward from quadrant one, you must find a breakthrough to motivate a visionary—you cannot simply "drop down" to quadrant four.

Using the Model as a Navigational Aid

While there are other forces that can affect life cycle placement besides paradigm shock and application breakthroughs, this system of coordinates allows for a good first approximation of where a technology *ought to be* in the life cycle, hence a place to start from and then modify as need be.

Let's try applying it to some of the cases mentioned already:

- Lotus Notes clearly has enabled work flow breakthroughs, so that puts it definitively on the right side of the diagram. The ambiguity in its positioning has to do with whole product paradigm shock, which is divided between the end users, who sense very little of it, and the IT community, which is reeling from it. As a result, demand dramatically exceeds supply, creating a tornado-like effect, but real market momentum is threatened by overly difficult constraints on the suppliers. Lotus should invest in Notes as something that desperately wants to fly up the tornado but is being held back, caught up in a tangle of complexity that keeps dragging it back to earth.

- Object-oriented databases clearly constitute a paradigm shock even a decade after their introduction. There are still few established standards and much experimentation is yet in progress. This means they are in the upper half of the diagram. At the same time, no one doubts the *theory* behind the application breakthroughs they promise—predominantly in the area of developer productivity and run-time performance—although the actual achievement of breakthrough has been limited to isolated cases. They are, therefore, in the upper-right quadrant, and the key question vendors of these systems must answer is, Are they in the early market or the chasm? This is a very practical question because every quarter they will have the opportunity to take yet another visionary deal, requiring them to build yet another special-case solution in return for a big check. When you are in the early market that proposition is a good deal, but when you are in the chasm, it will only sink you deeper. How can you tell the difference?

The issue is decided by how far you have progressed in the core product development that will be needed to support *any* chasm crossing. That is, the goal is to cross the chasm, work the bowling alley, and only then support general cases in the tornado. Building support for a customer application that will not be required for the bowling alley is a misuse of funds, a waste of time, and a prelude to chasm disaster. Building support, on the other hand, which will be needed for the chasm-crossing beachhead, is time and money well spent. The solution to the problem thus requires identifying where your beachhead is going to be, and what the whole product for that beachhead consists of, and then assessing how much core R&D is left to do and still applies *vs.* how much application-specific work is now needed. You do not want to transition to the application-specific work until you have your core engine running. As long as that is the primary issue, stay with the visionaries in the early market and pay the price of creating specials. Conversely, as soon as you have sufficient core to go forward, then you do not want to delay your progress by taking on even one more visionary project.

- In the case of the phone services, be they store-and-forward fax, conferencing, call forwarding, or caller ID, all represent significant paradigm shock for the Baby Bells, who are scurrying like mad to incorporate such capabilities, as well as for end users, who still have only a fifty-fifty chance of transferring a phone call without losing the person on the other end of the line. On the other hand, it is not yet obvious how any one of these features creates a significant application breakthrough. In other words, these technologies look like they are running into the wall between the upper- and lower-left quadrants—trying to use discontinuous innovations to improve, but not dramatically revolutionize, existing work flows. That dog won't hunt, according to this model at any rate, and the Baby Bells would be better served trying to find breakthrough applications instead, as VRUs (Voice Response Units) have so successfully done.

Another Kind of Barrier

All of the examples noted thus far involve *technological* shock. There also exists, however, *cultural* or *psychological* shock, where the barrier is not objective but subjective. But this too is part of paradigm shock. Consider the following pair of cases:

COLOR PRINTERS

Color printers put very little technological stress on the infrastructure. They work just like black and white printers, only with different color ink cartridges. Whatever paradigm shock there is, it is at the end-user level, not the technical support person's. That means we are in the lower half of the model. Moreover, color in business is well accepted as a niche application in the hands of trained graphic artists, but not as general purpose infrastructure for the rest of us, the "graphically challenged." Here end users are nervous about making fools of themselves (they recall what they did when they first got fonts) and economic buyers are even more nervous about lost productivity as users fiddle to get just the right shade of fuchsia for their upcoming presentation to top management.

So, we are stuck in the bowling alley with the unnerving thought that we might be here forever. Now what is actually happening is that the color-enabled printers are so inexpensive that they are proliferating anyway—people are just not using the color very much. This is fine if you are in the "razor" business of making printers: it is not so good if you are in the "blade" business of making ink cartridges. If the average user buys, say, four cartridges a year at $25 per cartridge, that is $100 million in revenue for every million printers in service. It is not hard to see how this can be a multibillion-dollar market, with color cartridges having premium pricing. So if you make these supplies, gaining general adoption of color is critical.

The need, then, is for a late bowling alley strategy that breaks out of the graphics ghetto and into the mainstream. One proposed strategy is to start a new alley, away from graphics, focused on using color to illustrate data. Color graphs, instead of graphics, is the focus of this campaign, the message being that people can see the patterns in the data far better if they are shown in color. Target customers include anyone who makes heavy use of spreadsheet graphs in reports or presentations—finance professionals, market researchers, strategic planners, quality-control managers, and the like. Alternatively, another target could be service providers such as insurance companies who pitch big-ticket items like HMO or benefits packages and find that their proposal document must carry a significant part of the selling load. Both groups have a compelling reason to buy, although the latter may have the edge for getting scarce funds.

In any case, there is no problem finding valid target customers. The issue is whole product. Specifically, the traditional showstopper to broader office use has been the absence of an affordable color copier. Color-based data and proposals don't just lose their charm in black and white; they lose information. But with the increasing speed of even low-cost printers, we will soon have a new option, called "print your copies." That way a single professional will be able to control the production process end to end, something that is critical for both ad hoc business reporting and proposal generation.

PRINTER COPIERS

"Print your copies," however, replaces one paradigm shock with another. One *copies* copies; one doesn't *print* them. It is a cultural paradigm, and it is about to take on tornado significance globally as the print and the copy paradigms are on a collision course. Both industries have known for some time that, with lower and lower cost digitization available, their underlying technologies have been converging. Now, going forward, they are virtually identical.

The paradigm shock, as we have seen, will be at the end-user level. People see copiers and printers as coming from completely different worlds, the former historically under the purview of administrative services, the latter computer services. From a work-flow point of view, we *print once* and *copy many*. We think *printing many* is weird. We also think scanning is weird, even though that is precisely what a copier does, so that while a printer with a color scanner is in fact a direct substitute for a color copier, our psychology simply has not yet caught up to the underlying technological convergence.

Now, given all of the above, where does a printer/copier fit on the life cycle? One's "natural" inclination is to put it in the lower-left Main Street quadrant, as each side makes continuous improvements to existing technology serving existing work flows. But that would be a grave mistake. In fact, the psychological discontinuity drives it all the way back into the upper-left quadrant because we simply cannot imagine the application breakthrough, *even though it is already enabled!* As a result, the only way "back home" to Main Street is to go "around the horn," first by focusing on work-flow breakthroughs to engage visionary adoption, then gaining pragmatist acceptance, and then accelerating back to Main Street. This journey should take much less time than a "genuine" adoption life cycle, because it is essentially psychological not technological, but it must follow the same curve.

Calibrating Marketplace Acceptance

The discontinuity analysis we have been conducting is based on applying a theoretical, predictive model to the marketplace. One can also take an empirical approach to the problem, working backward from the marketplace's actual behavior to date. Here you look for characteristic elements that signal life cycle status.

One such element is the press. Here are excerpts from three front-page articles in the same issue of *PC Week*, dated December 27, 1993, each followed with some commentary on life cycle positioning:

> **FIRST WINPAD-BASED MOBILE COMPUTERS DUE FROM HARDWARE VENDORS IN JUNE**
>
> The first WinPad devices . . . will run on Release 1.0 of WinPad, a 16-bit, standard-mode Windows derivative tailored for handheld systems, according to developers briefed on Microsoft's plans.
>
> Microsoft officials declined to comment on specific plans for WinPad. . . .
>
> WinPad's user interface will feature a table of contents, tabs, drag icons, a zoom-in lens, and a traylike clipboard, sources said.

One sure signal of an early market product is when its own developer declines to comment on it. Another is when the coverage focuses on technology and product features, the two items of greatest interest to early-market players. By contrast, mainstream markets are more interested in market and company information.

Compare this pre-chasm positioning of WinPad to the following *PC Week* article about Notes, remembering this is December of 1993:

NOTES ADMINISTRATORS MOVE SLOWLY ON ENTERPRISEWIDE MIGRATION PATH

"Network administrators and application developers are finding several hurdles on their path toward migrating Lotus Development Corp.'s Notes from the department to the enterprise.

"Although users are generally pleased with Notes 3.0 . . . corporate customers are finding it tough to develop robust enterprisewide applications that can be used throughout companies. Although Lotus officials tout the concept of 'living in Notes,' in reality most of the 500,000 installed base of users are, at the moment, just visiting.

"Notes not being available on Unix is a major concern to us."

KEVIN DAHENY, MANAGER, WORKGROUP APPLICATIONS DEVELOPMENT, MILIPORE CORP.

"We need better database connectivity, especially a good link from Notes to our large corporate databases on DB2."

JOHN MURPHY, DIRECTOR OF TELECOMMUNICATIONS, TRAVELERS CORP.

What we see here is a gradual migration to mainstream concerns. Note how much the article talks about people instead of product. The product has crossed the chasm, as indicated by the phrase "migrating . . . from the department to the enterprise" and also by the phrase "users are generally pleased," yet it is not quite ready for prime time, as indicated by the recurrent use of "although." Overall, the feeling is that the users want a tornado, but the IT people are saying that the whole product cannot stand up to a tornado-class infrastructure deployment.

As a result, we would conclude Notes is in the bowling alley by default, although there is no indication of niche marketing. Instead, there is an uneasy balance of tornado demand and near-chasm-like deficiencies in the whole product.

SYBASE DRAMATICALLY BOOSTS PERFORMANCE OF SQL SERVER

Answering the needs of corporate customers with very large databases, Sybase Inc., has improved the performance, functionality, and capacity of SQL Server 10, the database server core of the company's System 10 product group.

SQL Server 10, which started shipping in October at prices starting at $1,995, has dramatically improved performance for database creation, bulk data loading, and index creation. . . .

As companies move toward distributed systems, Sybase and competing vendors—such as The ASK Group Inc., Informix Software Inc., and Oracle Corp.—are all offering products similar to System 10. . . .

Here we are in the "safe as milk" category, somewhat ironic in light of subsequent revelations about the limitations of Server 10. The innovations presented here are all continuous—performance, functionality, and capacity—and a number of other mainstream vendors are "all offering products similar" to it. Note the emphasis on company and market issues as opposed to product and technology. All of this speaks to mainstream positioning, either tornado or post-tornado. Since there is not a lot of emphasis on cutthroat competition, which one always expects with tornado products, the conclusion one would draw here is that Sybase 10 is on Main Street.

Additional Indicators

Beyond press coverage, a second source of clues to market status comes from the behavior of other companies in the infrastructure. Lew Platt at HP, for example, realized that their commercial Unix server business was in the tornado when software vendors were calling him rather than the other way around. Going further, when a tornado is under way, the easiest way to spot the gorilla is to look for the company whose platform is first choice for other companies to support. If there is a lot of porting activity focused on a single vendor, even if that vendor is not you, it's a good sign that you and they are in a tornado market.

A second sign from the infrastructure is cloning. Most companies will not bother to emulate a product unless it is in the tornado and is the gorilla. There simply is not enough demand to warrant this behavior at other times in the market. This cloning goes hand in hand with a third type of tornado warning from the infrastructure, widespread price discounting within the product category—both for the gorilla product (as a loss leader to get customers into the store) and for clone products (to get the lowest possible price).

So, by reading business press, such as *BusinessWeek* and the *Wall Street Journal*, the IT industry press, such as *PC Week* and *Computerworld*, and keeping an ear out to the indirect channels through a magazine like *Computer Reseller News*, not to mention the ads in your daily newspaper, then analyzing actual press coverage in the terms modeled above, you can get a good composite view of where the marketplace thinks a technology is in the life cycle. In so doing guard against mistaking press enthusiasm for early-market products—after all, they are the only real news in the industry—with actual market acceptance of same. We have all lost count of the number of products that have won a product-of-the-year award posthumously. Also beware of drawing too many conclusions from price discounting as it is just as often attributable to bad marketing as market life cycle.

Making the Call as a Group

Whether or not you get your position relative to the life cycle absolutely correct, the critical success factor for any team is to come to a unanimous consensus and then act on that basis. If you all row in the same direction, it is much easier to course-correct as you go along.

The following are some "helpful hints" to keep your group on target:

- Just because a product has not yet been shipped doesn't mean it is in the early market. Instead, it should be placed where the group thinks it will *enter* the life cycle when it does ship. Every new generation of DRAM, for example, goes straight into the tornado.
- The same product can be at different points in the life cycle depending on global context. Typically, the markets in Japan, the United States, and Germany are not in sync with

each other. So specify geography when making a group choice.

- You can get to Main Street without ever going through a tornado. Sometimes we call these products "bowling alley forever." They just never become generic infrastructure. But their markets do mature, and the whole product does eventually become a commodity within the niches they serve. When it is clear to you that there is little chance of any tornado in the future, marketing should refocus itself to take a Main Street + 1 approach.

- Just because your product is going down the tubes doesn't mean you are in the chasm. Products can fail anywhere within the life cycle—although failing in a tornado takes special work.

- As already noted, you can have a "local tornado" within a single bowling alley segment. Demand exceeding supply will create tornado-like effects on your staff but will not generate the tornado returns to your shareholders. Treat this as a bowling pin market at its hottest.

At this point we are done with the material for this chapter, except for one last question that always seems to come up:

So How Do You Predict When a Tornado Will Start?

I don't suppose I can leave this chapter without at least addressing this question, because it is the one most on people's lips once they get into working with the life cycle model. On the other hand, I trust no one believes I can actually answer it—if I could, why would I not be firmly ensconced, piña colada in hand, gazing out into the Pacific blue over the top of a good novel perched on a well-shaded chest, eyes beginning to flutter as the morning nap approaches?

That being said, however, we can at least frame the problem as follows:

- First, bowling alley successes help tornadoes to start because they validate product architectures, albeit within limited circumstances. Without any such successes, the tornado wants to happen but has trouble getting off the ground. There are simply too many de facto standards that have yet to emerge. So one sign of tornado readiness is some niche market successes in place.

- Second, in retail markets, price point is a key indicator of tornado readiness. As a rule of thumb, getting under $1,500 gets one into the small office market where getting under $1,000 enables a tornado. Similarly, getting under $700 gets ones into the home market and getting under $300 enables a tornado. These are not fixed laws, of course, but when it comes to prediction, nothing is.

- More abstractly, tornadoes require the commoditization of the whole product. As long as there is even one significant component that requires scarce expertise to integrate, the market will struggle to get into the tornado phase. Conversely, once the last element is removed, if the market is ever going to tornado, it should happen almost immediately. If markets do not tornado under these circumstances, it usually means that there is no killer application, no compelling reason to buy.

- The big signal for the tornado is the "killer app." But it is not clear to me if tornadoes cause killer apps or vice versa. What we can say about these applications is that they supply universal infrastructure, are appealing to a mass market, and are commoditizable.

- You can know that a tornado has started when a gorilla company begins to emerge. By that point, however, it is normally too late to change history.

- Finally, betting on the tornado coming at a specific time is like buying a lottery ticket and expecting to win. There are simply too many variables to make this kind of bet make sense.

Conclusion to Part One, Transition to Part Two

In Part One, the Development of Hypergrowth Markets, we have been exploring the impact of market forces traceable to the Technology Adoption Life Cycle, and we have discussed in broad terms the course of action appropriate at each stage. All told, this has been an exercise in *navigation*, of building a map of the life cycle and learning how to read it properly. Our last act in this sequence has been to see how we could use the discontinuity model and the life cycle model as a kind of sextant or navigational aid.

Now we are going to turn to Part Two, Implications for Strategy, to integrate these ideas with the following traditional business strategy concerns:

- Strategic partnerships
- Competitive advantage
- Positioning
- Organizational leadership

What all these concerns share is a common interest in *power* and its distribution within marketplaces at large and within individual companies. When, as we move through a life cycle, critical success factors change, the power of different people and institutions rises and falls as well. As long as life cycles are relatively long-lived, our current market and managerial institutions are able to absorb these changes.

However, in the realm of high tech—and increasingly spreading to other high-change sectors as well—they can no longer do so. Life cycles are evolving too quickly, and there are too many of them. Power is changing hands far too often, and our traditional market mechanisms and management systems are not able to keep up with it. This is creating disillusion about strategic partnerships, confusion about sustainable competitive advantage, disorientation as to positioning, and resentment among our line organizations.

The way forward requires some drastic rethinking about how fundamental power relationships are defined and maintained in a rapidly shifting marketplace. That is the challenge the second half of *Inside the Tornado* seeks to address.

PART TWO

IMPLICATIONS FOR STRATEGY

CHAPTER 7

STRATEGIC PARTNERSHIPS

That strategic partnerships have become so integral to high-tech business strategy over the past decade is a function, in large part, of the migration toward *open systems*. The emergence of this paradigm is usually assumed to have grown out of customer frustration with vendor lock-in, but in fact it has had little real impact on switching costs and even less on customer loyalty. The walls of the corral may not be as high as they used to be, but the horses still tend to stay inside once they are penned. Instead, open systems' biggest impact has been on how vendors interact to complete whole products and compete for market leadership.

Under the old regime, embodied in IBM, DEC, Unisys, and the other major systems companies, vertical integration was the backbone of competitive strategy, and partners and allies, like pilot fish, were tolerated as long as they steered clear of the big fish's jaws. Whole product investment was so high that it restricted the market to only a few companies, and they in turn needed as many of the customers' dollars as they could get to recoup that investment. Marketing in this era was secretive, account development was exclusive, vendors were kept at arm's length, and the focus was on minimizing dependencies and maintaining control.

This system was undermined by the emergence of the microprocessor, enabling a much lower cost hardware investment model, which meant that vendors could actually share a market together to the profit of each. Indeed, no one vendor had sufficient capital to remove its dependence on others, and so a new paradigm of open architecture and inter-vendor cooperation developed, introduced by Apple in the Apple II, and then broadly disseminated by IBM's PC division and Sun Microsystems. These companies did not *allow* partners to fill the open slots inside their computer cases—they *recruited* them to do so—and marketing migrated toward a more open communications model, with a focus on sharing information for mutual success.

Within an open-architecture model, vendors are free to pursue a best-of-breed strategy, without having to take responsibility for the complete solution investment. This economic environment favors smaller, more nimble entrepreneurial entities while vendors successful under the old paradigm are put at a cost disadvantage. Whole products can get to market much faster if multiple companies compete to provide each part, and with work on all fronts going forward in parallel.

One of the first and most dramatic manifestations of the new strategy was Sun's extraordinary leapfrogging of Apollo in the technical workstation market. By all the rules of the tornado, this should not have been able to happen. Apollo was the established gorilla. The market should have stayed loyal to it instead of shifting its support to a substitute paradigm. So why did it? The answer is that Sun's open systems strategy allowed it to outmanufacture Apollo dramatically, and since in a tornado whoever "just ships" gets to take the sale, Sun was able to swamp its predecessor, despite the latter's market leadership advantages.

The reason Sun could outproduce Apollo was that its open systems strategy kept it from ever becoming the bottleneck in its whole product development. Instead it leveraged partnerships to outsource the needed components, relying on the natural mechanisms of a free market to bring together the whole product at the end. Sun *architected* and *orchestrated* these whole product solutions, but it did not actually manufacture or even purchase them. To partner, in other words, became a significant new option in what had heretofore been thought of as "make *vs.* buy" decisions. As a result of its partnering strategies, Sun enjoyed much more flexible lines of supply at essentially no cost to itself.

As an industry, high tech is still absorbing the enormity of this lesson and the swiftness with which it has realigned our relationships, and we are still exploring just how open systems partnering distributes power within the marketplace. To further penetrate these dynamics, let's take a look at how the Technology Adoption Life Cycle controls both the emergence and dissolution of partnership dependencies.

The Evolution of the Whole Product

One way to describe the life cycle is to say that it traces the increasing evolution and integration of the whole product, as the following diagram illustrates:

The Evolution of the Whole Product

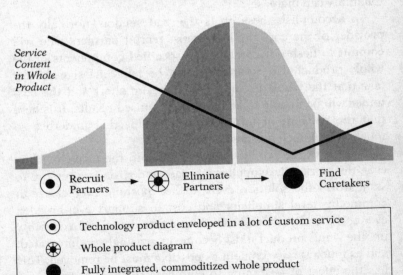

At the outset of the life cycle, the whole product consists of a barely complete core product surrounded by an envelope of custom services needed to make any particular application work. This is the era of the early market, when visionaries commit to take something perhaps 80 percent complete and use it as the foundation for fielding an application breakthrough. To create this result, they rely heavily on the services of systems integrators who pull the whole thing together. This is a challenging enterprise indeed, and the service content of any particular project typically outweighs the product investment by several times.

To cross the chasm and gain acceptance with pragmatist customers, vendors must institutionalize a whole product, initially for a specific niche of customers. This construct is an amalgam of existing products and services. What differentiates it from its early-market cousin is that every component preexists; none are created from scratch. To be sure, there is still some tailoring to be done, but there is no new design work. As a result, the product replicates with reasonable consistency and speed, the work can be leveraged from customer to customer, eventually from niche to niche, and thus costs can decrease and reliability can increase.

To accomplish these goals the lead vendor—normally the provider of the core product—must recruit partners who will commit to flesh out one or more specified components of the whole product. No component can be left "unassigned," for fear that the whole product will come up short and the customer will be unable to achieve the promised results. It is here that the network of informal partnerships that underlies so much of high-tech business is born.

Once a whole product gets sucked into the tornado, however, the marketplace applies stronger and stronger pressure to standardize the solution even further, pushing ever closer to commodity-level simplicity and cost to support ever-broader, ever-cheaper distribution. To drive costs down and reliability up, the whole product must become increasingly preintegrated, and as much service content as possible must be removed. This has the effect of beginning to eliminate the very partnerships that were launched seemingly moments ago.

This process continues throughout the tornado and into Main Street until an absolute nadir of partnering is reached and the whole product has been totally absorbed into the core product. At this point, +1 marketing is needed to differentiate what has now become a low-margin commodity. With it comes very modest opportunities to reopen partner relationships—assuming anyone is still on speaking terms.

Finally, at the end of life, service content reasserts itself in the form of the caretaker role. The infrastructure that used to service the product has passed on to newer paradigms, and customers still dependent on the older platforms need support. As we saw in the case of Computer Associates (chapter 5), these services can be profitable indeed.

Surfacing the Real Issue—*Power*

The point in all this is that partnerships, under the pressure of the evolution of the whole product, inevitably get into cross purposes, and the only way to manage them going forward is to surface the real issues. Ultimately those issues revolve around a single central concern—power. In order to manage and communicate effectively, and in order to set strategy realistically, we need to have a public model of how partner power is appropriately distributed within a market. As with everything else, these power relationships shift as the life cycle unfolds.

- *The Early Market*

  In the early market, power lies with the technology provider and the systems integrator. The former has the bait that brings visionary customers into range; the latter has the tackle necessary to land them.

  For example, consider a pair of early-market companies, Savi and Gyration, both of which are driven by visions of "location." In the case of Savi, they have a system of transmitters and receivers that allows transportation centers and warehouses to readily track and retrieve cargo containers and the specific contents within them. In the case of Gyration, they have a miniature solid-state gyroscope, about the size of a golf ball, weighing just a few ounces, which can, like any gyroscope, detect changes in movement and attitude and thereby be incorporated into any system that needs to track position or location.

Like many early-market products, both can support a myriad of applications from a whole host of business sectors. Thus while Savi is focused on intermodal transportation, specifically the yards where trains trade cargoes with trucks, it has been approached by an automobile company for intraplant container tracking and by a food co-op for perishable cargo tracking. Similarly, while Gyration is focused on "mice in free space"—hand-held devices that allow PC presenters, game machine players, and couch potatoes to interact with a pointer on a screen—they have been approached by automobile navigation vendors and video camera designers.

Now, in neither case does the early-market firm have the integration resources to capitalize on these opportunities. In the case of Gyration these might get supplied by the customer, but in the case of Savi they almost certainly call for the services of an independent systems integrator. Why? Because the visionary customer wants to deploy a novel infrastructure well in advance of the market and lacks both the technical know-how and the project management skills to do so. This is precisely the scarce expertise that integrators provide, and once they are on the scene, all power is ceded to them.

Next to the technology provider and the integrator, everyone else is a bystander, to be brought into the game at the call of the integrator. The reason why bystanders take an interest at this point is that visionary deals often drag along very large purchases of complementary infrastructure products and services. If these bystanders are market leaders in their own right, integrators acknowledge that power cautiously, seeking to co-opt their good standing with the customer without ceding account control. On the other hand, if the bystanders are simply commodity suppliers, integrators expect—and get—them to jump at a moment's notice.

- *The Bowling Alley*

In the bowling alley, as well as when crossing the chasm, power centralizes into the hands of the ringleader of the niche market attack. This is the company that has scoped out the target customer, understood the compelling reason to buy, and designed the whole product. These people *see* the market opportunity; nobody else does. In effect, then, they are recruiting partners for a mining expedition. They are the ones with the map to the gold, and that is what gives them their power.

The key to making these partnerships work, then, is leadership based on the ringleader's knowledge of the marketing opportunity. Conversely, it is not based on them having the image of being a much larger company. I stress this because many small companies feel they need the latter in order to gain the support of powerful allies. It simply isn't true.

In the example of Documentum cited earlier in chapter 2, their whole product for the pharmaceutical industry's CANDA application required the active support of Sun Microsystems, Oracle Corporation, and Computer Science Corporation, all three being multibillion-dollar enterprises who would have considered Documentum's annual revenues a rounding error in their own financial calculations. Yet all three let Documentum lead, and as a result all three gained what for them was a +1 expansion niche in their mainstream markets.

There is a curious form of symbiosis at work here, as follows: Small companies' bowling pins can be large companies' +1 extensions. Large corporations need these niche expansions to grow their Main Street businesses, but their management mechanisms make it hard to champion these efforts from within the company. The initial revenue results simply look too paltry to bother with. They are still suffering from post-tornado syndrome, where anything less than another home run seems not worth the bother.

When an energetic outsider comes in with a clear target and a good plan, it fills this leadership vacuum, dragging the

Main Street company into new areas of opportunity it cannot get to under its own power. The key to success here is to have early wins that escalate. Large vendors have short attention spans and many people competing for their attention, but nothing cuts through the clutter like success.

In short, the ringleader's power is a function of its ability to be a "ring giver" (the name Germanic tribes gave to their chieftains for the rewards they were expected to distribute to their warriors). The focus of the leader's efforts must be to make sure that each partner in the alliance makes money, particularly in the first few engagements. This money primes the pump for the partnership. Once the pump is running, it will feed itself, and the ringleader can sit back and reap the profits.

- *In the Tornado*

Power in the tornado centralizes in gorilla companies and their cronies—what we might call "The Club." Nominees for this roster are set by the contents of the whole product inventory, from which the market selects a leading candidate for each component. This slate of candidates is elected as the "institutionalized" solution set within which every component is guaranteed to be compatible with every other. Customers can always swap out component vendors from this set, and most sooner or later do, but they do so at their own risk.

Thus in the DOS era, the "PC Club" included Microsoft, Intel, IBM, Lotus, MicroPro, and Ashton-Tate. When the LAN era hit, it was expanded to included Novell and Compaq. When the interLAN era hit, it was further expanded to include Cisco and Synoptics. Meanwhile back in the corporate headquarters of *Fortune* 500 companies, the client/server revolution has pushed aside an Old Guard dominated by IBM for hardware and databases and application vendors like Dun & Bradstreet, with a new club, led by Oracle for the database, Hewlett-Packard for the server, and SAP for financial applications.

Surrounding this club of gorillas is a horde of monkeys running in and out, trying to play on intergorilla rivalries to gain opportunistic business. The temptation is to say that these monkeys have no power, and that is true if you look at any one of them individually. But as a group they act as a friction-reducing lubricant, providing adequate substitutes for teams where one or another of the gorillas cannot get along with the others. Also, as a group, monkeys have a considerable impact on market prices, particularly late in the tornado, which forces the gorillas into a design-out-the-partners mode that eventually breaks up the Club.

The biggest challenge in the tornado, however, is to correctly place the role of the chimp. How much partnership power does this company have? The answer is highly situational. Where it is operating in its own established accounts, it has the equivalent of gorilla power and is accepted as a "virtual member" of the Club. In this context, chimps are ceded the right to set the de facto standards for their portion of the solution set, and monkeys must defer to them just as they defer to the big apes. Outside its own installed base, however, a chimp has more the status of a monkey that "shows well," one that other Club members don't have to apologize for. Here the chimp must defer to the gorilla's standards and compete directly against monkeys who show it no respect whatsoever.

The point is that in a tornado a chimp's power is radically unstable. There is no real chimp role; it is always a substitute, oscillating between the two stable roles of gorilla and monkey. Solving this dilemma is the essence of a chimp's competitive strategy, something we will look at more closely in the next chapter.

- *On Main Street*

As markets move to Main Street, power, which has already been stripped away from the service vendors, now begins to be stripped from the product vendors as well. The beneficiary of this shift, the one to whom power is now migrating, is the distribution channel. And now for the first time, power relationships within partnerships have a propensity to become dysfunctional.

This pattern is readily visible in the PC industry, where the retail channel of choice for Main Street has become the computer superstore, such as CompUSA, Tandy's Incredible Universe, or Silicon Valley's local favorite, Fry's. Their power is based on controlling access to and shaping interactions with the customer. Their goal, of course, is to maximize the total number of transactions and to optimize profit margins on any individual transaction while keeping overhead costs to an absolute minimum. This objective often puts them in conflict with the interests of gorilla product vendors, and that is where the power struggles take place.

For example, retail channels routinely advertise one or more of the gorilla's products at the lowest possible price in order to attract customers into their stores. Once the customers are lured by this bait, the sales force is instructed to switch them to higher margin purchases. This behavior is encouraged by chimps and monkeys, often in the form of extra commissions or rebates to make their products more profitable to sell. Needless to say, all this drives gorillas crazy and has generated numerous tactical responses, none of which to date has proved particularly stable. The point is, all these responses acknowledge that the power has shifted to the channel.

In markets served by higher-end distribution channels, such as direct sales forces, this same pattern is at work, but it is masked by the fact that these channels appear to be under the product vendor's control. That "fact," however, is an illusion. Sales forces, like any other channel of distribution, will optimize for their own benefit. The inability to see this in action continues to cripple mainframe vendors like IBM and Unisys. Here's what's going on:

When whole products are of such complexity that they never commoditize, even on Main Street they generate high margins. In part this is because switching costs make competition at this point in the life cycle out of the question. This is vendor lock-in, and it is a sweet time for any distribution channel. The only threat to the status quo is an infrastructure swap-out based on a new paradigm. Therefore, the one thing a direct sales force will never do is bring in the new paradigm. Thus a company like IBM or Unisys, dependent on a single direct sales channel for interaction with its mainframe installed base, is effectively blocked from selling its new paradigm solutions and must watch in helpless frustration as competitors pillage their installed bases—*with impunity!*

The way forward out of this problem state, for PC vendors as well as mainframe vendors, is to break the back of the channel by finding alternate routes to the customer. It is a testimony to the power of the channel, however, that despite this being clear to many management teams, little has actually been accomplished to alter the situation.

Finally, in the PC industry there is a class of gorillas who are extremely well served by this whole turn of events—the core technology providers, including Intel for microprocessors, Microsoft for operating systems, Seagate and Conner for hard drives, and Toshiba and Samsung for DRAM memory. These vendors don't care whether the channel sells gorillas, monkeys, or chimps because all three must incorporate their products. The more the other vendors' portion of the whole product commoditizes, the higher the volume of total sales in the market, the more their stocks soar.

Such is the evolution of the distribution of power within partnerships over the Technology Adoption Life Cycle. In every case, the companies who control the customer relationship have the greatest leverage. In the early market, this was primarily the integrators. In the bowling alley, this is the ringleader. In the tornado, with the infrastructure buyer in particular, this is the club of gorillas. And on Main Street, it is the distribution channel itself.

So goes the theory, at any rate. In actual practice, localized forces and tactics shape events considerably, raising a host of interesting problems in strategy. Let us look at a sampling.

Five Questions of Strategy

1. *How do I know if a partnership is really strategic?*

This question comes up more often than one might expect, normally driven by a partner imposing demands on a resource-constrained operation. If the partnership is truly strategic, the management team intends to accommodate the request, but to do that it will have to deprioritize some less strategic relationship. So how do you tell which are which?

The key mistake to avoid is assuming that a partnership with a gorilla is more important than one with a chimp, or even a monkey. Instead, the initial question to ask is, are we partnering on a single revenue opportunity, partnering for a potential revenue stream, or partnering to capture market leadership? Of these three, market leadership is the only strategic objective.

To be sure, revenue, in and of itself, is the lifeblood of your company, but strategy is concerned with the future implications of a sale, not its immediate ones. Of these the most important is your progress toward becoming a market leader, whether it be in a niche or in a tornado. Market leadership is a territory capture game in which you overinvest resources in order to prioritize sales within the target segment. Partnerships that are focused on that segment are entitled to the extra support of these resources.

Since a single revenue opportunity has no strategic importance in this sense, it obviously is not entitled to this status, but how about an opportunity that also dangles the lure of a future stream of revenue? All of Venezuela will standardize on your product, and you will be collecting royalties for the next several decades. This is the ambiguous case, posing a "net present value" problem of whether the gamble is worth the risk. Consultant experience argues that it is almost never worth it. Revenue streams simply do not run up to your doorstep this easily. They ultimately go to the market leader, at least the profitable portions, and then to the others that have made structural commitments to the market.

So, to keep it simple, a partnership is only strategic when it is focused on the whole product necessary to win you the number one position in a target market.

2. *How do I manage strategic partnerships created with no specific whole product in view?*

We are seeing a lot of this sort of thing as we head into the latter part of the 1990s in the arena of *digital convergence,* with computer, telephony, broadcast, and entertainment companies all jumping into relationships. Indeed, there is something of a mad dash going on as companies not yet partnered rush in for fear of being left out of the dance altogether. So let me be clear about such activity: It is not *bad* strategy—it is *dreadful.*

Partnerships formed in absence of the focal point of a whole product are simply unmanageable. Extravagant in and of themselves—they consume resources like crazy as people rush about trying to figure out what they are supposed to do—they are horrendously expensive in terms of opportunity cost. That is because top management actually thinks something productive is going to come out of them. It won't. But by the time it doesn't, one or more years of opportunity to have been doing something actually productive will have been irrevocably lost.

Progress toward a whole product is the critical feedback mechanism of partnership. Recall that the whole product itself is defined as the minimum set of products and services needed for customers in the target segment to achieve the value proposition promised. Assuming this value is truly desired, adoption activity among these customers tells us whether or not we have achieved this goal. Absence of adoption means one or more components of the whole product is either missing or improperly integrated. This in turn allows the group of partners to focus on what remains to be done to activate this market.

All of the above results in coordinated market development activity with measurable results. Anything less than this kind of feedback results in a field trip of uncertain duration but all too predictable outcome. If you are in a partnership formed in advance of a commitment to a specific whole product, make target market selection your top priority. Otherwise run.

3. *How do I decide when to partner as opposed to make or buy?*

In the 1980s we learned that if you were considering a make-versus-buy decision, the right answer is almost always *buy*. It saves time, it avoids the risk of adding cost without adding commensurate value, and it allows you to focus all your energy where you can get the best marginal return on investment. It has taken high tech longer than one might imagine to absorb this lesson because we are an industry of engineers who resist anything not invented here—but for the most part we have this one under control.

The more challenging decision for us to make nowadays is whether or not to *partner* to gain a key component of our proposed whole product. Partnering really does go against the grain of engineering mentality. It entails coping with ambiguity and implies trust, neither one being the technical community's strong suit. Worse, it is something championed by marketing, a sure sign of ill to come.

Nonetheless, partnering is key to market development, and not just for all the leverage we explored in our discussion of open systems. Partnerships create the *market muscles* needed to actually move those levers. That is, in open systems solutions, everything is *assumed* to plug and play. In reality, at the outset nothing actually does. As a result, only those solutions that get special attention ever achieve the necessary final level of integration. Successful partnering gets a set of companies focused on a specific solution set to accomplish this goal.

Moreover, partnering, by spreading the rewards of market development among multiple companies, creates multiple sources of support in the marketplace. Other people now have a stake in your success. By contrast, when completely vertically integrated vendors win, no one else does. This means every hand in the market is turned against them.

So partnerships confer critical leverage. At the same time, however, they are expensive and exhausting to manage. As a rule, a total of two to three partners in any one opportunity is probably optimal. Within this team each partner needs something real and challenging to do along with a reward commensurate with doing it. When these conditions are met, it is normally best strategy to partner rather than buy or make.

4. *Tell me again why I shouldn't keep all the partnering revenue to myself if I can?*

To be sure, when a single vendor vertically integrates the whole product by itself, the initial impact is positive for everyone immediately involved. Not only does the vendor get to keep all the customer's money, but because it can exercise end-to-end quality control over the whole product, the customer gets a better solution. The long-term impact of this decision, however, can be negative, for two reasons:

1. No other vendors are attracted into the market, there being nothing there for them to gain, so the market grows only as fast as the dominating vendor, which can grow only as fast as its gating factor will let it. When the vendor is instead able to leverage its primary product assets across a broader base of allies, it eliminates this constraint and grows much larger much faster.

2. As we saw in our discussion of the bowling alley, juicy service margins seduce vendors into staying in the bowling alley instead of commoditizing the whole product for

a run at the tornado. This leaves the vendor vulnerable to an end run by a competitor who has nothing to lose, having no stake in the current market, as the Unix server vendors are now discovering at the hands of an emerging Microsoft NT community.

It turns out in an open systems market that partnering is almost always the optimal strategy, provided you can keep the partnership focused. Ultimately there is only one thing that will work here—*money*—and the only money that counts is the customer's. The responsibility of the market leader is to make a market for the other partners. Until money is actually made, the partnership is in a state of suspended animation and aging by the minute. It is as if a timer were set at the outset of the relationship, and to hold the interest of the parties involved, the first, second, and third pieces of business had better come in on schedule.

So if you have a piece of business in hand, and you have the choice of keeping it all to yourself or actually giving some of it away to feed another partner, ask yourself, is this a strategic partnership? If it is not, by all means keep it to yourself. Revenue is revenue, for goodness sakes. On the other hand, if the partnership really is strategic, then giving the business away to the right strategic partner is the lowest cost, highest return investment in market development there is.

5. *How do you dance with a gorilla in a tornado and come away in one piece?*

"May you live in interesting times," goes the Chinese curse. Interesting indeed is the fate of companies who fulfill subsidiary demands the gorilla product generates. These are the institutionalized whole product partners who now must play the game of musical chairs to see who stays in and who gets designed out as the commoditization of the whole product progresses. Once again, the strategic principle is, if we are not the gorilla it is not our market, and eventually we will be forced out. Therefore we must act accordingly.

To begin with, we must realize that as the tornado subsides, the gorilla company will begin to eye our business as really *their* business, and the customer, seeking an increasingly preintegrated whole product, will support the gorilla's effort to design us out. What we have, then, is a temporary permit to market our products within the gorilla's domain. As the permit approaches expiration, we need to migrate our business to some new, hopefully related, area, and cede the commodity portion of it back to the gorilla or over to the low-cost clones. In other words, instead of resenting the Microsofts and Intels and IBMs and Suns of this world for designing us out, we should leverage the business they create for us as long as we can, and then say thanks for the ride.

Why don't most companies act this gracefully? The problem is, the dollar volume generated in the tornado is so huge, we are hard put to imagine how we can ever replace it. So letting go of it seems ludicrous. After all, who is going to explain to our shareholders that all this revenue we generated was never really ours, that we were just sharecropping on the gorilla's plantation? Unfortunately, there is no good answer to this question—that *is* what we were doing, and if our investors thought differently, then they (and perhaps we) have been setting a false value on our equity.

The only viable way out of this dilemma, in the short to medium term, is to sustain enough ongoing innovation to keep us just outside the gorilla's reach. Longer term, of course, we have to find some place where we can be the gorilla.

Partnering as a Service Provider

Thus far we have looked at partnership challenges through the eyes of product vendors cooperating to make a whole product. Service providers also are needed to complete the whole product, and they must deal with this same life cycle as well. Here's how it looks through their eyes:

Value-Added Service Providers and the Life Cycle

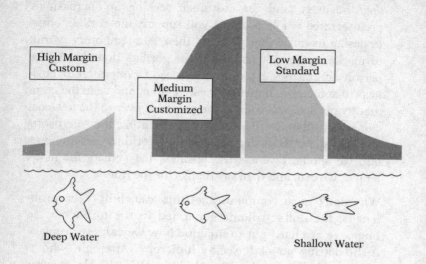

The service component of the whole product is inversely proportional to its state of preintegration. At the front of cycle, this preintegration is low, and the service vendor is a high-margin "deep water" fish. At the back end, preintegration is high, requiring the service vendor to be a "shallow water" fish. Indeed, at some point in the shallowing of margins, it behooves the service provider to merge with the sales channel because there is no longer sustenance for more than one service organization.

At every stage in this evolution, however, fish can thrive. They just need to evolve with different organizational structures to do so. Each of these providers, that is, has a "sweet spot" in the whole product's evolution where the level of service required directly matches their core competencies. These sweet spots are both temporary and permanent: they are temporary in that the current of whole product evolution flows perpetually from left to right, causing the whole product to drift up to them, through them, and eventually past them. They are permanent in that any given type of fish should seek to stay as close as possible to its sweet spot.

To survive and prosper, then, service providers must swim against the current of whole product evolution, keeping their position fixed relative to the life cycle, and not fixating on any specific whole product opportunity. Fixation on any particular whole product is disastrous, because each year as it evolves further to the right the service margins it can support decrease until eventually the fish is out of water.

In sum, the service provider's relationship to any specific whole product is always transient. Unfortunately, we humans do not like transience—particularly our own—so we tend to deny it, preferring instead to fixate on something as if it were permanent. This leads service providers to make the fatal mistake of defining themselves in relation to a particular whole product—desktop publishing, LANs, CAD, MRP—with the goal of staying in that market forever. This strategy simply will not work for all the reasons we have been examining. Instead, what a service provider must do is define themselves first and foremost by their relationship to the Technology Adoption Life Cycle.

Specifically, long-term stability in a service business, more than anything else, depends upon a single success factor—being able to earn the same gross profit margins year after year. These gross margins correspond to a place in the life cycle model, a sweet spot, a level of integration service that corresponds in market value to whatever margins the service provider needs to charge. Systems integrators understand this very well and keep their engagements very close to the front of the cycle in order to charge very high margins. Retail superstores also understand this very well, keeping their commitments as far to the back as they can, in order to keep their costs low enough to make money on very low margins. VARs and any other service providers "in the middle," on the other hand, rarely come to grips with this principle, with the result that they typically come into and go out of business on about a four- to seven-year cycle.

But VARs can stabilize their businesses if they recognize that every year they must renew their added value. That is, each year some part of the service offering they provided last year is no longer worth the margins they need to earn, and they must let go of this old business. At the same time, each year some service offerings that previously were beyond their level of expertise to provide have now drifted into their territory, and they must go capture this new business. If service providers grasp this principle of renewal, they can actually have businesses that are *more* stable than product providers, because they need never bet their future on producing a winning product. Instead, they can let the market identify the winners at no cost to them and focus themselves on completing their whole product integration.

A good example of how one executes this strategy has been passed on to me by John Addison, who managed a part of Sun's VAR business in the late 1980s. In 1987, if a Sun VAR could deliver AutoCad, that was good enough to earn them their required margins. The reason why was that AutoCad was a DOS program that had been ported to Sun's workstations but still did not run very well without special tuning. At the same time the AutoCad user base was totally PC-oriented and was not compatible with Unix. So there were plenty of ways a VAR could earn its money.

By 1988, however, VARs were also expected to be able to deliver the third-party extensions to AutoCad. And by 1989, they were expected to support in addition a desktop publishing interface to Frame or Interleaf. End users by this time were confident enough in the technology to want to be able to show their clients drawings that were dressed up to be more appealing. By 1990, the expectation had escalated further to include a drawings database for version control to keep track of engineering changes, and by 1991 had increased further still, to incorporate a relational database for passing bill of materials data from the drawings to an MRP system. Each year, then, the VAR was expected to take on new challenges in order to continue to justify the margins it needed to earn. By 1991 just reselling AutoCad on Sun was a task for low-touch, high-volume resellers—and VARs that could only provide this service came nowhere near the margins they used to be able to charge.

This "fish model" is an important tool for product vendors

to use in their communications with service partners, especially indirect channels of distribution. Instead of arguing about why discount margins are getting less and less favorable to the reseller, the conversation should instead be based on two key points:

1. What gross margins does the service partner need to make to have a healthy business?
2. Let us agree to do business only where those margins can be earned.

The net impact of these two principles is that it puts both the product vendor and the service provider on the same side of the table, helping to avoid a tendency to squeeze on the part of the former and to whine on the part of the latter. Both must now focus together on the reality that whole product evolution is changing their current relationship. The most constructive path forward is to pursue the following line:

- Taking the service provider's margin requirements as a constant, what whole products are now drifting out of its range?
- How in the short term can the service provider squeeze a last good year or two out of this business by "productizing" its experience into a form less costly to deliver?
- Looking to the future, what kind of opportunities are coming downstream to replace these lost sources of revenue?
- How in the short term can the product vendor accelerate the market development of these opportunities to increase deal flow for the service provider?

The key point overall is that product vendors and service providers, like siblings, share deep ties of mutual dependence in the long term but are seemingly in perpetual conflict in the short term. These short-term squabbles arise from the fact that whole products must flow along the life cycle while service providers must stay in one place relative to it. Until this dynamic is mutually acknowledged, relationships are plagued with resentment and suspicion. On the other hand, once it is out in the open, companies can begin to cooperate across whole product opportunities, seeking to bring a new one into range each time an old one drifts out.

Recap

Open systems business strategy puts a premium on partnerships to ensure rapid development of new technology markets. At the same time, however, the evolution of the whole product makes all such relationships transient. Learning how to partner, how to make and keep commitments, in such an environment is probably the second-biggest challenge for the current crop of high-tech executives.

Learning how to compete in such an environment, on the other hand, is probably the single biggest challenge. Hence the importance of the next chapter, to which we shall now turn.

CHAPTER 8

COMPETITIVE ADVANTAGE

Because all high-tech wealth has its origins in the tornado, and because the tornado fuels competitive intensity to its hottest flame, the issue of gaining *competitive advantage* is the single most talked about theme in Silicon Valley. At the heart of these discussions are three key variables, what consultants Michael Treacy and Fred Wiersema at CSC Index call in their 1995 bestseller, *The Discipline of Market Leaders*, "value disciplines":

1. Product leadership
2. Operational excellence
3. Customer intimacy

Achieving superiority in any one of these domains typically involves compromising the other two. Treacy and Wiersema argue therefore that no one company can expect to excel in all three areas, and that the better part of competitive strategy is to determine in which of these three lies your company's core competency and develop a strategy focused on excelling in the single dimension that plays most to your strengths.

As a devotee of focus, I think this a terrific idea, but in the case of high-tech marketing, the dynamics of rapidly maturing life cycles force you to take a more complex approach, as the following diagram indicates:

Value Disciplines and the Life Cycle

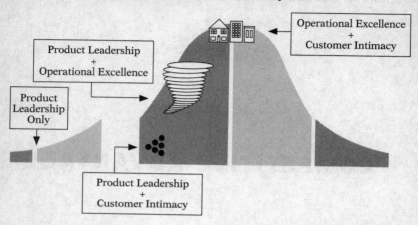

The claim this diagram makes is that the life cycle itself dictates which variables are critical at any given point, and you simply must execute these variables to win the competitions you are facing and earn the right to move on to the next stage. So let's play back through the life cycle and see how it looks in this context, beginning with the early market where the only variable that counts is *product leadership.*

At this point in the life cycle, the competition is not among alternative products—with discontinuous innovations there are no alternative products—but rather among *alternative breakthrough possibilities.* That is, visionaries are seeking to gain a dramatic competitive advantage by doing something outside the norm. The competition is other outside-the-norm alternatives competing for the visionaries' attention and cash.

This leads to a selling competition where charismatic salespeople vie to win the attention of the visionary with outrageous promises, which heroic sales-support specialists try to illustrate in demos invented more or less on the fly, and which R&D groups agree to make come true under the influence of contagious enthusiasm and too much caffeine. All this is done to win the competition for the visionary's endorsement.

Competitive advantage in this context is a function of two elements:

1. The capability of inducing radical change by completely bypassing the bottlenecks that restrict progress under the status quo.
2. The flexibility to adapt to the idiosyncracies of the visionary's specific plan.

The first of these two factors falls into the domain of product leadership. The power of a paradigm shift lies in the ability to cut through the Gordian knots that have stymied all previous attempts. The solution is always a function of new technology enabling a completely novel approach to the problem, and that is precisely what attracts the visionary's attention.

The other key factor, flexibility, is a function of the product being so new that it is not yet encumbered by other commitments. It offers a blank slate upon which the visionary can write. Since no other whole product as yet exists, the early market customers are free to create their own.

Ultimately, then, each closed sale comes down to a commitment to complete a whole product specific to a single customer's requirements, which entails a scope of work more like a custom service project than a product purchase order. This in turn sets in motion the forces that must ultimately bring the early market to a close:

1. Your product becomes increasingly encumbered with commitments, reducing its flexibility.
2. You run out of service resources allocable to special projects.

It is then that, like it or not, you must cross the chasm.

Crossing the Chasm and Competing in the Bowling Alley

The techniques used to beat the competition when you cross the chasm are identical to those used in the bowling alley, so we will treat the two as one. The goal in both cases is to establish market leadership within a well-defined niche, thereby earning the economic rewards that go to the leader and also establishing one's credibility as a long-term player in the market. The key to all bowling alley competitions is being the first to provide a *differentiated* whole product. Once this whole product is fielded, the niche customer base rallies around it, and no other solution paradigm has permission to compete.

So the critical success factors here are two:

1. Provide the *whole* product, because until you do, the customer base does not rally around, and the competition is still open.
2. Be first, because there is no second prize.

Whole product success in the bowling alley is a function of two competitive factors: *product leadership and customer intimacy.* The former enables the new whole product solution to differentiate itself from the status quo solutions to the customer's problem. The latter enables it to differentiate itself from other similar high-tech offerings that are not focused on this particular niche's requirements.

Take, for example, Silicon Graphics' workstation dominance in entertainment and multimedia animation. SGI's innovation was graphics-processing software and silicon that enabled it to rotate and move three-dimensional images in real time. These algorithms, however, were not unique to SGI. They were also in use, for example, by Cray in flight simulators. SGI was unique in driving down their costs because their visionary goal was to enable a new category of productivity enhancement called *visualization.* Unfortunately, there was not—nor is there yet—any visualization market, so to cross the chasm SGI had to target a segment. Many possibilities arose—industrial design, drug design through molecular modeling, animation, and others—and SGI sold into all these markets.

But it wasn't until it became customer-intimate with the entertainment market, understanding its peculiar blend of digital and analog technologies, that it was able to create a whole product to really close out the competition. The compelling reason to buy was to create and edit production-quality sequences that either could not be filmed or did not appear on the film actually shot. Many workstations might have provided the necessary computational horsepower, but only SGI persisted with the customer segment to fight through the innumerable hurdles to final production. Of course, until the last hurdle was surmounted, no money could come out the end of the value chain, and everything had to be justified as pilot work. Conversely, as soon as the last hurdle was past, money came flooding through the value chain—witness the returns on *Terminator 2* and *Jurassic Park*—and SGI was catapulted into prominence.

So who was SGI competing against? On the axis of customer intimacy, their competitors were companies like Ampex and Panavision, analog technology providers whose machines record to film and tape. These companies controlled the status quo through a long tradition of customer intimacy, and SGI's differentiation was product leadership based on digitizing imagery. On the axis of product leadership, on the other hand, its competitors were Sun, HP, and IBM, all of which had workstations that could also process digitized images. Here SGI's differentiation was its intimate engagement with the entertainment industry's editing and production problems.

From these two classes of competitor, when you are in the bowling alley, it is important to choose a customer-intimate and not a product-leadership competitor as your *reference competitor* for positioning purposes. First of all, you are looking to attract the attention of target customers who have never heard of you but who have a long-standing investment in the older paradigm. By referencing that paradigm, you make yourself immediately understandable to these people. Second, within that frame, you can set the value of your solution relative to that of an older, less-efficient approach, thereby escaping price competition with product-similar companies that share your technological advantages. Thus when Apple entered the desktop publishing market, for example, it did not reference IBM computers as the competition but rather Linotype printing systems, which cost an order magnitude more than a personal computer system. This not only kept IBM at bay, it kept Apple's prices up.

Indeed, one of the keys to competing in the bowling alley is that you can and should *pick your competition*. Failure to do so creates the opposite effect of the benefits we have just been touting. Thus those companies that assume their competition must come from products like theirs actually alienate their target customer, who is by definition someone who is not currently using a high-tech solution and thus cannot readily relate to high-tech issues and concerns. And should they overcome this alienation by an expensive market education campaign, achieving awareness and acceptance of the product category, they will have set a reference price based on the box, not on the solution, a price that will be far lower than the actual value delivered to the customer. This, in turn, will eradicate profit margins that should have been used to bring together a niche-specific whole product. Lacking these margins, the vendor cannot afford to undertake the whole product task, nor is there enough money in the sale to attract the right partners, so the whole product in fact never materializes, and the market never happens. But all this was the vendor's own fault.

In sum, in the bowling alley, winning or losing is absolutely under the control of the vendor. By focusing on the intersection of product leadership and customer intimacy, and by successfully deploying a whole product that fulfills the target customer's compelling reason to buy, vendors can create an unbeatable competitive advantage that will last for the duration of the new paradigm. Since no market is ever anxious to shift paradigms, this can be as long as a decade or more (witness Apple's success in desktop publishing and Autodesk's success with AutoCad). In a world of ever-shrinking product life cycles, winning market leadership in a bowling alley segment is a profound financial event, and it is accessible to any company that has made a successful product innovation. Moreover, once one has secured an initial beachhead market segment, one also has a privileged position to gain the same kind of rewards from additional segments through applying these same principles to bowling alley strategy.

Given all this, it is hard to overstate a consultant's frustration with the number of clients who simply refuse to commit to niche markets. In almost every case, it is because they have their eye on the tornado, so we had best turn our eyes in that direction as well.

Competing in the Tornado

The tornado's natural turbulence makes sorting out competitive strategy hard enough, since at any given moment it's hard to tell if a market response is due to your action or just hitting a thermal. It is made even more complex, however, in that principles for correct strategy depend upon whether the market has granted you gorilla, monkey, or chimpanzee status. We'll look at each of these alternatives in turn.

- *Competing as a Gorilla*

  The goal during the tornado for the gorilla is to maximize market share while sustaining privileged price points. As the market leader, it requires less effort to justify its purchase and it needs to leverage this advantage over its other competitors. In other words, it simply has to go out and win sales as fast as possible.

  The focal point of the competition, then, is the distribution channel. At the high end it is a competition for competent representation—feet on the street. The winner is the company who can outrecruit, outmotivate, and outcompensate the other firms. Tornado forces feed on themselves. Once a company starts getting a gorilla reputation, it finds it easier to recruit top-quality account executives, who in turn make it easier to gain an increasingly disproportionate share of sales, which reinforces gorilla status.

  At the low end, on the other hand, there is no sales representation, only shelves. Here the competition is to take up as much shelf space as you can, thereby putting more of your boxes in front of prospective customers and leaving less room for competitor's boxes. In the 1980s the personal computer industry worked out its mechanisms of distribution on the fly, and the gorillas of the 1980s were those companies who understood indirect sales channels and could manipulate them to their advantage. By contrast, companies like IBM and DEC that entered the market with gorilla status based on direct sales forces were badly served by their inability and unwillingness to work in this medium. And in the 1990s new variations on distribution have allowed companies like Dell, Gateway, and Packard Bell to compete for gorilla status.

In the fight for distribution channel domination, the critical success factors are *product leadership and operational excellence.* The role of product leadership when competing against monkeys is to reset the standard, temporarily making their offerings obsolete. This is Intel's fundamental strategy for retaining control over the microprocessor industry, keeping AMD, Cyrix, and Nexgen at bay. In so doing the gorilla regains a temporary monopoly via its new products and at the same time frees up its old inventory to be used in head-to-head price competition against the monkey's current product. With PC products, much of this competition takes place in catalogs, price clubs, and other low-cost channels—strategic turf in a tornado because of gaining expanded access to customers—where you can find fabulous prices for gorilla brands but normally only at the end of their product life cycles.

Against chimpanzees, on the other hand, product leadership is often a catch-up effort for gorillas, particularly late in the tornado. By this point, the dynamics of the gorilla's installed base have slowed down its ability to innovate, both from the sheer volume of customers to support and from an increasing conservatism that resists rocking the boat. Chimpanzees with smaller installed bases and less to lose from risk confiscate the innovation mantle. Thus, for example, IBM, Apple, and Motorola are currently challenging Intel with their Power PC RISC chip. Whenever such a challenge occurs, the market turns to the gorilla and asks, When are you going to have these features? As long as the answer is "in the next release," the gorilla's hegemony is secure. This need to catch up, however, drives an increasingly larger proportion of the gorilla's total release contents, causing even less innovation going forward. In this way gorilla products over time lose their technological edge, thereby earning the contempt of the technology enthusiasts, the loyalty of the pragmatist majority, and the devotion of their stockholders.

As the wheels of product leadership grind slowly to a halt, gorillas find it increasingly important to focus on *operational excellence*. From the outset this efficiency has been key to winning the gorilla battle in the first place. In a tornado, demand is rampant, and success is all about having supply. Glitches in operational excellence can be catastrophic, especially at tornado speeds and volumes, as the previously cited quality hiccups at Intel, Intuit, and HP can testify.

Operational excellence is also critical in order for the gorilla to maintain control over the tornado's high-volume commodity market and thereby retain its economies of scale. These economies, in turn, give it its primary weapon against the monkeys, aggressive pricing, which gives them no choice but to price lower still, even though their margins may go negative. At the same time, the discipline of efficiency gives the gorilla a profit margin edge against chimpanzees allowing it to outinvest them in R&D (the current ratio between Intel and its nearest rival, Advanced Micro Devices, is a staggering 4 to 1). By contrast, gorillas who disdain the fight for the low end, preferring instead to luxuriate under an umbrella of high prices in a bath of high margins, sooner or later find themselves under attack by a coalition of chimps and monkeys who have taken over leadership in the arena of operational excellence, leaving the gorilla with no viable response other than to retreat slowly but inexorably into a high-end-only product leadership strategy.

In all this competition, one might ask, who is the gorilla's primary competitor? The answer is, everyone. When Andy Grove says, "Only the paranoid survive," he is talking about what it takes for gorillas to retain their status. Everyone is aligned against them. The question then arises, for positioning purposes, who should be a gorilla's *reference competitor?* This is an interesting question, for to raise any one company to the status of a reference competitor gives more prominence to it than it deserves. But without a reference competitor, it is virtually impossible for a market to position any offering, even a gorilla's, correctly.

The winning strategy, it turns out, is for the gorilla to reference three different types of competition at different points during the tornado, as follows:

1. At the very outset, coming out of the bowling alley, gorillas should reference the older technology they are displacing. During this stage they are not yet aggressively preying on rivals but rather joining with them to put the final kibosh on the old paradigm.

2. Once the old paradigm is in full retreat, gorillas should then reference the "pack," consisting of all the other companies in their category, without singling out any one of them. If one particular chimpanzee threatens them, then they should call them out by name and focus everything on defeating them.

3. Finally, once their dominance is assured, gorillas should cease to reference other companies at all and instead reference their own products as competition. Thus, Intel positions the Pentium not against the Power PC but against the 486, and HP positions its color laser printer not against Canon but against its own high-end color inkjets.

- *Competing as a Monkey*

At the opposite end of the pecking order from the gorilla, the monkey plays a much more opportunistic game. Lacking the capital, the R&D, the marketing budget, the clout, and any number of other gorilla advantages, monkeys are in no position to compete for market share in the tornado. Moreover, even were they to gain it, they have not the resources to keep it, so it is of no use to them. Instead, their goal should be to take the money and run. That is, every day the monkey should be cashing out the business. Never should they take a stand. Here's why.

Tornadoes generate enormous spending, and even the greediest gorilla simply cannot fulfill the demand. Distribution channels demand competitive alternatives, both on the axis of innovation and the axis of price. It is typically the chimpanzee's role to provide the former and the monkey's the latter. All channels of distribution need to have a low-cost entry point, and they need monkeys to provide it. So there is always a structural demand for monkey participation in any mass market. What is missing is any brand loyalty or customer lock-in. Monkeys can only win the sale, never the market. That is, because they are a transparent clone of the gorilla, when they win a sale, they do *not* win a customer for life. There is no cumulative effect to their sales, no switching cost to hold in their customers, and hence no benefit of market share. Monkeys have nothing to gain except the sale itself.

How then can monkeys stay in business? Monkeys compete on *operational excellence* based on economies—not economies of scale, just economies. Consider their advantages. Monkeys need no R&D budget. All engineering is reverse engineering, conducted offshore with low-cost, highly educated personnel. They need no market development budget. All marketing is based on slipstreaming the gorilla's market development efforts, with the message always being the same: We're just as good as the leading brand at a fraction of the cost. They need no capital for building up inventory prior to a new product launch because there are no product launches. All they need is capital to get into the game and a cash flow that can cover their growth.

Within this framework a monkey's reference competitor is always the gorilla product. That is how they slipstream the leader's marketing efforts. But their real competition comes from other monkeys. Assuming comparable cost competition, further competitive advantage is primarily a function of access to the distribution channel. Where multiple companies can secure that, the ability to grant credit becomes a key differentiator. Unfortunately, granting credit runs counter to the economics of the monkey strategy, so at this point a smart monkey realizes the field is becoming overcrowded and moves on.

Monkeys are unbeatable if they play this game correctly, investing in nothing, defending nothing. When they get in trouble is after a run of success that causes them to decide they should grow up, become gorillas, and make a name for themselves. Typically this entails taking on a much higher cost structure without a commensurate gain in competitive advantage. The problem is they are trying to break the laws of evolution. By taking a bowling alley approach to some niche markets, you can evolve from a monkey to a chimp, and a chimp, in turn, can become a gorilla if one of its niches blossoms into the next-generation tornado market, but a monkey cannot become a gorilla. Since monkeys only focus on gorillas, however, they never even see the chimp playing its role, much less learn how to emulate it. Perhaps, then, the next section may prove of special assistance to them.

- *Competing as a Chimpanzee*

The subtlest strategy challenge in a tornado is to play the role of the chimpanzee correctly. This is the role of Informix and Sybase *vs*. Oracle in relational databases, of Wellfleet (now Bay Networks) *vs*. Cisco in routers, of Canon, Epson, and Lexmark *vs*. HP in PC printers, of Macintosh, Unixware, and OS/2 *vs*. Windows in PC operating systems, of Lotus and Novell *vs*. Microsoft in office automation suites, of Lawson, PeopleSoft, and Oracle *vs*. SAP in the client/server financials market. All of these companies have major investments in their own technologies. None of them can afford to play the hit-and-run game of the monkey. But equally true, none of them can go toe-to-toe with their respective gorillas and hope to come away victorious. So now what?

The first step to being a successful chimp is to be very clear about what you are competing for. As with all tornado markets, you are competing for distribution first and foremost, simply to get access to the pent-up customer demand. The real question is, what is the value of *market share* to you?

First of all, market share is a reflection of sales volume, so obviously from your point of view, the bigger the better. From the point of view of your partners and allies, also bigger is better, as this creates more total available market for them to serve. From the market's point of view, however, it wants you to grow *only so far and no further*. That is, the pragmatist community that dominates mainstream market purchase decisions wants, in addition to a clear market leader, several other companies to have enough market share to be substantial—and thus a safe alternative to the gorilla if one is needed—but not enough to upset the pecking order, specifically the gorilla's authority to set de facto standards. So much is riding on the de facto consensus—so many purchase decisions, so much wealth, so many plans and architectures—that the switching costs from a whole marketplace point of view are simply not bearable. As a result, a gorilla must repeatedly demonstrate suicidal tendencies or a terminal condition before the market will abandon it and elect a new leader.

Thus it is the market, and not the gorilla itself, that is preventing you from overtaking the gorilla and becoming number one—*and you cannot compete against a market!* That is, Apple Macintosh or IBM OS/2 have permission to take their share of the OS market from 10 percent to 12 percent or 15 percent, but they do not have permission to take it to 50 percent *under any circumstances*. Thus IBM's repeated attempts to position OS/2 as a "Windows 95 killer" are inherently futile. It simply cannot happen. This has nothing to do with the quality of the respective products. It has to do with the preexisting alignment of massive amounts of wealth, with powerful interest groups in corporate IT departments, software ISV companies, hardware vendors, distribution channels already precommitted. Changing this balance of power would be catastrophic to too many constituencies. The market simply will not permit it.

So the first rule of market share competition for chimps is *be aggressive, but only go so far*. There is another consideration to limit one's territory expansion into the tornado. Going forward, after the tornado lapses, this territory is going to be harder and harder to defend. That is, to retain market share going forward, chimps have to keep their products current with the market's evolving de facto standards. These standards, however, are under the control of the gorilla, who doesn't need much encouragement to figure out ways to keep the chimp chasing his tail. Recent antitrust actions against Microsoft, including a brief filed by five anonymous software companies in conjunction with the now defunct proposal to acquire Intuit, detail how Microsoft has used its advantaged position to create obstacles against fair competition.

This behavior, in my view, can be protested but cannot realistically be prevented. For one thing, it is impossible to determine the boundary line between a gorilla's right to take the architecture where it thinks best and the violation of that right, which is to introduce elements solely for the purpose of discoordinating a competitor's efforts. More important, however, behind the entire scene, bigger even than the gorilla's power, is the collusive behavior of the marketplace itself, bent on institutionalizing a coherent power structure regardless of its fairness. This behavior is not centralized in any one entity, it is pervasive, and thus it is not clear how it can be targeted for remedial action.

So what is a chimp to do? Let's look at OS/2, for example. IBM should, as it has been advised by countless consultants to do, forsake its gorilla ambitions at this time and concentrate on winning a dominant share of a well-defined subsegment of the market, one which is at best marginally served by the market-leading solution. Chimps—and we should note that there is no one more galled to be called a chimp than an ex-gorilla—must not fight the gorilla on its own turf. The system is rigged, the referee bribed. Instead, they must seek out some more neutral venue where by exploiting their chimp freedoms—namely, the ability to focus and innovate within a local segment—they can stake out turf that it is not yet committed to the gorilla.

This is essentially equivalent to adopting a bowling alley strategy during the tornado, and it is, to say the least, somewhat counter-intuitive. Why, if sales are plentiful and the market is growing faster than anyone can supply it, should any vendor voluntarily reduce its overall unit sales? For that is what focusing on a segment will cause, at least in the short term. In any given quarter, you can always sell more opportunistically than you can by focusing—so we cannot expect any allies on the sales force when we advocate this approach. Indeed, why would anyone support it?

The reason is that there is life after the tornado. If during the tornado you as a chimp pursue sales on a 100 percent opportunistic basis, and do not use this period to carve out a differentiated position for yourself, then as the market consolidates after the tornado, there is no place for you to retreat to, and no home base from which to conduct future market development. This is the fate that befell Ingres. Obsessed with fighting Oracle during the tornado, falling behind in growth numbers quarter after quarter, it could not imagine committing to any market focus, despite the recommendations of multiple consultants, for that would, at least in the short term, have restricted its sales volume and thus put it even further behind Oracle. Instead, Ingres continued to try to out-Oracle Oracle, even though everyone knew that could not be a winning strategy.

Then the tornado subsided. At this point, markets consolidate around fewer vendors—the gorilla, for sure, some monkeys, too, although far fewer than in the halcyon tornado days, and a handful of chimps—if they have a differentiated value proposition to offer. Thus Sybase was welcome for its technological leadership in distributed computing, and Informix still held the number-one position with VARs serving the low end of the Unix server market. But the market could find no comparable value proposition in the case of

Ingres. Challenged on its very reason to be, and having no market segment of its own to retreat to, and no future hegemony on which to build, the company floundered, and now they are no more.

Summing up, because of the market dynamics we have been tracing, for the chimp to fight the gorilla is not only a losing battle, it is the wrong battle. The right one is to capture available territory at the margins of the gorilla's domain, secure a base of operations, and plot for the next tornado. Gorillas make lots of enemies, and the next time there is a chance for payback, you can be sure of allies. But not during the current tornado, during which too many people have too much to lose to support a counterattack.

Inside the tornado, then, reverting to bowling alley principles, chimpanzees should resort to a combination of *product leadership* and *customer intimacy*. Product leadership will successfully differentiate them from the monkeys when competing for the gorilla's overflow business, which typically represents a substantial revenue flow. At the same time, customer intimacy, when focused on a segment, can be used to carve out a market leadership position within that restricted territory. One has to be careful here, however. *Unfocused* customer intimacy, while it generates lots of positive feedback, is a profound waste of a strategic resource. That is, generic "good customer service," will always win customers' praise but at the end of the day earns no higher margins and captures no lasting territory. It is critical instead to institutionalize customer intimacy in the form of segment-specific whole products that create defensible barriers to entry against future incursions by a post-tornado, market-hungry gorilla.

In closing this discussion of tornado competition, the key lesson is that the market forces at work are far more powerful than the explicit actions of any one individual vendor, even the gorilla, and it is these forces themselves, and not the players, that one needs to attend to first. You simply cannot fight a tornado.

Competing on Main Street

As we move from the tornado to Main Street, hypergrowth sales volumes subside, and competitors must readjust from focusing primarily on capturing new customers to extending and deepening their commerce with their existing installed base. It is not that there are no new customers to win; there are, and it is important to compete for them. It is just that there is now more money to be made from selling extensions to the current base. If we do not reorganize our operations to harvest this yield, we will leave an enormous amount of money on the table and be unable to fund our entry into the next tornado.

The question is how best we can refocus our energies to gain competitive advantage. Let us recall the lessons of chapter 5. Customers spend money on Main Street primarily to extend and enhance the infrastructure deployed during the tornado—adding compatible systems and upgrading older ones. In neither case is there substantial technological risk. Therefore, the technical buyers in the IT community are not particularly interested or concerned about Main Street buying decisions, provided they stay within corporate guidelines. Similarly, the economic buyers in the end-user community see little on Main Street that demands their attention, as long as this year's purchasing stays within budget. Infrastructure is infrastructure—there are no strategic issues for them to focus on.

This reduces the interested constituencies to two: the end user and the Chief Financial Officer. The latter, working through the means of a purchasing department, wants to drive expenditures down through substituting low-cost commodities for high-priced brands. End users, on the other hand, want to get products that give them added value, whether that value be greater utility or personal satisfaction. Like kids at Christmas they push back against the powers that be to see if they can get what they really want.

This tension defines marketing strategy on Main Street. If you are a monkey, your best strategy is to be the low-cost provider the purchasing agent seeks, leveraging your own version of *operational excellence*, which is based on delivering commodity products with minimum overhead. If you are a chimp, on the other hand, you must win over the end users to sponsor your added value. This is a *customer intimacy* strategy based on whole product +1 offerings targeted at specific end-user applications.

If you are a gorilla, you can play both sides of the street, attacking the commodity market with a low-end offering, and the premium market with a series of +1 niche offerings. At the same time, aggressive gorillas continue to innovate enough to keep the monkeys scrambling. That is, by shifting the de facto standards slightly, they present the customer base with an easy-to-absorb enhancement but force the clone provider into another round of reengineering. In the meantime, the clone product is now no longer a perfect clone, thereby forcing it to discount even further to be an acceptable value.

Chimps caught up in this process have to be careful. They can win temporary advantages by being the first to meet a new forecasted point in the continuous evolution of the category. Thus Canon beat HP to an under-$300 street price for ink-jet printers, Brother beat them to an under-$400 laser printer, and Lexmark beat them to 1,200 dots-per-inch output. Similarly, when Compaq was struggling to meet competitive price points from both Dell and Gateway, the latter companies made significant incursions into its installed base. In all these cases, however, while the invading companies enjoyed a burst of sales for their accomplishments, once the gorilla caught up, they could not maintain their market share advantage.

The overall lesson for Main Street, then, is that *operational excellence* and *customer intimacy*—and *not product leadership*—are the key success factors. The former supports low-cost value propositions, the latter +1 market development. Product leadership, by contrast, often results in only temporary market-share gains, achieved at considerable expense and unlikely to result in sustainable competitive advantage. As such they are not worth the cost—better to focus your investment either on marketing into +1 niches where you can retain the customer or on R&D investment in preparation for the next paradigm shift.

The underlying dynamics of Main Street market competition are defined by the monkey, the provider of the clone prod-uct, and not the gorilla. Monkeys establish the rules of engage-ment by setting the lowest price point in the market, which becomes in effect the reference price. If no competitor responds, and if the end users stay out of the decision process, then the monkey, along with the CFO and the purchasing agent, win. For chimps to defeat monkeys, they must insert additional requirements and specifications into the purchase decision, thereby changing the field of competition. Purchasing agents are expert at either ignoring such additions or insisting that they ought to be free. Hence the need for the chimp to engage the end user in sponsoring them during the purchase process.

In the bowling alley, this sponsorship came from the eco-nomic buyer because the buying decision had significant eco-nomic implications that went beyond the IT issues. On Main Street the issues do not warrant this level of attention, nor can vendors afford to pay for the kind of distribution channel that can capture the economic buyer's interest. Increasingly, instead, they must rely on lower-cost indirect means of commu-nication—advertising, merchandising, and direct mail—to make their case, and these materials should be directed straight at the end users.

This need to achieve customer intimacy through low-cost, indirect channels of communication defines the core compe-tence required for Main Street market success. At the surface it appears to be self-contradictory—how can one be intimate without ever having direct contact? The answer, as artists have known throughout the centuries and consumer package-goods marketing has demonstrated throughout this one, is through *shared fantasies*.

This mechanism is easiest to see whenever companies are successful in selling commodity products at premium prices—soft drinks, toothpaste, breakfast cereals, deodorants, fountain pens, running shoes, or cigarettes. It is extremely unusual for any of these campaigns to focus on the utilitarian benefits of the product (indeed, some have no utilitarian benefits). Instead, they cloak their communications in all sorts of literary effects—beautiful scenes, attractive characters, absorbing little plots, striking images—to attract niches of customers who identify with these representations. When the customers buy the product they get the benefit of the underlying commodity, of course, but they also get a reaffirmation of their own identity, a way of describing to themselves and to the world the values they ascribe to, the social class to which they belong.

All of this has been well-known for a long time. The question is, what relevance does it have to high tech? Prior to Main Street, the answer is darned little. There are simply too many utilitarian concerns in the air—reliability, compatibility, ease of use, return on investment—for customers to be entertaining any fantasies. But once Main Street has been reached, once the standards have been set and the whole product has been truly commoditized, then the opportunity reasserts itself. And that is where the PC industry—particularly the software component of it—stands today.

Exactly how we will go forward from here is not yet clear. The use of shared fantasies has been so abused by consumer package-goods marketing that customers no longer make themselves as accessible to it as they used to. Sophisticated purchasers screen out advertisements and deconstruct their attempts to manipulate them. On the other hand, part of any purchase decision is to imagine oneself using the product beneficially, and we all expect help from the vendor in this process. In the case of high-tech products, which can be so abstract, this imagining is often the key to getting the end user oriented, as the desktop metaphor of the Macintosh and the inbox metaphor of electronic mail have proved. These are shared fantasies, too, and without them we could not proliferate high-tech solutions.

In sum, the adaptation of consumer marketing's experience with achieving customer intimacy with end users through shared fantasies communicated through indirect means is fertile ground for marketing innovation in high tech. Companies who master this adaptation will have initial—and probably sustainable—competitive advantage on Main Street because of their superior marketing materials.

In light of our industry's history of product-based competition, this raises an interesting question: Who should be the reference competitor cited by these materials? Should, in fact, they be referencing a competitor at all? The actual competitor, the monkey, does not deserve to be called out by name—why give them name recognition that they cannot get for themselves? On the other hand, if you reference the gorilla or other chimps, you are reopening your installed base to competitors you have already bested. That makes no sense, either. So, by default, it turns out *the best reference competitor for Main Street is yourself.* In marketing communications, you should be referencing your older line of products, which you dignify in your competitive comparisons while at the same time showing how your current offerings have gone beyond them. Then if competition enters from the outside, it must compete on a turf defined entirely by your architecture, past and present.

Hypercompetitiveness

This concludes our survey of the strategies for achieving competitive advantage as they evolve over the Technology Adoption Life Cycle. As we have seen, the appropriate critical success factors—or the key value disciplines, as Treacy and Wiersema call them—change dramatically as we move from the bowling ally into the tornado and then on to Main Street. This creates problems in communication, both within the marketplace and within our own organizations, topics to which we shall turn our attention in chapters 9 and 10.

Before moving on, however, there is one last aspect of competitiveness to address, which is what happens when it goes awry. The proper name for this is *hypercompetitiveness.*

In medieval literature, there are a vast number of stories about knights dueling to the death for the hand of a fair lady. This is real competition. At first blush, it seems like an extraordinary expression of love for the lady, but the more you get into these stories, the more you realize the knights are far more interested in each other than her. There is page after page about their equipment, and their horses, and how they fight, and what they say, and only a line or two at the end about a "happily ever after" with the lady. She is simply the excuse for them to do what they love best, which is to bash each other's brains out.

Unfortunately, we often replicate this same pattern in our marketing efforts. We say we are customer-focused, but in fact we *act* competitor-focused. Our advertising talks more about how we are better than the other guy than how we are good for the customer. Our product releases are defined less from what the target customer needs and more from what the competitor's product has (or has announced). We court partners not because our target customer needs them but because our competitor might get them. At the end of the day, we know our competitors far better than our customers, and our language and ideas reflect it.

Why do we behave in such a self-defeating way? How is it that the need to beat the competitor overwhelms the goal of serving the customer? Usually it is simply out of fear of losing, escalated to a level where it supersedes all other objectives. This leads to a state of hypercompetitiveness. Indeed, it is the goal of a certain style of management to induce this state, and in sales-driven efforts during the tornado it can produce dramatically successful results. Elsewhere and in other organizations, however, it throws companies off track and should be guarded against. How to do this successfully depends on which part of the organization needs addressing.

- *Hypercompetitive Sales*

  In sales organizations, hypercompetitiveness consists of trying to win every sale at any cost. All prioritization is a function of the current deal on the table, which leads to a succession of massive fire drills and fragmentation of all resources. This is not a winning way. Instead, one must discriminate between strategic and opportunistic customers, and reduce one's investment to win the latter so that one can increase investment in gaining the former. Indeed, targeting and investing to gain market share with certain classes of customers is the whole point of marketing strategy.

Hypercompetitive sales forces, however, refuse to support such strategies. They insist on being allowed to fight any battle, and then complain that marketing has not armed them with the weapons they need. But no company can afford to arm its sales force for all battles, and the reason the competition is eating their lunch is that they are fighting on the competitors' turf, using weapons of the competitors' choice.

The only way to move forward from here is to instigate marketing initiatives to attack new opportunities where we can define our own turf. At first this should be presented to the hypercompetitive sales force as a "both/and" and not as an "either/or" proposition. Marketing's focus should be on ensuring the whole product advantage within the target market, and sales should be allowed to come to the party when it will. As more and more of the pipeline gets filled with "our" kind of deal instead of the competitor's, the sales force will feel comfortable redirecting its efforts to the more strategic turf. But until that happens, one has to endure the slings and arrows of outraged voice mail.

- *Hypercompetitive Engineering*

In engineering organizations, hypercompetitiveness consists of trying to outdo the competitor's product accomplishments, regardless of whether the target customer needs the additional capabilities. Again, this is not winning strategy. The correct approach is to invest in customer satisfaction, even when that means doing highly tedious tasks, such as writing a complete set of drivers to interface your Internet software product to every fax modem on the market, or fundamentally uninteresting ones, like pruning back existing functionality in order to design out cost and complexity.

In order to avoid such busywork, hypercompetitive engineers enter into an alliance with hypercompetitive sales forces who are complaining that the reason we are not selling is because the competitor's product has some feature that ours doesn't. This sparks another round of development and product releases. When these are no more successful in gaining the customer's approval, there is no one left to blame but marketing, which clearly has failed to present these new offerings in the correct light.

The fix here is to engage R&D in the marketing process, building a cross-functional consensus as to where we are in the life cycle and what our priorities should therefore be. Because engineers are skilled in systems analysis, if the market opportunity is presented in a systems context, as it is the goal of these models to do, this cross-functional effort can be highly productive.

- *Hypercompetitive Marketing*

  Marketing organizations, too, can be hypercompetitive in their approach to partners and allies, distribution, pricing, or positioning. Here the dysfunctional behavior is always some version of "me first" degenerating into "me only." It typically shows up in price and margin negotiations that often break off because one or another partner simply cannot live with what is being offered. People call this playing hardball.

  Open systems markets, however, punish this kind of behavior because when a needed partner or ally withdraws, the egocentric vendor cannot simply replace them through vertically integrating inside their own company. The market insists instead on being allowed best-of-breed choices and will disqualify proprietary alternatives. The vendor can always go seek another partner, of course, and if the lesson has been learned, all will be forgiven. But if hypercompetitiveness persists, the market will deliberately isolate the vendor, *even if they are a gorilla.*

  Recall some examples cited earlier in the book of companies who tried to control the tornado—Sony with Betamax, IBM with MicroChannel, Adobe with Level 3 PostScript. In every case the market worked to isolate these vendors and ultimately either expel them or get them to back down. These

were extraordinarily costly mistakes and were due entirely
to hypercompetitive marketing.

Recap

The issue of competitive advantage gets so much attention
from management and is so elusive in the context of hypergrowth markets that it deserves recap. The dominant theme is
that the life cycle calls into play different value disciplines at
different stages, as follows:

Bowling alley: Product leadership, customer intimacy
Tornado: Product leadership, operational excellence
Main Street: Operational excellence, customer intimacy

- In the bowling alley, one differentiates from the status quo
  solution through technology leverage (product leadership)
  and differentiates from similar technical products through
  segment focus (customer intimacy).
- In the tornado, competitive strategy is a function of whether
  you are a gorilla, a monkey, or a chimpanzee.

  - Gorillas use operational excellence to ship in high vol-
    ume, gaining the maximum amount of new customers
    possible and also driving their costs per unit down—an
    advantage they can capture either as margin or, by pass-
    ing it on to the customer, as increased market share. They
    use a stream of new product releases (product leadership)
    to keep customers engaged and their competitors off bal-
    ance.
  - Monkeys compete on low price. Their form of operational
    excellence is based on reducing overhead to an absolute
    minimum. They do not compete for product leadership,
    their core technology competence being rapid and accu-
    rate reverse engineering.
  - Chimpanzees compete with the gorilla using their own
    version of product leadership, but this alone will not
    result in sustainable competitive advantage, since the
    market is biased to favor the gorilla's feature set as the de

facto standard. To gain sustainable advantage, chimpanzees need to revert to bowling alley strategy, carving out niches of market leadership by using customer intimacy to create segment-specific whole products, even in the midst of the tornado.

- Main Street offers two grounds for sustainable competitive advantage, the low-cost commodity provider and the niche-oriented premium brand. Monkeys are well suited to the former, chimps to the latter, while gorillas can and should do both.
- Hypercompetitive behavior is as damaging as uncompetitive behavior. The goal of strategy is to win the game, not beat the competition. Only in the tornado are the two goals identical.

All these issues revolve around how power distributes itself relative to competitive advantage. The previous chapter looked at power relative to partnerships. Now we need to see how these power "positions" are negotiated and communicated within the marketplace. That is the real significance of *positioning*, the topic to which we shall now turn.

CHAPTER 9

POSITIONING

Positioning is one of the most misunderstood elements in business strategy, for all sorts of reasons, some profound, some superficial. The most profound, in my view, is that we continue to think our positioning is primarily a *statement about us*. It is not. Instead, it is primarily about the *place we occupy within two interrelated systems*, both of which predate our existence, and both of which can get along just fine without us. They are:

1. The system of purchase choices available to a customer
2. The system of companies interacting to make a market

There are numerous books out on how to conduct positioning relative to the first of these two systems, so I am going to confine myself here solely to the second context for positioning, the act of taking one's place within a system of companies interacting to make a market.

This second system, of course, is a means to get to the first. That is, if we do not have a place in the set of companies making a market, we cannot get access to the customers we wish to serve. In order to get financing, access to distribution, and the cooperation of partners and allies to make the whole product, we must first establish relationships with the market makers. What does it take, then, to succeed here?

First of all, we must recognize that market makers are not some hidden elite. They are simply the companies that are already successful in the marketplace. These companies are currently interlinked in supply chains or value chains to bring whole products to customers, and they are making money doing so. As such, they have a stake in whatever we propose. Our presence in a market can enhance existing chains and enable new ones, in both cases bringing us into natural alliance with other players. At the same time, we can threaten existing chains either with direct competition or with replacement via an alternative chain, in either case creating adversaries in the process.

Since no company can create or serve a market all by itself, we need to secure the cooperation of at least some market makers, not only to get started but to continue functioning successfully over time. In short, we are looking at a power structure, and the first goal of positioning is to secure a position within it.

So, what are the available positions within a typical market's power structure? Basically they can be laid out along what should be a familiar grid to any strategic planner:

Market-Maker's View of the Marketplace

	Established Product	New Product
New Market	Imperialists vs. Natives	Explorers & Forty-niners
Established Market	Old Guard: Gorillas Chimpanzees Monkeys	Barbarians vs. Citizens

This grid of products and markets, established *vs.* new, is normally used to organize strategic entry and investment decisions. But the same forces that impact those decisions impact positioning as well, so it is also useful to represent the fundamental power roles in a free market, as follows:

THE OLD GUARD

In the lower-left quadrant, established markets are dominated by established products from the Old Guard. This is a hierarchy of companies, the pecking order set by market share, by the rules of engagement discussed in the previous chapter. It comes into being during the tornado and it presides over the market throughout its Main Street phase.

Since this quadrant represents the bulk of the money in the market at any given time, its power relationships are extremely significant and are watched closely for change. These same players also dominate word-of-mouth communication within the marketplace so what they say about each other as well as any new entrant has enormous influence. Because their supply and value chains are well established, new entrants are presumed to be competitors, not allies. In this light, they are immediately classified by size, which in turn determines their subsequent range of response.

A welcome new entrant in this quadrant might be a monkey intent on underpricing the current market with clone products. Distribution channels at the low end constantly seek to stock lower and lower priced alternatives because low prices attract people into their stores where, it is hoped, they can actually be persuaded to buy a higher priced item from the same shelf. Gorillas and chimps are not threatened, because there is only a fixed amount of shelf space allocated to monkey products, and the new monkey will only displace an old monkey, a matter of little importance.

A far more disturbing event in this quadrant is when a gorilla from a neighboring market comes in and challenges the local gorilla on its own turf. Now everyone with a power position in the Old Guard is at risk. If the new gorilla wins, the old gorilla won't go away, so in order to make room, everyone else has to move down one in the pecking order, and the smallest chimp, unable to convert to a monkey, is often eliminated. This is what happened in the ECAD software market when Cadence challenged Mentor—companies like Daisy and Valid got shoved down a notch and eventually were eliminated, the latter becoming absorbed into Cadence. For most companies, then, it is better if the new gorilla does not win. In that case, it is more likely to retreat entirely rather than convert to chimp status. This is what Compaq did after its abortive attempt to challenge HP in the PC printer market, much to the relief of the chimps there— Canon, Lexmark, and Epson. If instead Compaq had chosen to stick it out, then all of them would have suffered new restrictions on their shelf space.

Competition for positions in the Old Guard quadrant, therefore, represent a zero sum game. There are a fixed number of positions that the market can support, and if one company moves in or up, it has to be at another company's expense. Change is normally for the worse, and the Old Guard is thus by nature a conservative club.

EXPLORERS AND FORTY-NINERS

By contrast, in the upper-right quadrant are the entrants into the early market. These people neither threaten nor enhance the position of the Old Guard. They are watched with curiosity and amusement, the assumption being that they will go bust in the chasm, but with interest nonetheless because of the possibility that one might strike it rich. The market can distinguish two types here—explorers, who are driven by technology interests, and forty-niners, who are in it for the money. Neither is assumed to have any power at present, but if a forty-niner can come back with a few gold nuggets and a map to the mother lode, all that will change.

Visioneer is a company that as of this writing is in this quadrant. It makes a scanner about the size of a cigarette carton that fits between your keyboard and your PC. Any time you want to incorporate a paper document into work you are doing on the computer, you simply feed it into the box and it appears on the screen as a bit-mapped image. From there you might drag it onto a fax icon to fax it off to someone, or put it into some e-mail you are sending, or copy it into a word-processing document as an appendix, or use OCR (Optical Character

Recognition) software to turn it into editable text for revision. For anyone who communicates a lot through PCs, it is an attractive bridge between the world of paper and the world of screens.

Because of its form factor, Visioneer is a new product, and because it targets the everyday PC user, it is going into a new market. Thus it is in the position of a forty-niner who has come back to town with some gold nuggets. The rest of the scanner providers at this point are just watching, which is what the mainstream market always does when events occur in the early market. What they are waiting for is definitive assay results on the nuggets—is there gold in them thar hills or not? If the early returns are positive, then the Old Guard will try to move in. Here Visioneer is significantly at risk, because unlike most players in the early market, it has few barriers to entry to protect it: the hardware technology it uses is pervasive, and the rest of the whole product—with the exception of its software— is available off the shelf. Thus its software is its map to the mother lode. The question is, having seen this software in action, can competitors—and will competitors—try to copy it and get to the mine before they do? Visioneer has got to stake its claim quickly and definitively to cut off this possibility.

What we see here is that the power positions in the early market quadrant are entirely a function of control over previously unknown and unclaimed sources of wealth. These positions are taken by technology leaders with market insight, with two questions pending:

1. Is their insight real?
2. If so, can they capitalize on it before the Old Guard jumps their claim?

In general, the farther the new territory is from the Old Guard's existing borders, the more secure the new entrant can feel. Thus Lotus Notes enjoyed quite a long gestation period because it was far from anything then in vogue. Now, however, it is clear that Ray Ozzie's insight was real, and the question has become, will Lotus (now IBM) be able to successfully defend this turf against Novell and Microsoft? This is clearly Lotus's game to lose, and to date, they have not misstepped. The one outstanding issue, in my view, is the continued complexity of Notes applications. In order to get fully into the tornado and ride it to new heights, they need to do more work on commoditizing the whole product. But this is a straightforward challenge well within their grasp, so I would argue they are in a reasonably stable power position.

Positions in the other two quadrants, by contrast, are inherently unstable, being outgrowths of conflict at the borders of the existing power structure—either established products entering new markets, or new products entering established markets. In either case the Old Guard is directly involved from the outset. True to its capitalist imperialist roots, this club sees its own expansion into new markets as manifest destiny—imperialists *vs.* the natives—whereas anyone else's forays into its space is viewed as an assault on virtue itself—barbarians *vs.* citizens.

IMPERIALISTS *VS.* NATIVES

Looking first at new market imperialism, power relationships in the New World are set by which member of the Old Guard arrives first in the new market and achieves sufficient market leadership and penetration to claim it. Thus in the relational database market, Informix is currently enjoying rapid growth in Central Europe, leveraging its strength in Germany based on a long-standing relationship with Siemens. In Japan, on the other hand, even though Informix was an early leader, it was unable to achieve significant market share and has now been displaced by Oracle, which forced its way in via a power relationship with Nippon Steel.

As Old Guard companies are able to stake claims in new markets, they become upwardly mobile within their existing hierarchy, displacing companies who have no new sources of wealth. In the PC industry, for example, the traditional Old Guard of IBM, Compaq, and Apple was startled to discover in 1994 that Packard Bell, a well-established supplier of highly undistinguished clones, no doubt a monkey or at best a junior chimp, was *number four in their market!* Worse, in the first half of 1995 they have actually jumped to number one in terms of units shipped! The effrontery! Where had they come from? Well, while other vendors eschewed low-price outlets like Costco and the Price Club, Packard Bell embraced them, focusing intensely on operational excellence to achieve strikingly low prices while maintaining good quality. This enabled them to claim a "new market" consisting largely of late adopters buying their first PC for the home or small office.

Because the Old Guard dominates the power relationships in the current marketplace, it normally has its way when it comes to entering new markets, but occasionally it can encounter devastating resistance from the natives. If you wanted to see a case study of such resistance in action, you could have had no better seat in the house than to have plugged into the Internet while Intel's debacle over the mathematical errors caused by the Pentium was going on. The "flaming" that Intel took over it was a direct result of its arrogant treatment of the Internet natives. Gleefully they struck back, roasting Intel to the point where even the stubborn Mr. Grove submitted. All the companies planning on "civilizing" the Internet, converting it into an Information Superhighway, and building its offramps, malls, trailer parks, or the like, had best take heed of Intel's experience, or they may be in for a rocky time indeed.

BARBARIANS *VS.* CITIZENS

Successful or no, power relationships growing out of the imperialist quadrant typically cause gradual rather than abrupt shifts in the status quo of the Old Guard. This is not so in the case of the fourth quadrant, new products entering established markets, or barbarians *vs.* citizens. This is the assault mainframe vendors faced from the minicomputer revolution of the early 1980s, what the minicomputers in office automation faced from the PCs in the mid-1980s, and what traditional applications are facing from client/server applications in the 1990s. In each case, the new product strikes right at the heart of an established market, routing the Old Guard, and putting all existing power relationships into turmoil. Such is the destructive power of the next tornado.

Consider, for example, the chaos created by the onslaught of the PC into office automation. Does anyone remember Smith Corona, Olympia, Remington, Olivetti, or the IBM Selectric? Once the proud flagships of the well-appointed office, they are now relegated to filling out Federal Express labels and multi-part forms. How about Wang, Lanier, NBI, and Four-Phase? Are there any word processing departments left? What about IBM's PROFS, DEC's All-in-One, Prime's CEO, or HP's Desk? Isn't e-mail now PC-based? And what about the two major channels of distribution into the office, NOPA (National Office Products Association) and NOMDA (National Office Machinery Distributor Association)? Have not all their sales reps given up in the face of Office Depot and other superstores? Has anyone seen Liquid Paper recently? How about carbon paper, ditto masters, or mimeograph machines?

Consider how much money has shifted from one set of suppliers to another, and still the carnage is not done. Today the fax business (more than $10 billion per year) and the copier business (more than $50 billion per year) are under siege, as are to varying degrees the U.S. Mail, 35mm slide presentation and the graphics houses that create them, and business forms suppliers.

With each new tornado, enormous sums of wealth shift as value chains and supply chains reconfigure and realign into new coalitions. These are the most dramatic power changes in business, and positioning in these times is a matter of life or death, fortune or fatality.

We should not think, however, that the Old Guard is never the victor in these encounters. At the end of the 1980s, after Intel had defeated the challenge of the Motorola 68000 through its now-famous Crush program, it was then besieged by a horde of barbarian RISC microprocessors—MIPS with the R3000, Sun with SPARC, HP with PA/RISC, IBM with the Power PC, and Motorola with the 88000. Despite massive onslaughts by one and all, Intel held its ground. Why was this possible? As long as the whole product is healthy, as long as each new release narrows the gap between the invader's advantage and the Old Guard's status quo, the current power positions will hold, with the Old Guard nourished by another year's strong revenues and the attackers having to live off the land as best they can. Intel had all the applications, and it was able to co-opt the paradigm shift sufficiently to defuse its threat.

Positioning Among Market Makers

So, to sum up, we have multiple positions within a market infrastructure, with the frame of reference set by the Old Guard, the established players in the established markets. All positions are a function of present wealth and future prospects, combined with whether one supports or threatens the current establishment. The marketplace, when confronted with any new company, will immediately try to position it into one of these four quadrants, and then, within that quadrant, into one of the various roles discussed. As soon as such a position is established, then all the players in the market know how to treat the new entity, and predictable market relations can resume.

Having surveyed the variety of positions available within a market infrastructure, we now want to revisit the idea of positioning. First of all, what is our goal? And second, how can we direct our communications to achieve it?

The goal of positioning within a market infrastructure is to take one's rightful place and no other. That place is determined by our ability to create or enhance a value chain or preempt another company's current position in one. Markets, that is, are as inherently cooperative as they are competitive, and they are continually on the lookout for opportunities to realign their current business processes into more efficient forms. At the same time, they are also always in search of new sources of revenue. As a new arrival, if you can provide either, you are of positive interest. If you cannot, the only remaining question is whether you are a threat, and if so, how much of one.

Your position, then, is a function of the money flow you affect. It is a place ceded to you by the other members of the market based on their perception of how you best fit into the total system. They, in turn, take their cues from what you say, verified by what you can actually do. Skepticism is the order of the day, and credibility is your most important asset. This is one time, in other words, where if you cannot walk the walk, you must not talk the talk.

Translating these principles into actual cases, the first question you must decide is within which quadrant do you best fit? That is, are your current and future prospects best understood by seeing you as a member of the establishment's Old Guard, be it gorilla, chimp, or monkey, or as an imperialist, a native, a barbarian, a citizen, an explorer, or a forty-niner? Each role implies different power relationships, seeks out different allies, and aligns against different competitors, so people do want to know. And if you say you are none of these, then you had best present a strong alternative position, else you will be tagged as just another no-name company whom people can afford to ignore since you won't be around for long (which is a self-fulfilling prophecy since staying around requires at least some support from someone).

Once you identify which archetype fits you best, you will be surprised to learn how much of your communications are pre-ordained for you. Market relations in this context are a bit like old-fashioned melodramas—"You must pay the rent!" "I can't pay the rent!"—the roles are well known, the lines well rehearsed, the variations modest. So, think back to every B-movie you have ever watched and in that context select from the following thumbnail sketches the role you are most suited to play:

The Cast
(IN ORDER OF APPEARANCE)

- *The Gorilla*

You are a dictator, and the only question is whether you are benevolent or cruel. As a benevolent one, you are revered for setting the standards that have allowed an entire market sector to prosper, and your ongoing investments from admittedly huge profits will benefit generations to come. As a cruel one, you demand unswerving loyalty from partners while being entirely capricious in your own movements, creating fear, hatred, and resentment among some players, but still arbitrarily making others dazzlingly rich, at least for a while—and even your worst enemies grudgingly admit that the trains are running on time. Either role is acceptable and stable. What cannot be tolerated is any suspicion that you are losing your grip on the reins of power.

Good ancillary roles for gorillas are imperialist and citizen, the former to show that you are not only strong enough to stay in power but to extend it, the latter to show that you are protecting the current market players from losing their franchises to the next paradigm. By contrast, simply standing pat is disconcerting as it makes you a stationary target for all sorts of conspiracies. It is just this concern that currently is making the market nervous about Novell, the current gorilla in the LAN market.

- *The Chimpanzee*

    Your role is the least stable, and you must always show yourself to be in motion. You became a chimpanzee because you were a candidate for gorilla in the last tornado market but were not selected. This means you are a perpetual threat to the gorilla and a ready target for monkeys. At the same time, you have a real power base in the established market and cannot afford to desert it. Here's what you must do instead:

    1. Secure your power base by retrenching into a subsector of the overall market, building up sufficient whole product advantage to ward off even the gorilla's attacks, and communicating to all that
        A. you are not interested in further expansion into the established market, but
        B. you will defend this turf to the death.

    2. Stake out a new claim, either as an imperialist or a forty-niner, with the goal of getting out from under the current gorilla. Your supporters will stick by you in the existing market if they think you can be the gorilla in the coming

one. Make sure you target something that the current gorilla cannot easily grab from you, remembering that it is in its interest to pick a fight with you now.

3. Keep the current gorilla occupied by playing the game of Let's-you-and-him-fight, whereby you throw other competitors into the fray. Phil White at Informix has succeeded brilliantly at this ploy, using first Ingres and then Sybase to keep Oracle occupied and keep himself out of Larry Ellison's immediate sights.

If you need additional coaching in this role, and can take time out from all your duties, watch Shakespeare's history plays—their whole subject is the machinations of chimpanzees, each seeking to be the next gorilla.

- *The Monkey*

This is an easy role, as long as you don't put on airs of being something else. Your primary audience is the distribution channel and the purchasing agent, neither of whom are much impressed with gorilla or chimpanzee claims, both of whom are more impressed with a percentage point or two of margin. Do not waste marketing communications dollars on PR or image advertising—that is for chimps and gorillas who need to establish relationships with end-user customers and investors. You are strictly a middleman.

Your goal is to be the low-cost supplier who is easiest to do business with. You should understand from the outset that this status is inherently transient, and that you yourself are inherently transient. When confronted for a fight, run immediately for the highest tree. Then, when the attacker gets bored and goes away, come back down and continue to do business, taking heart in the knowledge that of all the species of primate, yours is the one that will endure the longest.

- *The Explorer*

You are a walk-on in the drama of the marketplace, interesting for the information you may dig up, but otherwise a blank because you are not motivated by immediate profits.

This is a confusing role if it is your primary identity—as it is, for example, for not-for-profit industry consortia like Sematech, the CAD Framework Initiative, or the Open Systems Foundation. People simply do not know how seriously to take any of the standards these groups promulgate, and many development cycles are wasted in the process.

The role of explorer is much more interesting if it is an ancillary role of a gorilla or chimpanzee, who can afford to finance such expeditions in hopes of finding a Northwest Passage or its economic equivalent, a prelude to coming out as a forty-niner.

- *The Forty-niner*

Your role is the one that most differentiates high tech from other markets. You are claiming to have found gold, and your primary goal now is to recruit a team of partners to go cross the chasm and mine it. You lead the team because you are the only one who truly knows where the gold lies, the only one able to define the target application and the whole product, and because you have proprietary control over at least one key element of the value chain.

To get people to follow you is no mean feat, and you had best be represented by a charismatic leader whom people want to believe. This leader must paint a picture of the future so vividly that otherwise prudent people forsake their current security in favor of this new quest. Lacking any historical evidence, the arguments presented must be elegant, consistent, and coherent, allowing people to believe because the explanation is so, well, believable. And when it comes time to lead your team across the chasm, you will bolster your credibility by focusing on a specific target customer with a compelling reason to buy and absolutely nail the whole product for that one application.

- *The Imperialist*

This role is open to any member of the Old Guard who can extend the market for their established products into new territory, whether it be through geographical expansion, or being first to port to a new computing platform, or through deeper vertical market penetration. The assumption is that the existing infrastructure, or natives, serving these new markets will have nothing in its armament to counter the new technology you bring.

Whether this is true or not, you will find that the real power of the natives lies in their control of access to the customer through both the distribution and communication channels. For you to be successful, you may have to abandon some of your imperialist arrogance and subordinate yourself to the local culture, building partnerships of mutual benefit and dependence. If you do so, you will secure a strong position in the new market, defensible against even the strongest competitor.

Imperialist development is key to sustaining Old Guard viability. As your fellow market makers brush up against the boundaries of current markets, they need to know where you—and they—go from here. Stay-at-homes tend to lose ground in the pecking order when competing against expansionist arrivals whose coffers are swelled with New World wealth.

- *The Native*

This role is the mirror opposite of the imperialist. Instead of having the new technology, you have the existing relationships, and you can choose either to support or resist the imperialist's arrival, depending on which is more to your advantage. Responding passively and doing neither, on the other hand, is a losing game.

Whether you resist or support, you play the role the same way, positioning yourself as a member in good standing of the native market infrastructure and interpreting the imperialist's moves in that light. The key is to be the first to recognize and appreciate the imperialist's capability and its significance and then use that understanding to position yourself as a knowledgeable spokesperson. Either way, this can be a breakthrough opportunity for a heretofore unheralded company to gain major market clout.

For example, when IBM decided to enter the CASE (Computer-Aided Software Engineering) market with a comprehensive architecture called AD/Cycle, it threw into prominence a little known vendor called Bachman, who overnight had the inside track for repository-based application development. Bachman positioned itself as the native market spokesman. As it turned out, IBM was unable to deliver on its vision, and Bachman subsequently suffered at the hands of this association, but that does not detract from the brilliance of this move. It was a superb native response.

- *The Barbarian*

This is the most aggressive role in the marketplace because once you embark upon it, there is no retreat. The good news is that normally you do not invade the Old Guard's established market without first gaining momentum elsewhere, so you have a lot of control as to when you actually declare war. In fact, the most successful strategy is not to declare war at all but instead to work the edges of the established market, eroding it away bit by bit.

Sooner or later, however, the Old Guard will sound the alarm, and when that happens, your role is to rally a horde of invaders—the new tornado market makers—to attack a contested piece of market territory. Success depends on realizing that you are fighting a long-term war—the Old Guard is not going away ever, as it has no place to go to—so you must manage your attack carefully.

Microsoft is a barbarian when it attacks the world of server-centric computing with its NT operating system. Its best initial target is the LAN, where it will come directly in conflict with Novell. If it wins there, it will then gradually move upstream, attacking first the low-end Unix market, working eventually to surround the high-end servers in much the same way the Unix barbarians, led by HP, are now surrounding the IBM mainframes. But even Microsoft must be careful in executing this strategy, for as we shall see, the local citizenry have strong weapons at their disposal as well.

- *The Citizen*

What do you do when your core markets are under attack by an intimidating horde of barbarians led by some ruthless albeit mopheaded and bespectacled leader? First you must sound the alarm, drawing the invaders out into the open so that their strategy of erosion no longer works. Then you must marshal your own market-making allies into mounting a defense.

The key to your strategy is not to counterattack but rather to fight a war of attrition over the issue of completing the whole product. Positioning yourself as a spokesperson for the Old Guard, you declare the utmost respect for the new technology but express reservations over its lack of a complete solution for your marketplace. Cluck at the absence of utility software, standards and procedures, and all the other mundane elements that make up a mature operating environment. Since the barbarians, by definition, must play on your turf, you can set up any number of these hurdles for them to jump over, consuming time and resources and discouraging their allies. At the same time, see what you can do to foment rebellion back in the invader's home market, working with disaffected chimpanzees to undercut the gorilla barbarian's power base.

All this buys time for your ultimate response, which must be a counteroffensive based on you yourself bringing new technology to the fray, thereby moving the battle definitively out of the barbarian's reach. IBM is currently taking this approach in the mainframe market based on its new lower cost high-end processors, and we'll see if it can successfully lead the resurgence of centralized computing that analysts like the Gartner Group are predicting.

So much for the guided tour through a B-movie version of *The Valley of High Tech*. If the characterizations do shade into caricatures, the underlying point is a crucial one: market makers understand each other's presence in the market through just this kind of scenario-based role playing. To have a credible presence in a market, therefore, you must present yourself as playing a familiar role within a familiar plot. This is the sole goal of positioning within the market infrastructure.

Many such positioning efforts fail for one of two reasons. The more common is that the company in question "overcasts" itself—unwilling to accept the bit part that fits its station, it insists on being the lead. Such companies the market simply dismisses as naive and foolish. Less common, but more worrisome, are good companies with strong market-making potential that simply fail to signal the market as to their intentions. Instead, they spend all their time talking about their products. Market makers are not interested in anyone else's products; all they are interested in is the market for their own. Your positioning in a market, therefore, is not really about you at all; it is about how you impact the rest of the market's ability to make money.

It is hard for human beings to realize that the positioning statements they make about themselves are not intended as acts of self-expression, but realize they must if they are to coopt the market's mechanisms to serve their ends. This challenge, however, is but a subset of a whole host of daunting obstacles that face companies competing for a place in hypergrowth markets. Taken as a whole, the challenge is to continually adopt new tactics, often reversing the very approaches that have proved successful to date, in order to keep pace with the next stage of the life cycle's demands. Effectively this means you can never get comfortable, never get set in your ways. How to manage groups under these conditions, how to stabilize them so that they can keep their bearings in the midst of disorienting change, is the subject of the next and final chapter of *Inside the Tornado*.

CHAPTER 10

ORGANIZATIONAL
LEADERSHIP

Having reached the last chapter of this book, let us take a moment to reflect on how far we have come.

In Part One we surveyed the Technology Adoption Life Cycle from end to end (chapter 2), isolating six inflection points where market forces essentially reverse themselves and business strategies must change dramatically in order to adapt. Of these six, we focused on three—the bowling alley (chapter 3), the tornado (chapter 4), and Main Street (chapter 5)—digging into each to see the forces driving the marketplace outside our companies and then taking that knowledge back inside to help set strategic priorities. Seeing again and again how these priorities not only shift but actually reverse themselves, we saw the importance of accurately placing oneself on the life cycle and in that context reviewed tools for helping us do so correctly (chapter 6).

Over the course of Part Two we have been examining the impact of rapidly changing life cycle forces on the distribution and management of power in the marketplace. In chapter 7, "Strategic Partnerships," we looked at their impact on our interactions with allies, and in chapter 8, "Competitive Advantage" on our interactions with competitors. Then we looked at the two coming together in the previous chapter, "Positioning," which focused on how to take one's place within the total system of market makers, partners, and competitors alike.

At every stage we have emphasized the need to play the role the market dictates, to transition between roles smoothly, to let go of old behaviors that no longer serve and take up new ones that were until recently forbidden. Now we are left with but a single question to answer: How in the world can anyone actually make this work?

All the World's a Stage

People are not like Legos. We do not readily reconfigure ourselves, nor do we take kindly to such reconfigurations being imposed upon us. Our organizations cannot function effectively if they are continually being rechartered and redirected. Yet all this is precisely what sustainable hypergrowth market success requires.

To lead and manage in this context we must provide a layer of stability underlying all this change. Fortunately there exists an institution from which we can learn, one which has perfected the rapid switching of roles. It is the theater troupe, and though the analogy is bound to create a few grins, it is not as far-fetched as you might think.

Begin with the idea of change. On Tuesday the troupe is performing *Othello*, and everyone knows that Herman plays a great Iago. But on Friday, when they put on *The King and I*, he's just a stagehand because he can't sing a note. Now, does anybody have any trouble with this? Is anybody confused about the direction of the troupe or Herman's role in it? Absolutely not. This group *does* reconfigure itself readily, *does* take kindly to having such reconfigurations imposed upon it, and is *happy* to be continually rechartered and redirected.

What stabilizes the group are the notions of *scripts*, *roles*, *direction*, and *casting*, and we can co-opt every one of these ideas to build an effective organization for hypergrowth markets. Begin with scripts or what in business are commonly called scenarios. This entire book can be understood as the working out of three scenarios: "In the Bowling Alley," "Inside the Tornado," and "On Main Street." Moving in and out of these stories are an extraordinary cast of characters—gorillas and monkeys, forty-niners and imperialists, barbarians and chimpanzees. We didn't take these roles all that seriously at the time, nor were we intended to, but they *are* roles and we absolutely understood them as such.

And so the question arises, If we did take all this seriously, how far can we take this idea? Here we must tread carefully. Life is not literature. Nothing is predestined. We use scripts and roles to help find our way, but it is more like improvisation than a formal play. As long as we keep a light touch with this analogy, then we can go forward with it. As soon as we get heavy-handed with it, it will fail.

So proceeding with this caveat in mind, we can now turn back to the theater troupe, specifically one that specializes in "improv," to see how it's approach to *casting* and *direction* can shed light on the business problem of organizations' leadership. Actually, this idea is not all that far afield from the manager-as-symphony-conductor metaphor that was in vogue a few years ago. The idea of blending talents and getting the most from the group are common to both. But there are key differences that are telling:

- Improv direction comes from within the cast, spontaneously emerging as the situation clarifies. By contrast, a symphony conductor is simply a kinder, gentler representation of command and control management.
- As a result, the role of improv director "floats." Unlike the symphony conductor, it is not a job assigned to a single individual but rather a function that adheres to the first person who "recognizes" the script unfolding.
- Finally, whereas in an orchestra musicians each play their assigned instrument, in an improv cast roles are taken up

and put down rapidly. The actors are not expert, the lines are never perfected, and the goal is to generate the best effect you can and then get on with it.

There are additional aspects to this comparison that we will take up later, notably the inability of improv groups to scale up in size, but for now let us make the connection back to the business of hypergrowth markets.

Organizing Hypergrowth

The key institution for hypergrowth management is the cross-functional team brought into being by the development of a new category of product. At its core is a product marketing manager, the center point at which all forces converge, whose challenge is first to get the product into the early market and then across the chasm. Supporting the team are the standard institutions of functional line management—engineering, marketing, manufacturing, sales, and finance—from which the various team members have been drawn.

The team's first task is to create a market-based scenario, a script for how the market might go forward given the current players, changing needs, and the entry of the new category of product. Drawing on their own experience, along with whatever research they can lay their hands on, and using models from books like this one, the team projects a possible future and builds a plan around it. Each represented function interacts with the others to check assumptions and catch problems before they arise. It is as close to rehearsal as they are ever going to get.

The play starts and almost immediately it becomes clear it is an improvisation. Nothing follows script, many projections prove false, but still the team presses forward and, God willing, the beginnings of a market emerge. These are nurtured going forward and, until such time as tornado warnings loom, this form or organization remains stable.

Within this stability, however, different players take center stage over the course of the front half of the Technology Adoption Life Cycle. In the early market, R&D engineers, sales support engineers, evangelists, and charismatic salespeople are out front. When the chasm hits the team calls a brief intermission, huddling around the marketing and finance people, after which they launch into Act II, where vertical market managers, partner managers, and market-focused sales teams play to the house. All this time manufacturing, purchasing, quality control, and human resources work diligently backstage.

But all this changes once the tornado looms, and the objective of *customer intimacy* is replaced by that of *operational excellence*. Now for the first time the line institutions must engage with full force, each operating relatively independently and to its own rhythms to ensure maximum efficiency. All the heretofore "backstage" functions now take center stage as operations scale up dramatically to respond to tornado demand.

At this point there is a temptation to disband the original team. Its informal mode of operation is deemed unsuitable for the massive deployment of resources underway, and its members are deemed too junior given the extraordinary financial impact of management decisions. Both these concerns are warranted, but disbanding the team is not. Instead it should be rechartered from a tiger team action force to a product marketing council charged with ensuring ongoing communication and problem resolution among the various line functions. For left to their own devices these line functions will optimize exclusively for their local processes, creating a far from optimal total effect.

Not until the market has transitioned onto Main Street and the strategy of *product leadership* has been supplanted by a return to *customer intimacy* is it safe to disperse this council. But once this transition does occur, then the hypergrowth forces have subsided and companies can realign themselves along traditional Main Street models. Key roles going forward are product marketing and marketing communications to target margin-rich +1 opportunities and product management to keep driving down base costs. But none of these roles requires special organization to execute.

Managing Hypergrowth

Each phase of the drama of hypergrowth makes special demands on skills and expertise. The organizational structure of the improv theater troupe creates flexibility so that people with the pertinent skills can shuffle in and out of play. But behind the scenes there still needs to be a higher level of leadership and management, someone to sponsor the local team within the larger structures of the corporation, partnerships, investors, and the like. What does it take to be successful in this role?

Here is where the full force of hypergrowth change is felt, for what the following pages make clear is that no one personality is likely to be effective over all three stages of the mainstream market's development. The full consequences of this conclusion will be discussed at the end of this chapter, but for now let us at least characterize our ideal candidate for each phase.

To help us get started, let us revisit the principle that each stage in the mainstream portion of the life cycle brings to the fore two value disciplines while asking the third to recede. This notion is neatly captured by the following diagram:

Organizational Imperatives

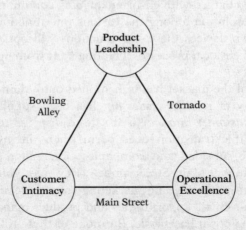

By working our way around this triangle we can summarize the managerial imperatives at each stage of the life cycle.

Management in the Bowling Alley

The goal of bowling alley strategy is to gain adoption of a discontinuous innovation by mainstream customers in advance of a widespread market acceptance. The recommended strategy for so doing is to focus on vertical market segments that have compelling needs, paying particular attention to building a complete whole product that fulfills the economic buyer's ROI agenda.

Now by virtue of promoting this discontinuous innovation, we are automatically bringing product leadership into this market. What differentiates our strategy is that we are yoking it to customer intimacy. That is what our commitment to a segment-specific whole product really means. It cannot be executed without a deep understanding of the customer's business application. In fulfilling this commitment, something else has to give, and in this case it is operational excellence. The bowling alley is no time to introduce process management or control systems. Our work flow lacks both the volume and the repeatability necessary to pay back investments in operational excellence. Rather, it is a time to accommodate the customer instead of ourselves, to spend more time on their site than at home, on their application than on our processes.

The knowledge that is most in demand in the bowling alley is *business expertise* in the vertical market. The whole product must deliver achieved ROI, and for that to happen, it must be architected by someone who genuinely understands the customer's business dynamics. Given how much their customers depend upon the systems they provide, high-tech companies are continually chagrined by how little they actually understand about how customers' businesses actually work. During the bowling alley, however, this embarrassment turns into acute anxiety as management teams realize they must direct bowling pin strategy based on careful evaluation of just this kind of knowledge.

Once a segment is targeted, then the most sought-after market expertise is *application engineering*, the ability to pull together segment-specific solutions in the field, to get a class of customers up and running, and begin to institutionalize a whole product that is reliable and replicable. This takes a special blend of discipline and imagination that is a far cry from the R&D brilliance and heroic on-the-fly invention that won the day in the early market. Customer intimacy in the bowling alley is not based on bonding with a single visionary champion but rather internalizing and responding to the issues that bind together a whole segment.

In progressing through this development, management should not be process-oriented but rather *event-driven*. The critical issue in the bowling alley is not efficiency but time. We are on a trek to the tornado. The more market segments we can have under our belt before the tornado hits, the better our starting position. There needs to be a sense of urgency to balance the urge to cherish each individual opportunity. This is not the time to sacrifice the one to the many, but it is a time to make a great cluster of the ones.

The bowling alley is also a time for bringing new people into the organization, and *recruiting* expertise is crucial here. The new people should not only set the standard for new-hires going forward but also should reset the bar for people who have been on board from the beginning. Pre-mainstream companies acquire staffing opportunistically and often carelessly, leading to highly variable talents. The lower end of this talent base must not be allowed to hire people who do not threaten them. Instead, they must be spurred by the new hiring to move up or out.

Finally, from a financial point of view, the number-one success measure in the bowling alley is *revenues within target segment*. This is even more important than total revenues, as the latter can be inflated by taking a visionary deal that actually hurts the enterprise's go-forward program. The biggest challenge to tracking segment revenues is post-sales revision of the target or "bull's-eye" marketing, where you draw a bull's-eye target around whatever you actually hit. Management needs to be savvy to prevent this, normally by getting a list of approved companies within segment in advance, with the entire team's compensation tied to meeting a specified within-segment revenue target.

Bringing all these factors together, the management profile that emerges is of a hands-on leader who spends more time with the customer and the troops than reviewing reports or winning points with top management. People in this role must be team leaders. They need not be particularly senior but should be very focused and disciplined in their approach to goal attainment. They must have a strong sense of quality control, but one rooted in customer satisfaction, not process metrics. They should be charismatic and personable with colleagues and customers alike. Above all, they must have an unwavering commitment to the end objective while retaining a high degree of flexibility about how it is attained.

Contrast all this with the management style needed for the tornado.

Management in the Tornado

The goal of tornado strategy is to capture as many "customers for life" as possible during a relatively brief flurry of infrastructure change-over. The recommended strategy for so doing is to ignore end users and economic buyers, focusing instead on infrastructure buyers and the channels of distribution needed to reach them. The whole value proposition is based on offering a rapid, risk-minimized transition to the new paradigm.

The fact that it is a new paradigm means we are still operating in the domain of product leadership. Indeed, over the course of the tornado, competitive pressure will force all vendors to continuously upgrade their offerings through frequent new product launches, each time ratcheting up the critical price performance measures. What differentiates this period from the bowling alley is the homogenization rather than individualization of the whole product, the desire for a common global infrastructure instead of a segment-specific business solution. This demand forces vendors into a mass-market mode where operational excellence is demanded in order to meet the "just ship" imperative without generating returned merchandise. Taking time out to customize a solution for a particular customer is anathema now, slowing down the tornado and introducing the risk of a glitch, so customer intimacy must take a backseat. The goal instead is first to institutionalize, then to standardize, and then to commoditize.

The knowledge that is most in demand in the tornado is *systems expertise*. This applies to both external and internal systems. Externally, customers need help in meshing the old and new paradigms together to create an operational infrastructure that has appropriate performance characteristics. Simply put, they have no choice but to make these systems work. All kinds of arcane technical issues get in the way here, and the vendors who can field the needed expertise to get their customers up and running quickly are able to then run off and get some more customers. At the same time, looking inside at itself, the company must also ramp up its own internal systems so as to handle the high-volume workload descending rapidly upon it.

In addition to strong systems engineering expertise, tornado companies also require strong *sales management*. The problem in a tornado is not to close *a* sale but to close *many* sales. Undisciplined sales teams cherry-pick markets, jealously guarding the size of their territories in order to preserve this convenient modus operandi. Sales management must continually push up the yield per acre if the company is going to come out on top in the tornado battle.

This kind of yield improvement imperative is but one of many organizational challenges that call out for a *process-driven* management style. In a tornado the one must always be subordinated to the many, and the many must be managed not as a series of discrete events but as a process flow. Doing it right the first time is critical because we are setting precedents for the 100th and 1,000th time as well. And building in metrics to make processes self-correcting in real time is mandatory because, as tornado volumes increase, inspection-based quality control becomes impossible. Organizations that must continue to fall back on fire drills simply have not sufficiently abandoned their bowling alley ways. In the tornado, while events clamor for attention, what rewards attention is process.

During this period of rapid expansion enormous numbers of people are hired. The critical expertise here is *new-hire orientation*, the art of getting people off to the right start. The goal here is to communicate the core values in which the company's culture is grounded, a set of deep-seated guidelines that allow people to navigate the myriad decisions of a tornado without always having to ask permission, seek supervision, or beg forgiveness. The medium of communication cannot be a handbook or a training class or a video. It must be communicated by direct interpersonal contact. Given the volume, this has to be a process, but it must not feel like one—hence the challenge.

And last, on the financial side, the critical discipline is *cash flow management*. Revenues skyrocket in a tornado, leading to bulging accounts receivable and draining the company of current capital. Most tornado companies go through at least one cash crisis where despite meteoric success they come within inches of missing payroll. Again, process discipline is the core requirement.

From all this we can infer a leadership profile that contrasts starkly with the bowling alley. Where there we want hands-on leaders who will roll up their sleeves, here we want executives who can stay above the fray, see the forest rather than get caught up in the trees, and eschew fire fighting in favor of fire prevention. To do this requires a seasoned professional, someone who has experienced the tornado before, and who understands not only the value but the implementation of business processes during a high-pressure period. We are looking for people more unflappable than charismatic, more disciplined than personable, who have a firmer grasp on priorities than on details, and who can maintain their heads—and their processes—while all about them are losing theirs.

Such are the bulwarks that hold companies firmly on course amid the eddying currents of the tornado—and run them just as firmly aground if they are allowed to continue in these ways on Main Street.

Management on Main Street

The goal of Main Street strategy is to capitalize on the two market development opportunities inherent in any newly adopted infrastructure—to continue to deploy the core commodity at the market's boundaries reaching out into secondary geographies, and to deepen penetration at its center, drilling down into secondary applications. The recommended strategy for so doing is to continue to commoditize the base whole product and to layer on top of it +1 initiatives for addressing niche-based value propositions. Because the former strategy, which continues to play to the infrastructure buyers, generates increasingly low margins, the latter +1 strategy, which plays to specific needs of end users, tends to be the defining element.

As we are continuing to play in a commodity business, operational excellence continues to be a critical value discipline. What differentiates our strategy from the tornado is that now there is no longer an adequate return from further R&D investment in the core price-performance factors. As a result, for the first time in the life cycle, product leadership is set aside as a critical success factor, to be replaced by a reawakened interest in customer intimacy. But this intimacy is a far cry from what we knew in the bowling alley. There it was based on a deep appreciation of the economic buyers' view of ROI in their particular segment. Here it is based on the *end users'* view of their own performance, the goal being to improve either productivity or personal gratification or both. It is these end users whom we seek to serve and whom we expect will champion our higher margin +1 offerings.

Now, since no single program is expected to be a home run, Main Street strategy requires us to field an ongoing stream of +1 offerings into the marketplace. Thus once again we want to adopt a process, not an event, orientation. But unlike the process orientation of the tornado, which is largely internally focused to ensure supply, Main Street processes are focused externally on creating additional demand based on a deepened understanding of end-user behavior and a more sensitive appreciation of the distribution channel's needs.

The knowledge that is most in demand at this time is typically associated with successful consumer packaged goods marketing, but the discipline itself, I suggest, should be called *convenience engineering*. The +1 programs must deliver genuine added value but at very little added cost. To do so, they must either eliminate an annoying element in the current paradigm or liberate for productive use some previously hard-to-use product feature—neither task requiring significant additional R&D investment in product leadership. Instead we want increased expertise in dissecting the behavior of end users, in human factors design and ergonomics, and in the psychology of personal gratification. At the same time, in the distribution channel, a different sort of convenience engineering is needed to get +1 offerings on the shelves in a distinctive but cost-effective and non-disruptive fashion.

Because much of what +1 programs deliver actually transpires inside the head of the end user—is of subjective rather than objective value—the most sought after marketing expertise is *marketing communications*. What previously was perceived as a tactical effort now becomes the arena in which value itself is defined, the venue in which companies conduct their relationships with end users. Less and less of the purchase's value comes from the mechanics of our product and more and more from the user's experience of it. Sensitivity to the factors that shape that experience, along with the ability to manipulate those factors, is critical to +1 strategy. At the same time, in the channel, marketing communications becomes the single most valued element, creating demand for much-needed higher margins in what is otherwise rapidly becoming a commodity category.

All of the above argues for a wholesale redeployment of talent, both from sheer downsizing to drive costs continually lower as well as from shifting emphasis from the team disciplines of vertical market development and tornado supply chain management to the individual disciplines of brand management and channel management. It is a time of reassignment and renewal, and it is critical to ensure that people get properly aligned with new work. For one of the great assets of flexible team organization is the opportunity to use new assignments for *staff development.*

Throughout this process the top priority financial discipline is *margin management,* for the goal of Main Street is to serve as a cash cow. R&D investment, while not ceased, should be stretched out, with fewer more widely spaced releases, and manufacturing and logistical cost controls must continue to contribute to reaching the next lower commodity price point. Greater spending on marketing programs to gain +1 customers needs to be continually validated by monitoring achieved margin increases above the commodity price level. It goes without saying that team compensation should now be tied to profits, not revenues or growth.

The Main Street management profile, in contrast to the tornado, portrays a people-oriented individual focused on customer satisfaction and staff development. Unlike the bowling alley manager, who focuses on task analysis in vertical markets to help economic buyers attain objectively measurable ROI, the Main Street manager must be adept at subjective value propositions targeted at end users from varying demographic segments. This requires an exceptionally secure ego, for effective communications programs require management to let go of what they would want to say in order for the program to be able to communicate what the customer wants to hear. Similarly, when it comes to staff development, success is a function of seeing people in their own terms more than molding them to fit one's own. Finally, Main Street managers must be sufficiently process-oriented to keep a constant flow of programs and assignments moving forward, continually taking the pulse of the people they serve to ensure variety and satisfaction.

Leading Hypergrowth

We can readily express the leadership challenge of hypergrowth by recapping the contrasts in management styles just surveyed:

Bowling Alley	Tornado	Main Street
Economic Buyer	Infrastructure Buyer	End-User
Vertical Markets	Horizontal Markets	Secondary Markets
Product Leadership	Product Leadership	Operational Excellence
+	+	+
Customer Intimacy	Operational Excellence	Customer Intimacy
Not Operational Excellence	Not Customer Intimacy	Not Product Leadership
Event-Driven	Process-Driven	Process-Driven
(External/Internal)	(Internal)	(External)
Key Disciplines:	Key Disciplines:	Key Disciplines:
• Business Knowledge	• Systems Engineering	• Convenience Engineering
• Application Engineering	• Sales Management	• Marketing Communications
• Recruiting	• New-Hire Orientation	• Staff Development
• Revenues Within Target	• Cash Flow	• Margin Management

Now, perhaps there are a few rare individuals who are up to the challenge of leading organizations throughout all three of these modes, but for most of us, that simply is unrealistic. So instead, let us try to solve the problem first personally, and then institutionally.

Recall Treacy and Wiersema's advice for companies was to focus on a single discipline to create a foundation for excellence. If we cannot follow that advice precisely as an enterprise, there is nothing to stop us from doing so as individuals. Which of the three value disciplines, then, most inspires us? If we answer product leadership, then we can be sure that Main Street is not our time to shine. Instead, we should look to make our best contributions either in the bowling alley or the tornado, the former if we gravitate toward application-specific solutions, the latter if we prefer general-purpose systems.

Similarly, if operational excellence is our forte, then we should leave the bowling alley to others and seek to assert ourselves once a high volume of transactions gets under way, either in the tornado or on Main Street. The former is better suited to people who like to invent and impose process in relatively chaotic times, the latter to those who prefer focusing on the people side of the equation once the dust has settled.

Or finally, if we see ourselves as champions of customer intimacy, then we must willingly take a back seat during the tornado, when the operational rule is "ignore the customer" and assert ourselves either earlier during the bowling alley or later on when the market has moved to Main Street. The former is better for people who enjoy using systems analysis to help bridge the gap between technology products and business objectives, the latter for those who can imaginatively participate in the domain of end-user experience and creatively shape subjective perception.

Taking the above as a whole, it is intended as no more than a place to start a self-diagnostic process that should also include peer-level feedback and outside counseling. Properly facilitated, this exercise can generate insightful discussion and individual revelation, the sort of team-building that really does build teams.

At the end of the day, however, we must bring the discussion back to power: How can we continually realign leadership responsibility freely without dislocating people, threatening their position, and polarizing the organization? In this context, while models of desired attributes can help us target the people we would like to be in charge, only an institutionalized organizational discipline can actually allow power to transfer itself situationally. The question is, Is such a discipline possible? And even if it were shown to be possible, locally in the context of a single project or group, how in the world could you ever scale up such a practice so that it could operate globally?

The Example of HP

Actually, over the past several years I have been witnessing such a global discipline operate successfully at Hewlett-Packard, and in particular in its Consumer Products Operation where all the PCs and printers are made. There both the laser printer and ink-jet printer divisions have been through multiple tornadoes, during the course of which I have watched a surprisingly broad and varied set of individuals come to the fore, make their contributions, and then step back into the fabric of the organization as a whole. Power and influence in HP's culture redistribute themselves relatively smoothly—certainly so in comparison to the other global enterprises I have had a chance to observe. Interestingly enough, however, I do not think this success is altogether intentional. Rather it is a by-product of the firm's strong commitment to *consensus management* and *decentralization*.

Consensus management is normally touted for its ability to empower contributions from less aggressive team members, to achieve higher quality through more complete and balanced planning and review, and to ensure widespread buy-in and support for critical initiatives. It is also criticized for its inability to react swiftly to transitory opportunities and to sponsor unconventional programs. In the context of hypergrowth markets, this translates into strength in the bowling alley and inside the tornado and weakness on Main Street, a good trade-off for high tech where tornadoes are recurrent and Main Streets foreshortened.

But there is another property of consensus management that is typically overlooked. Within its forums of continual, sometimes seemingly incessant, team meetings, leadership, power, and influence can shift back and forth subtly without disturbing the management hierarchy. Decision-making gravitates toward expertise rather than job title without challenging the latter's authority. Thus product and customer champions can come to the fore during the bowling alley, and systems champions during the tornado, and the group as a whole, knowingly or not, succeeds in navigating the changes that strategy hypergrowth markets impose.

Compare this to a more traditional command-and-control style of management where questions are routed to the person with the proper authority, everyone in between functioning as an information provider or advisor, or simply as an intermediary. Within this system decisions must be made at the proper point of control and nowhere else. This leads to operational excellence champions making customer intimacy decisions, customer intimacy champions making product leadership decisions, and so forth. When the market requirements and the manager's talents are in sync, on the other hand, this mechanism proves exceptionally effective, and since it also scales up readily, it is the system of choice for global organizations serving stable long-term Main Street markets. It is not well suited, however, to high-tech or other hypergrowth industries.

How can consensus management scale to global scope? Only through systematic decentralization. For a long time the operating rule at HP was, once a division gets to $100 million in revenues, break it in two. Even now, when the scale of operations is an order of magnitude higher, there are six independent divisions in the ink-jet business and four on the laser side of the house.

To appreciate the competitive advantage of decentralized organizations over centralized ones, consider the relationship between the surface area and the volume of a sphere. Let the surface area represent all the employees in a company who have direct contact with the customer and the marketplace, and let the volume represent the number of employees all told. If you double the volume of this sphere—doubling the total number of employees—you increase the surface area by only 70 percent. The rest of the new employees will be consumed in dealing with other employees. But if you first break the sphere into two pieces and then double its volume, you will also double the total surface area—more than 30 percent more new employees can make a direct contribution to the marketplace. The more you break things apart, the higher the ratio of surface area to volume—it's just that simple.

Now, in a rapidly changing environment such as that generated by hypergrowth markets, maximizing the ratio of employees who have direct interactions outside the company increases the chances of timely market intelligence, be it about customers, partners, or competitors, thereby improving the enterprise's overall odds of success. To be sure, such decentralization also requires some replication of internal functions, negatively impacting economies of scale, but it turns out that in rapidly changing markets, processes do not stay constant long enough for such economies to take effect. The large-scale system is instead continually in start-up or tear-down mode, constantly reorganizing, and never able to bring its full might to bear.

What is not often recognized in all this is the inherent support decentralization gives to consensus management. This came to a head at HP in the late 1980s when Packard and Hewlett stepped back in to dismantle a set of centralized committees charged with overseeing the matrix management of corporate resources. They rightly saw that such structures jeopardized the HP way, threatening to convert consensus management from an asset into a liability. The slow pace of consensus-based decision-making was frustrating enough; to centralize and bureaucratize it would be nightmarish indeed.

What lies at the center of the HP way, what Hewlett and Packard championed and executives like Dick Hackborn and Lew Platt carried forward, is an unswerving commitment to trust the HP employee. There is a great story from the early days of Bill Hewlett taking a fire ax to the door of a supply room because it was locked and some employees working over the weekend needed to get some supplies. If we trust our employees to make decisions for the company, Hewlett seemed to be saying, then by God we better trust them with the supplies as well. And indeed the phrase "we trust our employees" holds a prominent position in HP's mission statement. I have never seen it in any other.

This commitment to trust is mandatory if the leadership strategies of consensus management and decentralized operations are going to work. The problem is that business culture has not given much thought to this idea, and when it has, has tended to become obsessed with its obverse: how to keep from getting screwed. As soon as such thoughts raise their ugly heads, oversight mechanisms, command and control, and centralization are sure to follow. But what is one to do? The world is full of dishonesty, fraud, and malice—blind trust really *is* a loser's game. So how does one proceed?

It is here that executive leadership and example can make its biggest impact, It starts with the hiring process, which in turn starts with a profile of the desired employee. Microsoft hires for brains, Oracle for brains and ambition, Intel for a streak of combativeness that can contribute to its confrontational culture. HP hires for *trustworthiness*. Cavalier attitudes and personal disrespect can run rampant at any of these other companies, but not at HP. It is a question of values, of what you put first.

A Thought in Closing

At the end of the day, valuing trustworthiness is not in itself enough. Well-meaning people can still go far astray, even by consensus (indeed, perhaps especially by consensus). They need information systems and other feedback mechanisms to alert them to the need for course corrections. The question is, Who will these information systems be designed to serve first, you or them? The executive role is a command-and-control position. No one will fault you if you appropriate the feedback mechanisms and other information systems to ensure you are getting the most timely data possible. Nor will anyone mistake where it is you are putting your trust.

Trust, it turns out, is a complicated and challenging relationship, as much so in business as in parenting or marriage. Like everything else we have been discussing in recent chapters, it is ultimately about power. The paradox of trust is that by intelligently relinquishing power, one gains it back many times over. Once you reach your personal limits, this is the only economy of scale that can help. And because hypergrowth markets will push you to your personal limits faster than most other challenges in business, this is a fitting thought on which to close this book.

INDEX

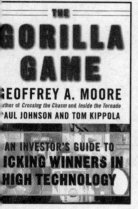